GENKI

AN INTEGRATED COURSE IN ELEMENTARY JAPANESE

THIRD EDITION

初級日本語［げんき］

げんき I

［第3版］

坂野永理・池田庸子・大野裕・品川恭子・渡嘉敷恭子

Eri Banno / Yoko Ikeda / Yutaka Ohno / Chikako Shinagawa / Kyoko Tokashiki

the japan times PUBLISHING

Hiragana　ひらがな

	a	i	u	e	o
	あ a	い i	う u	え e	お o
k	か ka	き ki	く ku	け ke	こ ko
s	さ sa	し shi	す su	せ se	そ so
t	た ta	ち chi	つ tsu	て te	と to
n	な na	に ni	ぬ nu	ね ne	の no
h	は ha	ひ hi	ふ fu	へ he	ほ ho
m	ま ma	み mi	む mu	め me	も mo
y	や ya		ゆ yu		よ yo
r	ら ra	り ri	る ru	れ re	ろ ro
w	わ wa				を o
	ん n				

g	が ga	ぎ gi	ぐ gu	げ ge	ご go
z	ざ za	じ ji	ず zu	ぜ ze	ぞ zo
d	だ da	ぢ ji	づ zu	で de	ど do
b	ば ba	び bi	ぶ bu	べ be	ぼ bo
p	ぱ pa	ぴ pi	ぷ pu	ぺ pe	ぽ po

	a	*u*	*o*
ky	きゃ *kya*	きゅ *kyu*	きょ *kyo*
sh	しゃ *sha*	しゅ *shu*	しょ *sho*
ch	ちゃ *cha*	ちゅ *chu*	ちょ *cho*
ny	にゃ *nya*	にゅ *nyu*	にょ *nyo*
hy	ひゃ *hya*	ひゅ *hyu*	ひょ *hyo*
my	みゃ *mya*	みゅ *myu*	みょ *myo*
ry	りゃ *rya*	りゅ *ryu*	りょ *ryo*
gy	ぎゃ *gya*	ぎゅ *gyu*	ぎょ *gyo*
j	じゃ *ja*	じゅ *ju*	じょ *jo*
by	びゃ *bya*	びゅ *byu*	びょ *byo*
py	ぴゃ *pya*	ぴゅ *pyu*	ぴょ *pyo*

Katakana カタカナ

	a	i	u	e	o
	ア a	イ i	ウ u	エ e	オ o
k	カ ka	キ ki	ク ku	ケ ke	コ ko
s	サ sa	シ shi	ス su	セ se	ソ so
t	タ ta	チ chi	ツ tsu	テ te	ト to
n	ナ na	ニ ni	ヌ nu	ネ ne	ノ no
h	ハ ha	ヒ hi	フ fu	ヘ he	ホ ho
m	マ ma	ミ mi	ム mu	メ me	モ mo
y	ヤ ya		ユ yu		ヨ yo
r	ラ ra	リ ri	ル ru	レ re	ロ ro
w	ワ wa				ヲ o
	ン n				

g	ガ ga	ギ gi	グ gu	ゲ ge	ゴ go
z	ザ za	ジ ji	ズ zu	ゼ ze	ゾ zo
d	ダ da	ヂ ji	ヅ zu	デ de	ド do
b	バ ba	ビ bi	ブ bu	ベ be	ボ bo
p	パ pa	ピ pi	プ pu	ペ pe	ポ po

	a	*i*	*u*	*e*	*o*
ky	キャ *kya*		キュ *kyu*		キョ *kyo*
sh	シャ *sha*		シュ *shu*	シェ *she*	ショ *sho*
ch	チャ *cha*		チュ *chu*	チェ *che*	チョ *cho*
ny	ニャ *nya*		ニュ *nyu*		ニョ *nyo*
hy	ヒャ *hya*		ヒュ *hyu*		ヒョ *hyo*
my	ミャ *mya*		ミュ *myu*		ミョ *myo*
ry	リャ *rya*		リュ *ryu*		リョ *ryo*
gy	ギャ *gya*		ギュ *gyu*		ギョ *gyo*
j	ジャ *ja*		ジュ *ju*	ジェ *je*	ジョ *jo*
by	ビャ *bya*		ビュ *byu*		ビョ *byo*
py	ピャ *pya*		ピュ *pyu*		ピョ *pyo*

	a	*i*	*u*	*e*	*o*
w		ウィ *wi*		ウェ *we*	ウォ *wo*
kw	クァ *kwa*	クィ *kwi*		クェ *kwe*	クォ *kwo*
ts	ツァ *tsa*	ツィ *tsi*		ツェ *tse*	ツォ *tso*
t		ティ *ti*	テュ *tyu*		
f	ファ *fa*	フィ *fi*	フュ *fyu*	フェ *fe*	フォ *fo*
d		ディ *di*	デュ *dyu*		
v	ヴァ *va*	ヴィ *vi*	ヴ *vu*	ヴェ *ve*	ヴォ *vo*

Other less frequently used *katakana* combinations include: イェ (*ye*), グァ (*gwa*), トゥ (*tu*), ドゥ (*du*), ヴュ (*vyu*).

本電子書籍は、書籍のデータを電子化したため、電子書籍にはそぐわない表現や、不要な情報を含んでいる場合があります。また著作権処理の都合上、一部データが差し替えられていることがありますので、ご了承ください。

本書は、2020 年 3 月 5 日に発行された『初級日本語 げんき I　GENKI: An Integrated Course in Elementary Japanese I』第 3 版を電子化したものです。
本電子書籍の全部または一部を無断で複写（コピー）あるいは、送信・配信することを禁じます。

初級日本語 げんき I　GENKI: An Integrated Course in Elementary Japanese I

1999 年 5 月 20 日　初版発行
2011 年 3 月 20 日　第 2 版発行
2020 年 3 月 5 日　　第 3 版発行

著　者：坂野永理・池田庸子・大野裕・品川恭子・渡嘉敷恭子
発行者：伊藤秀樹
発行所：株式会社 ジャパンタイムズ出版
　　　　〒 102-0082 東京都千代田区一番町 2-2　一番町第二 TG ビル 2F
　　　　電話 (050)3646-9500 (出版営業部)
ISBN978-4-7890-1730-5

First edition: May 1999
Second edition: March 2011
Third edition: March 2020

Illustrations: Noriko Udagawa and Reiko Maruyama
Photos: Pakutaso, Pixta, PhotoAC, and Photolibrary
English translations and copyreading: Umes Corp. and Jon McGovern
Narrators: Miho Nagahori, Kosuke Katayama, Toshitada Kitagawa, Miharu Muto, and Rachel Walzer
Recordings: The English Language Education Council, Inc.
Typesetting: guild
Cover art and editorial design: Nakayama Design Office (Gin-o Nakayama and Akihito Kaneko)
Printing: Nikkei Printing Inc.

Published by The Japan Times Publishing, Ltd.
2F Ichibancho Daini TG Bldg., 2-2 Ichibancho, Chiyoda-ku, Tokyo 102-0082, Japan
Phone: 050-3646-9500

Website: https://bookclub.japantimes.co.jp/
Genki-Online: https://genki3.japantimes.co.jp/

ISBN978-4-7890-1730-5

Printed in Japan

はじめに

本書は『初級日本語げんき』の改訂第3版です。『げんき』は長年、世界中の日本語学習者に愛用されてきました。

『げんき』は関西外国語大学で教えていた同僚の私たちが、教師にとっても学習者にとっても使いやすく、楽しく日本語を学べる教科書を目指して作ったものです。テキストのほか、ワークブック、音声教材、教師用指導書など必要な教材が揃っています。そして、豊富なイラストで楽しく練習しながら、基本から応用へと無理なく日本語能力が身に付く教材になっています。また、『げんき』では日本に留学しているメアリーとその仲間のストーリーが展開されます。彼女たちは多くの学習者に日本語学習の友達として愛されてきました。

社会の変化、学習者の多様化に伴い、『げんき』も変化してきました。この改訂版では、語彙、練習などの改訂に加え、教科書の電子版や音声アプリを提供することにしました。また、登場人物の多様性にも留意しました。私たちが、初版から目指していた「学びやすさ」「教えやすさ」が、さらに改善できたと感じています。

この改訂は『げんき』を使用してくださった多くの先生方や学習者の方々の貴重なご意見なしではかないませんでした。心より感謝いたします。また、本書のトレードマークとも言えるイラストを描いてくださった宇田川のり子さん、愛らしいメアリーさんの声をご担当の永堀美穂さん、ジャパンタイムズ出版の皆様、そして、初版以来ずっと労を注いでくださったジャパンタイムズ出版の関戸千明さんに、著者一同心より感謝いたします。さらに新しくなった『げんき』で、いっそう楽しく日本語を学んでいただけることを心から願っています。

2020年2月　著者一同

Preface

This book is the third edition of *GENKI: An Integrated Course in Elementary Japanese*, which has long been a favorite textbook for Japanese-language learners around the world.

We were inspired to create *GENKI* during our days as language instructors at Kansai Gaidai University. Our idea was to conceive a textbook that not only would be easy to use for both teachers and students, but also would make learning Japanese fun. We also developed workbooks, audio material, a teacher's manual, and other resources for making the most of the textbook lessons.

By offering many fun illustrations and other user-friendly features, *GENKI* provides a stress-free approach for learners to advance their Japanese skills from the basics to applied communication. To help learners more closely identify with the material presented, *GENKI* is framed as the story of Mary, an international student living in Japan, and her friends and acquaintances. For many learners, these characters have come to be bosom buddies on their Japanese language journey.

Over the years, *GENKI* has evolved to stay in step with the changing times and the diversification of learners. The third edition continues this evolution with enhancements such as revisions to vocabulary and practices, and with the addition of an e-book version and an audio app. Also, the cast of characters has been made more diverse. We believe that these changes have brought *GENKI* closer to our original goal by making it even easier to study and teach.

This new edition was made possible by the valuable feedback provided by many teachers and learners who have used *GENKI*. We are also very grateful to Noriko Udagawa, whose illustrations have become a trademark feature of this series, Miho Nagahori, who provided the adorable voice of Mary, and The Japan Times Publishing's Chiaki Sekido, who has tirelessly edited *GENKI* from day one. We hope that this edition and its new enhancements will make studying Japanese more fun than ever before!

The Authors
February 2020

初級日本語 [げんき] I

もくじ

会話・文法編 かい わ ぶん ぽう へん	Conversation and Grammar

第1課 LESSON 1　あたらしいともだち New Friends　　36

第2課 LESSON 2　かいもの Shopping　　56

読み書き編　　　Reading and Writing
よ か へん

Introduction

 I **What's _GENKI_?**

GENKI: An Integrated Course in Elementary Japanese is a study resource for people who are starting to learn Japanese. The book is intended mainly for use in university courses, but is also effective for high school students and adults who are beginning to learn Japanese either at school or on their own. It is designed to comprehensively build communication competencies across all four skill areas—listening, speaking, reading, and writing. Emphasis has been placed on balancing accuracy, fluency, and complexity so that students using the material will not end up speaking accurately yet in a stilted manner, or fluently but employing only simple grammatical structures.

GENKI consists of 23 lessons, divided into two volumes of textbooks and workbooks. Vol. 1 contains Lessons 1–12, and Vol. 2 covers Lessons 13–23. The audio material of the textbooks and workbooks can be downloaded and played on mobile devices by using an app called OTO Navi. Information on how to acquire this app can be found on the last page of this book.

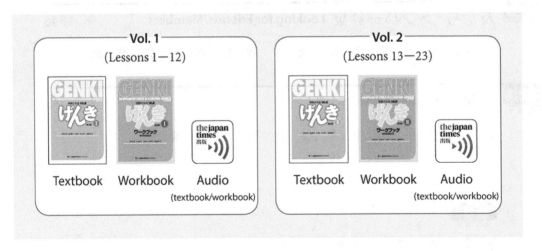

Completion of Vol. 1 should place you at a skill level on par with JLPT N5 or CEFR A1. Vol. 2 is intended to further raise your abilities to N4 or A2.

Textbook Structure

Each textbook volume is divided into two main sections: Conversation and Grammar, and Reading and Writing.

> **Conversation and Grammar:**
> Develops speaking and listening skills while building grammar knowledge and vocabulary.
> **Reading and Writing:**
> Cultivates reading and writing skills, including mastery of *hiragana*, *katakana*, and kanji.

Textbook 1 presents Lessons 1–12 in both of those sections. The overall structure of Textbook 1 is as follows.

GENKI Textbook Vol. 1   ♪ Audio files available

Pre-lesson	◆Japanese Writing System ♪		
Conversation and Grammar	Greetings ♪ Numbers (1 to 100) ♪		
	Lessons 1-12	Lesson Goals (In this lesson, we will...) **Dialogue** ♪ **Vocabulary** (50-60 words per lesson) ♪ **Grammar** **Practice** ♪	
		(Additional Information/Tasks) ● Culture Notes ● Useful Expressions ● Let's Find Out (Research topics)	
Reading and Writing	Lesson 1	*Hiragana* Chart *Hiragana* Practice ♪ / Reading Practice ♪ / Writing Practice	
	Lesson 2	*Katakana* Chart *Katakana* Practice ♪ / Reading Practice ♪ / Writing Practice	
	Lessons 3-12	Kanji List (14-16 kanji per lesson) Kanji Practice / Reading Practice ♪ / Writing Practice	
Appendix	Grammar Index Vocabulary Index 1 & 2 (J-E / E-J) Map of Japan Numbers Conjugation Chart		

 How to Use *GENKI*

1. Conversation and Grammar / Reading and Writing

As noted earlier, this textbook is divided into two main sections: Conversation and Grammar, and Reading and Writing. For each lesson, first go through the lesson in the Conversation and Grammar section, and then proceed to the corresponding lesson in the Reading and Writing section. However, if you do not need to work on reading and writing, you can study the Conversation and Grammar section on a stand-alone basis.

2. Orthography

The Conversation and Grammar section does not use kanji in Lessons 1 and 2; instead, the Japanese text is written only in *hiragana/katakana* with their romanized readings. From Lesson 3 onward, this section uses kanji but stops providing romanized readings, so you should strive to become able to read all *hiragana* and *katakana* by the end of Lesson 2. However, the readings of all kanji are given in *hiragana* so that this section can be studied by those who do not need to learn kanji. The Reading and Writing section does not provide readings in *hiragana* for kanji already studied.

3. Studying the Japanese script

Try to master all *hiragana* as you work through Lesson 1, and then do the same with *katakana* in Lesson 2. Start by reading the "Japanese Writing System" section (pp. 20–27) to familiarize yourself with the basics of Japanese orthography. Afterwards, begin practicing how to read and write *hiragana/katakana*, using the following resources.

Flashcards: The *hiragana/katakana* charts in the Japanese Writing System section can be cut up into flashcards to aid your practice. (Workbook: see pp. 11–12 for *hiragana*, pp. 23–24 for *katakana*.)

Kana **writing practice:** Lessons 1 and 2 of the workbook's Reading and Writing section provide exercises for writing *hiragana* and *katakana*. (Workbook: see pp. 121–127 for *hiragana*, pp. 128–132 for *katakana*.)

Reading Practice/Writing Practice: Lessons 1 and 2 of the textbook's Reading and Writing section include practices for reading and writing *hiragana/katakana* as part of words and sentences.

Kanji are studied from Lesson 3 onward in the Reading and Writing section.

4. Using the Conversation and Grammar section

● Dialogue

The dialogues contain the lesson's new learning targets. Learn them after studying the vocabulary and grammar items presented in the lesson.

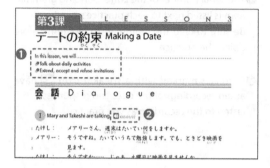

❶ Every lesson begins with a preview of the skills it will teach.

❷ Each dialogue has two audio recordings. The first is recorded as a normal conversation, and the second adds a pause after each sentence for practice.

● Vocabulary

This is a list of the words and expressions that appear in the dialogues and practices. A good way to learn them is to repeatedly go over a handful at a time.

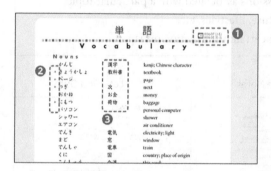

❶ There are two audio recordings of the vocabulary and English translations. The first presents each Japanese entry followed by its English equivalent, and the second is in the opposite order. Use the recordings to help you learn the words with your ears.

❷ Words that appear in the dialogues are marked with an asterisk.

❸ There is no need to memorize the kanji listed.

● Grammar / Expression Notes

The Grammar section explains the grammar items presented in the lesson. The Expression Notes at the end provide commentary on expressions and words not included among the grammar points.

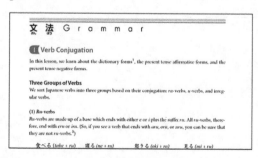

● Practice

The Practice section contains exercises dealing with the points covered in the Grammar section. The workbook also provides practices for the grammar points covered in the lesson. First do the practices in the textbook, and then check your mastery by doing the ones in the workbook.

❶The serial number of the corresponding grammar item is listed next to each practice's heading. Be sure to read the grammar explanation before doing the practice.

❷Exercises marked with a speaker icon 🔊 have audio recordings of the cues and responses. Listen to the recording as you practice.

● Additional Information

Some lessons include the following extra content.

> **Useful Expressions:** Lists of words and expressions associated with a particular topic.
> **Culture Notes:** Commentary on Japanese culture, lifestyles, etc.
> **Let's Find Out:** Tasks that require you look up certain information on Japan.

Useful Expressions	Culture Notes	Let's Find Out

5. Using the Reading and Writing section

The Reading and Writing section covers *hiragana* in Lesson 1, *katakana* in Lesson 2, and kanji in the remaining lessons.

● Kanji List

Lesson 3 and subsequent lessons present a table of kanji at the beginning. Try learning the characters by repeatedly going over a few at a time. Readings and words that are shaded should be memorized.

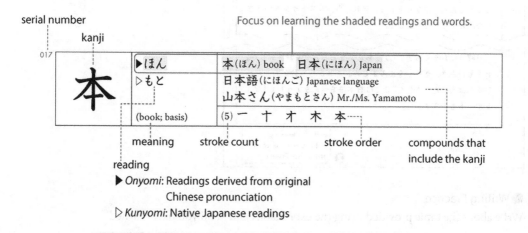

▶ *Onyomi*: Readings derived from original
Chinese pronunciation
▷ *Kunyomi*: Native Japanese readings

The workbook's Reading and Writing section includes kanji practice sheets.

● Kanji Practice

Do these exercises after memorizing the target kanji of each lesson.

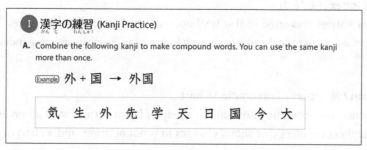

● Reading Practice

The reading practices assume that you have learned the grammar points and vocabulary presented in the corresponding lesson in the Conversation and Grammar section.

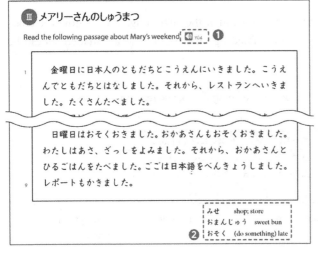

❶An audio recording is available for each reading.

❷English translations are provided for words not yet covered.

● Writing Practice

Write about the topic provided using the expressions and kanji you have learned.

> ### Ⅳ 書く練習 (Writing Practice)
>
> **A.** You are going out. Write a memo to someone in your house, telling when you will be back and whether you will have dinner at home.
>
> **B.** Write about your weekend. Use the above passage as a model.

6. Appendix

● Grammar Index

This index lists the Grammar entries of all lessons, as well as grammatical items from Expression Notes, Useful Expressions, and Culture Notes.

● Vocabulary Index (J-E / E-J)

The vocabulary entries presented in this textbook are listed in Vocabulary Index 1 (a Japanese-English index in *a-i-u-e-o* order) and Vocabulary Index 2 (an English-Japanese index in alphabetical order).

● Map of Japan / Numbers / Conjugation Chart

For your reference, the appendix also includes a map of Japan with a list of all prefectures, a table of Japanese numbers/counters that shows changes in pronunciation, and a chart of verb conjugations.

IV Fonts Used in This Book

The Japanese text in this book is mainly set in the Textbook font, which closely resembles hand-writing. Note that there are many different fonts used in Japan (a few examples are shown below), and that the shape of a particular character can vary depending on the font used. For example, certain fonts depict the two strokes of さ as a single stroke.

Example	Textbook font	さ	う	り	ふ	や
	Mincho font	さ	う	り	ふ	や
	Gothic font	さ	う	り	ふ	や
	Handwriting	さ	う	り	ふ	や

 V Other *GENKI* Resources

● GENKI-Online (https://genki3.japantimes.co.jp/)
GENKI-Online is a website providing additional *GENKI* materials for both teachers and learners.

● GENKI Apps
The following apps are also available to assist your study of *GENKI*.

GENKI Vocab Cards 3rd Ed. (iOS/Android)
Digital vocabulary flashcards that help you learn all the words and expressions studied in *GENKI* I and II.

GENKI Kanji Cards 3rd Ed. (iOS/Android)
Digital flashcards that aid your study of the readings and shapes of 317 kanji covered by *GENKI* I and II. The cards feature around 1,100 kanji words, plus illustrations that help you memorize kanji shapes.

GENKI Conjugation Cards 3rd Ed. (iOS/Android)
An app for mastering the conjugation of verbs and adjectives. Audio recordings, example sentences, and illustrations help you to efficiently learn 28 conjugation patterns.

Note: The apps for the 3rd edition will be sequentially released, starting in September 2020.
See GENKI-Online or The Japan Times Publishing website for updates.

Japanese Writing System

There are three kinds of characters in Japanese: *hiragana*, *katakana*, and kanji.[1] All three characters can be seen in a single sentence.

テ　レ　ビ　を　見　ま　す。　　　*I watch television.*

<u>katakana</u>　　　　kanji <u>hiragana</u>

Hiragana and *katakana*, like the alphabet, represent sounds. As you can see in the above example, *hiragana* has a roundish shape and is used for conjugation endings, function words, and native Japanese words not covered by kanji. *Katakana*, which has rather straight lines, is normally used for writing loanwords and foreign names. For example, the Japanese word for "television" is written in *katakana* as テレビ (*terebi*). Kanji, or Chinese characters, represent not just sounds but also meanings. Mostly, kanji are used for nouns and the stems of verbs and adjectives.

❶ H i r a g a n a

1. Basic *Hiragana* Syllables

There are forty-six basic *hiragana* syllables, which are listed below. Once you memorize this chart, you will have the skill to transcribe all of the Japanese sounds. (The romanization is given for general pronunciation reference.)

🔊 JWS-01

あ *a*	い *i*	う *u*	え *e*	お *o*
か *ka*	き *ki*	く *ku*	け *ke*	こ *ko*
さ *sa*	し *shi*	す *su*	せ *se*	そ *so*
た *ta*	ち *chi*	つ *tsu*	て *te*	と *to*
な *na*	に *ni*	ぬ *nu*	ね *ne*	の *no*
は *ha*	ひ *hi*	ふ *fu*	へ *he*	ほ *ho*

* The syllables し, ち, つ, and ふ are romanized as *shi*, *chi*, *tsu*, and *fu*, respectively, to closely resemble English pronunciation.

---

[1] There is another writing system called *rōmaji* (Roman letters), which is used for station names, signs, and so on.

ま ma	み mi	む mu	め me	も mo
や ya		ゆ yu		よ yo
ら ra	り ri	る ru	れ re	ろ ro
わ wa				を **o
ん n				

** を is also pronounced as "*wo*."

2. *Hiragana* with Diacritical Marks

You can transcribe 23 additional sounds by adding diacritic marks. With a pair of short diagonal strokes (゛), the unvoiced consonants *k, s, t,* and *h* become voiced consonants *g, z, d,* and *b*, respectively. The consonant *h* changes to *p* with the addition of a small circle (゜).

JWS-02

が ga	ぎ gi	ぐ gu	げ ge	ご go
ざ za	じ ji	ず zu	ぜ ze	ぞ zo
だ da	*ぢ ji	*づ zu	で de	ど do
ば ba	び bi	ぶ bu	べ be	ぼ bo
ぱ pa	ぴ pi	ぷ pu	ぺ pe	ぽ po

* ぢ (*ji*) and づ (*zu*) are pronounced the same as じ (*ji*) and ず (*zu*), respectively, and have limited use.

3. Transcribing Contracted Sounds

Small や, ゆ, and よ follow after letters in the second column (*i*-vowel *hiragana*, except い) and are used to transcribe contracted sounds. The contracted sound represents a single syllable.

きゃ kya	きゅ kyu	きょ kyo	ぎゃ gya	ぎゅ gyu	ぎょ gyo	JWS-03
しゃ sha	しゅ shu	しょ sho	じゃ ja	じゅ ju	じょ jo	
ちゃ cha	ちゅ chu	ちょ cho				
にゃ nya	にゅ nyu	にょ nyo				
ひゃ hya	ひゅ hyu	ひょ hyo	びゃ bya	びゅ byu	びょ byo	
みゃ mya	みゅ myu	みょ myo	ぴゃ pya	ぴゅ pyu	ぴょ pyo	
りゃ rya	りゅ ryu	りょ ryo				

4. Transcribing Double Consonants

There is another small letter, っ, which is used when transcribing double consonants such as *tt* and *pp*.

(Example) JWS-04

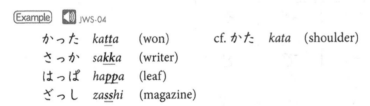

かった *katta* (won)   cf. かた *kata* (shoulder)
さっか *sakka* (writer)
はっぱ *happa* (leaf)
ざっし *zasshi* (magazine)

Note double consonant *n*'s as in *sannen* (three years) are written with ん + a *hiragana* with an initial *n* sound (な, に, ぬ, ね, and の).

(Example) JWS-05

さんねん *sannen* (three years)
あんない *annai* (guide)

5. Other Issues Relating to Transcription and Pronunciation

A. Long Vowels

When the same vowel is placed one right after the other, the pronunciation of the vowel becomes about twice as long as the single vowel. Be sure to hold the sound long enough, because the length of the vowel can change one word to another.

🔊 JWS-06

aa	おばあさん	*obaasan*	(grandmother)	cf. おばさん	*obasan*	(aunt)
ii	おじいさん	*ojiisan*	(grandfather)	cf. おじさん	*ojisan*	(uncle)
uu	すうじ	*suuji*	(number)			

ee   The long *ee* sound is usually transcribed by adding an い to an *e*-vowel *hiragana*. There are a few words, however, in which え is used instead of い.

えいが	*eega*	(movie)
おねえさん	*oneesan*	(big sister)

oo   The long *oo* sound is in most cases transcribed by adding an う to an *o*-vowel *hiragana*. There are, however, words in which the long vowel is transcribed with an お, for historical reasons.

ほうりつ	*hooritsu*	(law)
とお	*too*	(ten)

B. Pronunciation of ん

ん (*n*) is treated like a full syllable, in terms of length. Its pronunciation varies, however, depending on the sound that follows it. Japanese speakers are normally not aware of the different sound values of ん. Therefore, you do not need to worry too much about its pronunciation.[2]

C. Vowels to Be Dropped

The vowels *i* and *u* are sometimes dropped when placed between voiceless consonants (*k, s, t, p,* and *h*), or at the end of an utterance preceded by voiceless consonants.

(Example)   🔊 JWS-07

     すきです   *s(u)kides(u)*   (I like it.)

D. Accent in the Japanese Language

Japanese has pitch accent: all syllables are pronounced basically either in high or low pitch. Unlike English stress accent in which stressed syllables tend to be pronounced longer and louder, in Japanese each syllable is pronounced approximately in equal length and stress. The pitch patterns in Japanese vary greatly, depending on the region of the country.

---

[2]One variety of the ん pronunciation merits discussing here. When it is followed by a vowel or at the end of an utterance, ん indicates that the preceding vowel is long and nasalized. (Nasalized vowels are shown here with a tilde above vowel letters. You hear nasalized vowels in French words such as "bon," or the English interjection "uh-uh," as in "no.")

     e.g. れんあい   *rẽai*   (romance)   ほん   *hõ*   (book)

Followed by *n, t, d, s,* and *z* sounds, ん is pronounced as "n."   **e.g.** おんな   *onna*   (woman)

Followed by *m, p,* and *b* sounds, ん is pronounced as "m."   **e.g.** さんぽ   *sampo*   (stroll)

Followed by *k* and *g* sounds, ん is pronounced as "ng" as in "song." **e.g.** まんが   *maŋga*   (comics)

Example 🔊 JWS-08

あさ $\overset{a}{\underset{sa}{\rule{0pt}{1em}}}$ (morning)

なまえ $\underset{na}{\overset{ma\ e}{\rule{0pt}{1em}}}$ (name)

たかい $\underset{ta}{\overset{ka}{\rule{0pt}{1em}}}\ i$ (high)

Ⅱ K a t a k a n a

1. Basic *Katakana* Syllables

🔊 JWS-09

ア *a*	イ *i*	ウ *u*	エ *e*	オ *o*
カ *ka*	キ *ki*	ク *ku*	ケ *ke*	コ *ko*
サ *sa*	シ **shi*	ス *su*	セ *se*	ソ *so*
タ *ta*	チ **chi*	ツ **tsu*	テ *te*	ト *to*
ナ *na*	ニ *ni*	ヌ *nu*	ネ *ne*	ノ *no*
ハ *ha*	ヒ *hi*	フ **fu*	ヘ *he*	ホ *ho*
マ *ma*	ミ *mi*	ム *mu*	メ *me*	モ *mo*
ヤ *ya*		ユ *yu*		ヨ *yo*
ラ *ra*	リ *ri*	ル *ru*	レ *re*	ロ *ro*
ワ *wa*				ヲ *o*
ン *n*				

*The syllables シ, チ, ツ, and フ are romanized as *shi*, *chi*, *tsu*, and *fu*, respectively, to closely resemble English pronunciation.

2. *Katakana* with Diacritical Marks

🔊 JWS-10

ガ *ga*	ギ *gi*	グ *gu*	ゲ *ge*	ゴ *go*
ザ *za*	ジ *ji*	ズ *zu*	ゼ *ze*	ゾ *zo*
ダ *da*	*ヂ *ji*	*ヅ *zu*	デ *de*	ド *do*
バ *ba*	ビ *bi*	ブ *bu*	ベ *be*	ボ *bo*
パ *pa*	ピ *pi*	プ *pu*	ペ *pe*	ポ *po*

*ヂ (*ji*) and ヅ (*zu*) are pronounced the same as ジ (*ji*) and ズ (*zu*), respectively, and have limited use.

3. Transcribing Contracted Sounds

🔊 JWS-11

キャ *kya*	キュ *kyu*	キョ *kyo*
シャ *sha*	シュ *shu*	ショ *sho*
チャ *cha*	チュ *chu*	チョ *cho*
ニャ *nya*	ニュ *nyu*	ニョ *nyo*
ヒャ *hya*	ヒュ *hyu*	ヒョ *hyo*
ミャ *mya*	ミュ *myu*	ミョ *myo*
リャ *rya*	リュ *ryu*	リョ *ryo*

ギャ *gya*	ギュ *gyu*	ギョ *gyo*
ジャ *ja*	ジュ *ju*	ジョ *jo*

ビャ *bya*	ビュ *byu*	ビョ *byo*
ピャ *pya*	ピュ *pyu*	ピョ *pyo*

4. Other Issues Relating to Transcription and Pronunciation

The pronunciation of *katakana* and its combinations are the same as those of *hiragana*, except for the following points.

A. Long Vowels

The long vowels are written with ー.

(Example) 🔊 JWS-12

カー	kaa	(car)		ケーキ	keeki	(cake)
スキー	sukii	(ski)		ボール	booru	(ball)
スーツ	suutsu	(suit)				

When you write vertically, the ― mark needs to be written vertically also.

ボール → ボ
　　　　　 ｜
　　　　　 ル

B. Transcribing Foreign Sounds

Additional combinations with small vowel letters are used to transcribe foreign sounds which originally did not exist in Japanese.

(Example) 🔊 JWS-13

ウィ	ハロウィーン	harowiin	(Halloween)
ウェ	ハイウェイ	haiwee	(highway)
ウォ	ミネラルウォーター	mineraruwootaa	(mineral water)
シェ	シェフ	shefu	(chef)
ジェ	ジェームス	Jeemusu	(James)
チェ	チェック	chekku	(check)
ファ	ファッション	fasshon	(fashion)
フィ	フィリピン	Firipin	(Philippines)
フェ	カフェ	kafe	(cafe)
フォ	フォーク	fooku	(fork)
ティ	パーティー	paatii	(party)
ディ	ディズニーランド	Dizuniirando	(Disneyland)
デュ	デュエット	dyuetto	(duet)

The sound "v" is sometimes written with ヴ. For example, the word "Venus" is sometimes written as ビーナス or ヴィーナス.

Ⅲ Kanji

Kanji are Chinese characters which were introduced to Japan more than 1,500 years ago when the Japanese language did not have a writing system. *Hiragana* and *katakana* evolved later in Japan based on the simplified Chinese characters.

Kanji represent both meanings and sounds. Most kanji possess multiple readings, which are divided into two types: *on-yomi* (Chinese readings) and *kun-yomi* (Japanese readings). *On-yomi* are derived from the pronunciations used in China. Some kanji have more than one *on-yomi* due to temporal and regional variances in the Chinese pronunciation. *Kun-yomi* are Japanese readings.

When people started to use kanji to write native Japanese words, Japanese readings (*kun-yomi*) were added to kanji.

By the time of high school graduation, Japanese are expected to know 2,136 kanji (called Joyo Kanji), which are designated by the Ministry of Education as commonly used kanji. A total of 1,006 kanji are taught at the elementary school level, and most of the remainder are taught in junior high school.

There are roughly four types of kanji, based on their formation.

A. Pictograms
Some kanji are made from pictures:

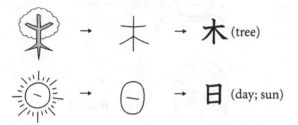

B. Simple ideograms
Some kanji are made of dots and lines to represent numbers or abstract concepts.

二 → 三 (three)　　　·　→ 上 (up)

C. Compound ideograms
Some kanji are made from the combination of two or more kanji.

日 (day; sun)　+　月 (moon)　→　明 (bright)

人 (person)　+　木 (tree)　→　休 (to rest)

D. Phonetic-ideographic characters
Some kanji are made up of a meaning element and a sound element.

Meaning element	Sound element	On-yomi
氵 (water)	+ 青 *sei* (blue)	→ 清 *sei* (clean)
日 (day; sun)	+ 青 *sei* (blue)	→ 晴 *sei* (clear sky)

Main Characters in This Book

登場人物紹介
とう じょう じん ぶつ しょう かい

メアリー・ハート
Hart, Mary

An exchange student
from the U.S.

木村たけし
き むら
Kimura, Takeshi

A Japanese student

ソラ・キム
Kim, Sora

An exchange student
from Korea

ロバート・スミス
Smith, Robert

An exchange student
from the U.K.

ジョン・ワン
Wang, John

An exchange student
from Australia

山下先生
やました せんせい
Prof. Yamashita

A Japanese teacher

鈴木健
すず き けん
Suzuki, Ken

A Japanese student

山川ゆい
やま かわ
Yamakawa, Yui

A Japanese student

お父さん
とう
Mary's host father

お母さん
かあ
Mary's host mother

会話・文法編
かい わ ぶん ぽう へん
C o n v e r s a t i o n   a n d   G r a m m a r

あいさつ

 K00-01

G r e e t i n g s

おはよう。
Ohayoo.

おはよう ございます。
Ohayoo gozaimasu.

こんにちは。
Konnichiwa.

こんばんは。
Konbanwa.

おやすみなさい。
Oyasumi nasai.

さようなら。
Sayoonara.

ありがとう。
Arigatoo.

ありがとう ございます。
Arigatoo gozaimasu.

おはよう。	Ohayoo.	Good morning.
おはよう ございます。	Ohayoo gozaimasu.	Good morning. (polite)
こんにちは。*	Konnichiwa.*	Good afternoon.
こんばんは。*	Konbanwa.*	Good evening.
さようなら。	Sayoonara.	Good-bye.
おやすみ（なさい）。	Oyasumi (nasai).	Good night.
ありがとう。	Arigatoo.	Thank you.
ありがとう ございます。	Arigatoo gozaimasu.	Thank you. (polite)
すみません。	Sumimasen.	Excuse me.; I'm sorry.
いいえ。	Iie.	No.; Not at all.
いってきます。	Itte kimasu.	I'll go and come back.
いってらっしゃい。	Itterasshai.	Please go and come back.
ただいま。	Tadaima.	I'm home.
おかえり（なさい）。	Okaeri (nasai).	Welcome home.
いただきます。	Itadakimasu.	Thank you for the meal. (before eating)
ごちそうさま（でした）。	Gochisoosama (deshita).	Thank you for the meal. (after eating)
はじめまして。	Hajimemashite.	How do you do?
〜です。	. . . desu.	I am . . . .
よろしく おねがいします。	Yoroshiku onegai shimasu.	Nice to meet you.

*The last syllable of *konnichiwa* and *konbanwa* is spelled with は instead of わ.

あいさつと おじぎ Greetings and Bowing
Aisatsu to ojigi

Japanese people greet each other by bowing, which has many other functions, such as expressing respect, gratitude, or apologies. There are different ways of bowing, ranging from a small nod of the head to a 45-degree bend at the waist. Generally, the longer and the deeper you bow, the more formal and respectful it appears to others.

Many Japanese tend to feel uncomfortable with physical contact, although handshaking is becoming quite common in business situations, especially those involving foreigners.

When meeting someone in a business situation for the first time, it is customary to exchange *meeshi* (business cards) with a small bow. Etiquette guides list a vast number of rules and pointers, but just remember that the important thing is to clearly show your respect when exchanging *meeshi*.

表現ノート
ひょう げん

おはよう/ありがとう ▶ *Ohayoo* is used between friends and family members, while *ohayoo gozaimasu* is used between less intimate acquaintances, similar to *arigatoo* and *arigatoo gozaimasu*. The rule of thumb is: if you are on a first-name basis with someone, go for the shorter versions. If you would address someone as Mr. or Ms., use the longer versions.

   Ohayoo is the greeting used before noon, but some people use it in casual settings in the afternoon or even at night when they see their classmates or co-workers for the first time that day.

さようなら ▶ There are several good-bye expressions in Japanese, the choice among which depends on the degree of separation. *Sayoonara* indicates that the speaker does not expect to see the person spoken to before she "turns a page in her life"; not until a new day arrives, or until fate brings the two together again. It sounds dramatic and ritualistic, and its daily use is largely restricted to school children taking leave of their teachers.

   じゃあ、また。   Jaa, mata.
   (between friends, expecting to see each other again fairly soon)

   しつれいします。   Shitsureeshimasu.
   (taking leave from a professor's office, for example)

すみません ▶ *Sumimasen* means (1) "Excuse me," to get another person's attention, (2) "I'm sorry," to apologize for the trouble you have caused, or (3) "Thank you," to show appreciation for what someone has done for you.

いいえ ▶ *Iie* is primarily "No," a negative reply to a question. In the dialogue, it is used to express the English phrase "Don't mention it," or "You're welcome," with which you point out that one is not required to feel obliged for what you have done for them.

いってらっしゃい/いってきます/ただいま/おかえりなさい ▶ *Itte kimasu* and *itterasshai* is a common exchange used at home when a family member leaves. The person who leaves says *itte kimasu*, which literally means "I will go and come back." And the family members respond with *itterasshai*, which means "Please go and come back."

   Tadaima and *okaeri* are used when a person comes home. The person who arrives home says *tadaima* (I am home right now) to the family members, and they respond with *okaerinasai* (Welcome home).

● れんしゅう Practice

A. Act out the following situations with your classmates.

1. It is one o'clock in the afternoon. You see your neighbor Mr. Yamada.

2. You come to class in the morning. Greet your teacher. Greet your friends.

3. On a crowded train, you stepped on someone's foot.

4. You dropped your book. Someone picked it up for you.

5. It is eight o'clock at night. You happen to meet your teacher at the convenience store.

6. You are watching TV with your host family. It is time to go to sleep.

7. You are leaving home.

8. You have come back home.

9. You are going to start eating.

10. You have finished eating.

B. Class Activity—Meeting someone for the first time

Walk around the classroom and introduce yourself to your classmates using the example below. Meet as many classmates as possible.

(Example) A : はじめまして。きむらたけしです。よろしくおねがいします。
Hajimemashite.   Kimura Takeshi desu.   Yoroshiku onegaishimasu.

B : ほんだあいです。よろしくおねがいします。
Honda Ai desu.   Yoroshiku onegaishimasu.

すうじ

🔊 K00-02

N u m b e r s

0 ゼロ／れい
zero　ree

1	いち ichi	11	じゅういち juuichi	30	さんじゅう sanjuu
2	に ni	12	じゅうに juuni	40	よんじゅう yonjuu
3	さん san	13	じゅうさん juusan	50	ごじゅう gojuu
4	よん／し／（よ） yon　shi　(yo)	14	じゅうよん／じゅうし juuyon　juushi	60	ろくじゅう rokujuu
5	ご go	15	じゅうご juugo	70	ななじゅう nanajuu
6	ろく roku	16	じゅうろく juuroku	80	はちじゅう hachijuu
7	なな／しち nana　shichi	17	じゅうなな／じゅうしち juunana　juushichi	90	きゅうじゅう kyuujuu
8	はち hachi	18	じゅうはち juuhachi	100	ひゃく hyaku
9	きゅう／く kyuu　ku	19	じゅうきゅう／じゅうく juukyuu　juuku		
10	じゅう juu	20	にじゅう nijuu		

● れんしゅう Practice

A. Read the following numbers. 🔊 K00-03

(a) 5　　(b) 9　　(c) 7　　(d) 1　　(e) 10

(f) 8　　(g) 2　　(h) 6　　(i) 4　　(j) 3

B. Read the following numbers. 🔊 K00-04

(a) 45　　(b) 83　　(c) 19　　(d) 76　　(e) 52

(f) 100　　(g) 38　　(h) 61　　(i) 24　　(j) 97

C. What are the answers? 🔊 K00-05

(a) 5＋3　　(b) 9＋1　　(c) 3＋4　　(d) 6－6　　(e) 10＋9

(f) 8－7　　(g) 40－25

第1課
だい　いっ　か

あたらしいともだち New Friends

In this lesson, we will ....

◉ Introduce ourselves
◉ Ask and tell people names, majors at school, time, etc.

かいわ D i a l o g u e

Ⅰ　Mary, an international student who just arrived in Japan, meets a Japanese student Takeshi at a school orientation. 🔊 K01-01/02

1　たけし：　　こんにちは。きむら　たけしです。
　Takeshi　　　Konnichiwa　　Kimura　　Takeshi desu.

2　メアリー：　メアリー・ハートです。あのう、りゅうがくせいですか。
　め あ り い
　Mearii　　　Mearii Haato desu.　　　Anoo,　　ryuugakusee desu ka.
　　　　　　　　　　　　　　　　　　は あ と

3　たけし：　　いいえ、にほんじんです。
　Takeshi　　　Iie,　　　nihonjin desu.

4　メアリー：　そうですか。なんねんせいですか。
　め あ り い
　Mearii　　　Soo desu ka.　　Nannensee desu ka.

5　たけし：　　よねんせいです。
　Takeshi　　　Yonensee desu.

Ⅱ At the orientation, Mary introduces herself to everyone. 🔊 K01-03/04

1 メアリー： はじめまして。メアリー・ハートです。
Mearii   Hajimemashite.   Mearii Haato desu.

2 アリゾナだいがくの がくせいです。にねんせいです。
Arizona daigaku no   gakusee desu.   Ninensee desu.

3 せんこうは にほんごです。じゅうきゅうさいです。
Senkoo wa   nihongo desu.   Juukyuusai desu.

4 よろしく おねがいします。
Yoroshiku   onegai shimasu.

Ⓘ

Takeshi: Hello. I am Takeshi Kimura.

Mary: I am Mary Hart. Um . . . are you an international student?

Takeshi: No, I am Japanese.

Mary: I see. What year are you in college?

Takeshi: I am a fourth-year student.

Ⅱ

Mary: How do you do? I am Mary Hart.

I am a student at the University of Arizona. I am a second-year student.

My major is Japanese. I am 19 years old.

Nice to meet you.

たんご

K01-05 (J-E)
K01-06 (E-J)

V o c a b u l a r y

S c h o o l

✳ だいがく	daigaku	college; university
こうこう	kookoo	high school
✳ がくせい	gakusee	student
だいがくせい	daigakusee	college student
✳ りゅうがくせい	ryuugakusee	international student
せんせい	sensee	teacher; Professor . . .
✳ 〜ねんせい	. . . nensee	. . . year student
いちねんせい	ichinensee	first-year student
✳ せんこう	senkoo	major

P e r s o n

わたし	watashi	I
ともだち	tomodachi	friend
〜さん	. . . san	Mr./Ms. . . .
✳ 〜じん	. . . jin	. . . people
にほんじん	nihonjin	Japanese people

T i m e

いま	ima	now
ごぜん	gozen	A.M.
ごご	gogo	P.M.
〜じ	. . . ji	o'clock
いちじ	ichiji	one o'clock
はん	han	half
にじはん	niji han	half past two

O t h e r s

✳ にほん	Nihon	Japan
アメリカ（あめりか）	Amerika	U.S.A.
✳ 〜ご	. . . go	. . . language
にほんご	nihongo	Japanese language
✳ 〜さい	. . . sai	. . . years old
でんわ	denwa	telephone
〜ばん	. . . ban	number . . .

✳ Words that appear in the dialogue

ばんごう	bangoo	number
なまえ	namae	name
* なん／なに	nan/nani	what

Expressions

* あのう	anoo	um...
はい	hai	yes
そうです	soo desu	That's right.
* そうですか	soo desu ka	I see.; Is that so?

ADDITIONAL VOCABULARY

K01-07 (J-E)
K01-08 (E-J)

Learn words that are relevant to your life.

Countries (くに kuni)

イギリス	Igirisu	Britain
オーストラリア	Oosutoraria	Australia
かんこく	Kankoku	Korea
カナダ	Kanada	Canada
ちゅうごく	Chuugoku	China
インド	Indo	India
エジプト	Ejiputo	Egypt
フィリピン	Firipin	Philippines

Majors (せんこう senkoo)

アジアけんきゅう	ajia kenkyuu	Asian studies
けいざい	keezai	economics
こうがく	koogaku	engineering
こくさいかんけい	kokusaikankee	international relations
コンピューター	konpyuutaa	computer
せいじ	seeji	politics
せいぶつがく	seebutsugaku	biology
ビジネス	bijinesu	business
ぶんがく	bungaku	literature
れきし	rekishi	history

Occupations (しごと shigoto)

いしゃ	isha	doctor
かいしゃいん	kaishain	office worker

かんごし	kangoshi	nurse
こうこうせい	kookoosee	high school student
しゅふ	shufu	housewife
だいがくいんせい	daigakuinsee	graduate student
べんごし	bengoshi	lawyer

F a m i l y (かぞく kazoku)

おかあさん	okaasan	mother
おとうさん	otoosan	father
おねえさん	oneesan	older sister
おにいさん	oniisan	older brother
いもうと	imooto	younger sister
おとうと	otooto	younger brother

ぶんぽう Ｇｒａｍｍａｒ

1 ＸはＹです

"I am a student." "My major is the Japanese language." "It is 12:30": These sentences will all be translated into Japanese using an appropriate noun and the word *desu*.

〜です。　　　　*It is ...*

がくせいです。 Gakusee desu.	*(I) am a student.*
にほんごです。 Nihongo desu.	*(My major) is the Japanese language.*
じゅうにじはんです。 Juuniji han desu.	*(It) is half past twelve.*

Note that none of these sentences has a "subject," like the "I," "my major," and "it" found in their English counterparts. Sentences without subjects are very common in Japanese; Japanese speakers actually tend to omit subjects whenever they think it is clear to the listener what or who they are referring to.

If it is not clear from the background situation or the preceding context what is being talked about, you can start a sentence with a "topic" marked by *wa*. Note that when we write in *hiragana*, we use the letter は for topic *wa* following the classical orthography.[1]

ＸはＹです。　　　*X is Y. As for X, it is Y.*

せんこうは　にほんごです。 Senkoo wa　　nihongo desu.	*(My) major is the Japanese language.*
わたしは　ソラ・キムです。 Watashi wa　Sora Kimu desu.	*I am Sora Kim.*
やましたさんは　せんせいです。 Yamashita san wa　sensee desu.	*Mr. Yamashita is a teacher.*
メアリーさんは　アメリカじんです。 Mearii san wa　　amerikajin desu.	*Mary is an American.*

---

[1] The *hiragana* は therefore has two pronunciations: *wa* (in the topic position) and *ha* (in most other positions). There are few exceptions, such as *konnichiwa* (good afternoon) and *konbanwa* (good evening). They are usually written with こんにち<u>は</u> and こんばん<u>は</u>.

Wa is a member of the class of words called "particles." So is the word *no*, which we will turn to later in this lesson. We add particles to noun phrases to indicate how the phrases relate to the rest of the sentence.

Note also that nouns like *gakusee* and *sensee* in the above examples stand alone, unlike their English translations "student" and "teacher," which are preceded by "a." In Japanese, there is no item that corresponds to "a," nor is there any item that corresponds to the plural "-s" at the end of a noun. Without context, a sentence like *gakusee desu* is therefore ambiguous in terms of the singular and plural interpretations.

2 Question Sentences

You can just add *ka* at the end of a statement and turn it into a question.

りゅうがくせいです。
Ryuugakusee desu.
(I am) an international student.

りゅうがくせいです<u>か</u>。[2]
Ryuugakusee desu ka.
(Are you) an international student?

The above sentence, *Ryuugakusee desu ka*, is a "yes/no" question. Question sentences may also contain a "question word" like *nan*[3] (what). In this lesson, we learn how to ask, and answer, questions using the following question words: *nanji* (what time), *nansai* (how old), *nannensee* (what year in school), and *nanban* (what number).

A : せんこうは <u>なん</u>ですか。
　　Senkoo wa　　nan desu ka.
　　What is your major?

B : (せんこうは) <u>えいご</u>です。
　　(Senkoo wa)　　eego desu.
　　(My major) is English.

A : いま <u>なんじ</u>ですか。
　　Ima　　nanji desu ka.
　　What time is it now?

B : (いま) <u>くじ</u>です。
　　(Ima)　　kuji desu.
　　It is nine o'clock.

A : メアリーさんは <u>なんさい</u>ですか。
　　Mearii san wa　　nansai desu ka.
　　How old are you, Mary?

B : <u>じゅうきゅうさい</u>です。
　　Juukyuusai desu.
　　I'm nineteen years old.

A : <u>なんねんせい</u>ですか。
　　Nannensee desu ka.
　　What year are you in college?

B : <u>にねんせい</u>です。
　　Ninensee desu.
　　I'm a sophomore.

---

[2] It is not customary to write a question mark at the end of a question sentence in Japanese.

[3] The Japanese question word for "what" has two pronunciations: *nan* and *nani*. *Nan* is used immediately before *desu* or before a "counter" like *ji* (o'clock). The other form, *nani*, is used before a particle. *Nani* is also used in the combination *nanijin* (person of what nationality).

A：でんわばんごうは　なんばんですか。　　B：867-5309です。
Denwa bangoo wa　　　nanban desu ka.　　　　　Hachi roku nana go san zero kyuu desu.
What is your telephone number?　　　　　　　*It is 867-5309.*

3 Noun₁ の Noun₂

No is a particle that connects two nouns. The phrase *Sakura daigaku no gakusee* means "a student at Sakura University." The second noun *gakusee* provides the main idea[4] (being a student) and the first one *Sakura daigaku* makes it more specific (not a high school, but a college student). You can use *no* like the possessive ("Takeshi's") in English, as in the first example below. Here are some examples of *no* between two nouns. The main idea is always the noun₂, with the noun₁ providing restrictions, specifications, etc.

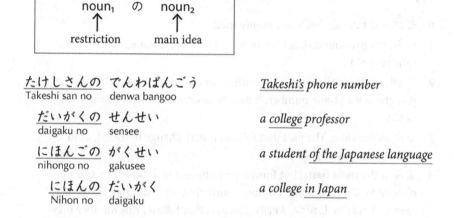

たけしさんの　でんわばんごう　　　　　*Takeshi's phone number*
Takeshi san no　denwa bangoo

だいがくの　せんせい　　　　　　　　　*a college professor*
daigaku no　sensee

にほんごの　がくせい　　　　　　　　　*a student of the Japanese language*
nihongo no　gakusee

にほんの　だいがく　　　　　　　　　　*a college in Japan*
Nihon no　daigaku

A phrase of the form "noun₁ *no* noun₂" acts more or less like one big noun. You can put it wherever you can put a noun, as in the following example:

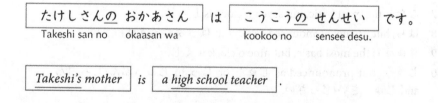

| たけしさんの　おかあさん | は | こうこうの　せんせい | です。 |
| Takeshi san no　okaasan wa | | kookoo no　sensee desu. | |

| *Takeshi's mother* | *is* | *a high school teacher* | . |

---

[4] Here is what we mean by the "main idea." In the phrase *Takeshi san no denwa bangoo* (Takeshi's phone number), the noun *denwa bangoo* (phone number) is the main idea, in the sense that if something is Takeshi's phone number, it is a phone number. The other noun *Takeshi san* is not the main idea, because Takeshi's phone number is not Takeshi.

表現ノート
ひょう　げん

あのう ▶ *Anoo* indicates that you have some reservations about saying what you are going to say next. You may be worried about interrupting something someone is currently doing, or sounding rude and impolite for asking personal questions, for example.

そうですか ▶ *Soo desu ka* acknowledges that you have understood what was just said. "Is that so?" (with rising intonation) or "I see" (with falling intonation).

Numbers ▶ Many number words have more than one pronunciation. Refer to the table on pp. 380-381 for a general picture.

0 ゼロ and れい are both commonly used.

1 いち, but pronounced as いっ in いっぷん (one minute) and いっさい (one year old).

2 に all the time. When you are reading out each digit separately, as when you give your phone number, it may be pronounced with a long vowel, as にい.

3 さん all the time. The part that follows it may change in sound, as in さんぷん, instead of さんふん.

4 よん is the most basic, but fourth-year student is よねんせい and four o'clock is よじ. In some combinations that we will later learn, it is read as し (as in しがつ, April). The part that follows this number may change in sound too, as in よんぷん.

5 ご all the time. When read out separately, it may be pronounced with a long vowel, as ごう.

6 ろく, but pronounced as ろっ in ろっぷん.

7 なな is the most basic, but seven o'clock is しちじ.

8 はち, but usually pronounced as はっ in はっぷん and はっさい.

9 きゅう is the most basic, but nine o'clock is くじ.

10 じゅう, but pronounced as じゅっ or じっ in じゅっぷん/じっぷん and じゅっさい/じっさい.

せんせい ▶ The word *sensee* is usually reserved for describing somebody else's occupation. *Watashi wa sensee desu* makes sense, but may sound slightly arrogant, because the word *sensee* actually means an "honorable master." If you (or a member of your family) are a teacher, and if you want to be really modest, you can use the word *kyooshi* instead.

さん ▶ *San* is placed after a name as a generic title. It goes both with a given name and a family name. Children are referred to as *chan* (and boys in particular as *kun*), rather than *san*. Professors, doctors, lawyers and others in "high-status occupations" are usually referred to with the title *sensee* rather than *san*. *San* and other title words are never used in reference to oneself.

Referring to the person you are talking to ▶ The word for "you," *anata*, is not very commonly used in Japanese. Instead, we use the name and a title like *san* and *sensee* to refer to the person you are talking to. Therefore, a sentence like "Ms. Hart, are you Canadian?" should be:

ハートさんは カナダじんですか。
Haato san wa   kanadajin desu ka.

instead of ハートさん、あなたは カナダじんですか。
Haato san,   anata wa   kanadajin desu ka.

Culture Notes

にほんじんの なまえ Japanese Names
Nihonjin no namae

When Japanese give their name, they say their family name first and given name last (middle names do not exist). When introducing themselves, they often say only their family name. Here are some typical Japanese names.

Family name		Given name			
		Men		Women	
さとう	Satoo	ゆうと	Yuuto	さくら	Sakura
すずき	Suzuki	かいと	Kaito	ゆい	Yui
たかはし	Takahashi	そうた	Soota	あおい	Aoi
たなか	Tanaka	はるき	Haruki	りん	Rin
いとう	Itoo	だいすけ	Daisuke	かな	Kana

Most Japanese names are written in kanji. For example, Tanaka is usually written as 田中, which means "middle of the rice field." Family names are often related to nature or geographical features. Because many kanji share the same reading, names with the same pronunciation may be written with different kanji, such as 裕子 and 優子 for the feminine name *Yuuko*.

れんしゅう P r a c t i c e

Ⅰ メアリーさんは アメリカじんです ☞Grammar 1

	Hart, Mary	きむら たけし Kimura Takeshi	Kim, Sora	Smith, Robert	やましたせんせい Yamashita sensee
Nationality	American	Japanese	Korean （かんこくじん） kankokujin	British （イギリスじん） igirisujin	Japanese
Year	2nd year	4th year	3rd year	4th year	
Age	19	22	20	22	47

A. Look at the chart above and describe each person's nationality. 🔊 K01-09

[Example] メアリーさん → メアリーさんは アメリカじんです。
Mearii san　　　Mearii san wa　　amerikajin desu.

1. たけしさん　　2. ソラさん　　3. ロバートさん　　4. やましたせんせい
Takeshi san　　　Sora san　　　Robaato san　　　Yamashita sensee

B. Tell which year they are in school. 🔊 K01-10

～ねんせい （. . . year student)
nensee

1	いちねんせい ichinensee	3	さんねんせい sannensee	5	ごねんせい gonensee
2	にねんせい ninensee	4	よねんせい yonensee	6	ろくねんせい rokunensee

[Example] メアリーさん → メアリーさんは にねんせいです。
Mearii san　　　Mearii san wa　　ninensee desu.

1. たけしさん　　2. ソラさん　　3. ロバートさん
Takeshi san　　　Sora san　　　Robaato san

C. Tell how old they are. 🔊 K01-11

~さい　(... years old)
sai

1	いっさい issai	6	ろくさい rokusai	11	じゅういっさい juuissai
2	にさい nisai	7	ななさい nanasai	20	はたち／にじゅっさい* hatachi　nijussai
3	さんさい sansei	8	はっさい hassai	21	にじゅういっさい nijuuissai
4	よんさい yonsai	9	きゅうさい kyuusai	35	さんじゅうごさい sanjuugosai
5	ごさい gosai	10	じゅっさい* jussai	40	よんじゅっさい* yonjussai

*じゅっさい (jussai), にじゅっさい (nijussai), etc., are also pronounced じっさい (jissai), にじっさい (nijissai), etc.

(Example) メアリーさん → メアリーさんは じゅうきゅうさいです。
Mearii san　　　Mearii san wa　　juukyuusai desu.

1. たけしさん　2. ソラさん　3. ロバートさん　4. やましたせんせい
Takeshi san　　Sora san　　　Robaato san　　　Yamashita sensee

D. Group Work—Tell your group members (1) your name, (2) your nationality, (3) your year in school, and (4) your age.

(Example) （わたしは）メアリーです。アメリカじんです。
(Watashi wa)　Mearii desu.　　Amerikajin desu.

にねんせいです。じゅうきゅうさいです。
Ninensee desu.　　Juukyuusai desu.

II メアリーさんは アメリカじんですか ☞Grammar 2

A. Ask and answer questions using the given cues. 🔊 K01-12

(Example 1) メアリーさん／アメリカじん
Mearii san　　amerikajin

→ Q：メアリーさんは アメリカじんですか。
Mearii san wa　　amerikajin desu ka.

A：はい、そうです。
Hai,　soo desu.

(Example 2) メアリーさん／さんねんせい
Mearii san　　　sannensee

→　Q：メアリーさんは さんねんせいですか。
　　　　Mearii san　　　　sannensee desu ka.

　　A：いいえ、にねんせいです。
　　　　Iie,　　ninensee desu.

1. メアリーさん／いちねんせい
   Mearii san　　　ichinensee

2. たけしさん／にほんじん
   Takeshi san　　nihonjin

3. たけしさん／じゅうきゅうさい
   Takeshi san　　juukyuusai

4. ソラさん／アメリカじん
   Sora san　　amerikajin

5. ロバートさん／よねんせい
   Robaato san　　　yonensee

6. ロバートさん／にじゅういっさい
   Robaato san　　　nijuuissai

7. やましたせんせい／にほんじん
   Yamashita sensee　　nihonjin

B. Ask about their age and year in school.

(a) Age 🔊 K01-13

(Example) メアリーさん　→　Q：メアリーさんは なんさいですか。
　　　　　　Mearii san　　　　　　Mearii san wa　　nansai desu ka.

　　　　　　　　　　　　　　A：じゅうきゅうさいです。
　　　　　　　　　　　　　　　　Juukyuusai desu.

1. たけしさん　　2. ソラさん　　3. ロバートさん　　4. やましたせんせい
   Takeshi san　　　Sora san　　　Robaato san　　　Yamashita sensee

(b) Year in school 🔊 K01-14

(Example) メアリーさん　→　Q：メアリーさんは なんねんせいですか。
　　　　　　Mearii san　　　　　　Mearii san wa　　nannensee desu ka.

　　　　　　　　　　　　　　A：にねんせいです。
　　　　　　　　　　　　　　　　Ninensee desu.

1. たけしさん　　2. ソラさん　　3. ロバートさん
   Takeshi san　　　Sora san　　　Robaato san

C. Look at the chart about Mary's host family and answer the questions. 🔊 K01-15

Mary's host family

	おとうさん otoosan (father)	おかあさん okaasan (mother)	おにいさん oniisan (elder brother)	いもうと imooto (younger sister)
Occupation/ School	かいしゃいん kaishain (works for a company)	かんごし kangoshi (nurse)	だいがくいんせい daigakuinsee (graduate student)	こうこうせい kookoosee (high school student)
Age	48	45	23	16

1. おとうさんは　かいしゃいんですか。
   Otoosan wa　　　kaishain desu ka.

2. おとうさんは　なんさいですか。
   Otoosan wa　　　nansai desu ka.

3. おかあさんは　せんせいですか。
   Okaasan wa　　　sensee desu ka.

4. おかあさんは　なんさいですか。
   Okaasan wa　　　nansai desu ka.

5. おにいさんは　かいしゃいんですか。
   Oniisan wa　　　kaishain desu ka.

6. おにいさんは　なんさいですか。
   Oniisan wa　　　nansai desu ka.

7. いもうとは　だいがくせいですか。
   Imooto wa　　　daigakusee desu ka.

8. いもうとは　なんさいですか。
   Imooto wa　　　nansai desu ka.

Ⅲ にほんごの がくせいです ☞Grammar 3

A. Translate the following phrases into Japanese using の (*no*). 🔊 K01-16

(Example) student of the Japanese language → にほんごの がくせい
                                               nihongo no   gakusee

1. my teacher
2. my telephone number
3. my name
4. Takashi's major
5. Mary's friend
6. student at the University of London
7. teacher of the Japanese language
8. high school teacher

B. Look at the chart and describe each person using the given cues.

	Hart, Mary	きむら たけし Kimura Takeshi	Kim, Sora	Smith, Robert	やましたせんせい Yamashita sensee
School	U. of Arizona	Sakura Univ.	Seoul Univ.	U. of London	Sakura Univ.
Major	Japanese	history (れきし) rekishi	computer こんぴゅうたあ (コンピューター) konpyuutaa	business びじねす (ビジネス) bijinesu	(Japanese teacher)

(a) School 🔊 K01-17

(Example) メアリーさん → メアリーさんは アリゾナだいがくの
        Mearii san   Mearii san wa   Arizona daigaku no

                  がくせいです。
                  gakusee desu.

1. たけしさん   2. ソラさん   3. ロバートさん   4. やましたせんせい
  Takeshi san   Sora san   Robaato san   Yamashita sensee

(b) Major 🔊 K01-18

(Example) メアリーさん → メアリーさんの せんこうは にほんごです。
        Mearii san   Mearii san no   senkoo wa   nihongo desu.

1. たけしさん   2. ソラさん   3. ロバートさん
  Takeshi san   Sora san   Robaato san

C. Answer the following questions. 🔊 K01-19

1. メアリーさんの せんこうは ビジネスですか。
    Mearii san no　　　　senkoo wa　　　　bijinesu desu ka.

2. たけしさんは アリゾナだいがくの がくせいですか。
    Takeshi san wa　　　Arizona daigaku no　　　　gakusee desu ka.

3. たけしさんの せんこうは なんですか。
    Takeshi san no　　　senkoo wa　　　nan desu ka.

4. ロバートさんは ロンドンだいがくの がくせいですか。
    Robaato san wa　　　　Rondon daigaku no　　　　gakusee desu ka.

5. ロバートさんの せんこうは なんですか。
    Robaato san no　　　　senkoo wa　　　nan desu ka.

6. ソラさんの せんこうは けいざい (economics) ですか。
    Sora san no　　　senkoo wa　　　keezai desu ka.

7. やましたせんせいは にほんだいがくの せんせいですか。
    Yamashita sensee wa　　　Nihon daigaku no　　　sensee desu ka.

D. Group Work—Ask group members questions as in C above.

Ⅳ でんわばんごう (Telephone Numbers)

A. Pair Work—Read the dialogue below with your partner. 🔊 K01-20

A : でんわばんごうは なんばんですか。
    Denwa bangoo wa　　　nanban desu ka.

B : 283-9547です。
    Ni hachi san kyuu go yon nana desu.

A : 283-9547ですね。* 　　　(*ね＝right?)
    Ni hachi san kyuu go yon nana desu ne.

B : はい、そうです。
    Hai,　　　soo desu.

B. Group Work—Use the dialogue above and ask three classsmates their telephone numbers.

name	telephone number
( )	( )
( )	( )
( )	( )

Ⅴ じかん (Time)

🔊 K01-21

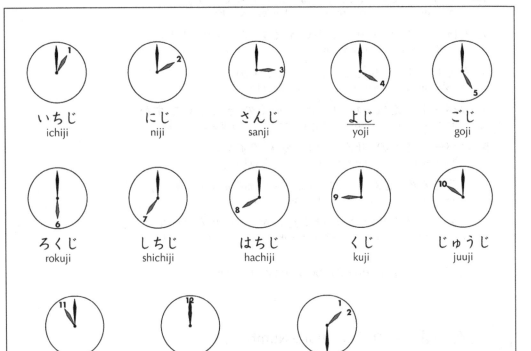

いちじ ichiji	にじ niji	さんじ sanji	<u>よじ</u> yoji	ごじ goji
ろくじ rokuji	しちじ shichiji	はちじ hachiji	くじ kuji	じゅうじ juuji
じゅういちじ juuichiji	じゅうにじ juuniji	いちじはん ichiji han		

A. Look at the following pictures and tell the time. 🔊 K01-22

(Example) いちじはんです。
Ichiji han desu.

e.g.

(1)

(2)

(3)

(4)

(5)

(6)

(7)

(8)

B. Pair Work—Using the pictures in A, ask the time as in the example.

(Example)　A：すみません。いま なんじですか。
　　　　　　Sumimasen.　　Ima　　nanji desu ka.

　　　　　B：いちじはんです。
　　　　　　Ichiji han desu.

　　　　　A：ありがとう ございます。
　　　　　　Arigatoo　　　　gozaimasu.

　　　　　B：いいえ。
　　　　　　Iie.

C. Look at the map and answer the questions. 🔊 K01-23

(Example)　Q：とうきょうは いま なんじですか。
　　　　　　Tookyoo wa　　　ima　　nanji desu ka.

　　　　　A：ごぜん さんじです。
　　　　　　Gozen　　sanji desu.

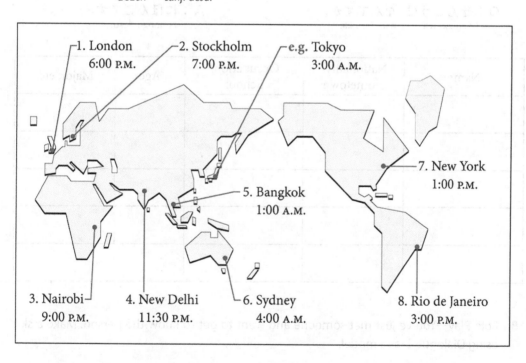

1. London
6:00 P.M.

2. Stockholm
7:00 P.M.

e.g. Tokyo
3:00 A.M.

7. New York
1:00 P.M.

5. Bangkok
1:00 A.M.

3. Nairobi
9:00 P.M.

4. New Delhi
11:30 P.M.

6. Sydney
4:00 A.M.

8. Rio de Janeiro
3:00 P.M.

Ⅵ まとめの れんしゅう (Review Exercises)

A. Class Activity—Ask five classmates questions and fill in the chart below. 🔊 K01-24

(Example)

Q：おなまえは？ (What is your name?)
　Onamae wa?

A：メアリー・ハートです。
　Mearii Haato desu.

Q：ごしゅっしんは？ (Where do you come from?)
　Goshusshin wa?

A：アリゾナです。
　Arizona desu.

Q：おしごとは？ (What is your occupation?)
　Oshigoto wa?

A：がくせいです。
　Gakusee desu.

Q：なんねんせいですか。
　Nannensee desu ka.

A：にねんせいです。
　Ninensee desu.

Q：なんさいですか。
　Nansai desu ka.

A：じゅうきゅうさいです。
　Juukyuusai desu.

Q：せんこうは　なんですか。
　Senkoo wa　　nan desu ka.

A：にほんごです。
　Nihongo desu.

Name	Nationality/Hometown	Occupation/School	Age	Major, etc.

B. Role Play—You've just met someone and want to get to know the person. Make a skit using Dialogue Ⅰ as a model.

C. Self-introduction—Using Dialogue Ⅱ as a model, introduce yourself to the class.

Useful Expressions

じかん
T i m e

Hours
1 いちじ ichiji
2 にじ niji
3 さんじ sanji
4 よじ yoji
5 ごじ goji
6 ろくじ rokuji
7 しちじ shichiji
8 はちじ hachiji
9 くじ kuji
10 じゅうじ juuji
11 じゅういちじ juuichiji
12 じゅうにじ juuniji

Minutes	
1 いっぷん ippun	11 じゅういっぷん juuippun
2 にふん nifun	12 じゅうにふん juunifun
3 さんぷん sanpun	13 じゅうさんぷん juusanpun
4 よんぷん yonpun	14 じゅうよんぷん juuyonpun
5 ごふん gofun	15 じゅうごふん juugofun
6 ろっぷん roppun	16 じゅうろっぷん juuroppun
7 ななふん nanafun	17 じゅうななふん juunanafun
8 はっぷん／ happun	18 じゅうはっぷん／ juuhappun
はちふん hachifun	じゅうはちふん juuhachifun
9 きゅうふん kyuufun	19 じゅうきゅうふん juukyuufun
10 じゅっぷん * juppun	20 にじゅっぷん * nijuppun
	30 さんじゅっぷん * sanjuppun

* じゅっぷん (juppun), にじゅっぷん (nijuppun), さんじゅっぷん (sanjuppun), etc., are also pronounced じっぷん (jippun), にじっぷん (nijippun), さんじっぷん (sanjippun), etc.

ごぜん くじ じゅうはっぷん
gozen kuji juuhappun

ごご さんじ
gogo sanji

いちじ ごじゅうごふん
ichiji gojuugofun

よじはん／よじ さんじゅっぷん
yoji han yoji sanjuppun

第2課
だいにか

かいもの Shopping

L E S S O N 2

In this lesson, we will . . . .

🍡 Ask and answer how much things cost
🍡 Do shopping
🍡 Order food in a restaurant

かいわ D i a l o g u e

I 🔊 Mary goes to a flea market. K02-01/02

1	メアリー： Mearii	すみません。これは いくらですか。 Sumimasen.　　Kore wa　ikura desu ka.
2	みせのひと： Mise no hito	それは さんぜんえんです。 Sore wa　sanzen en desu.
3	メアリー： Mearii	たかいですね。じゃあ、あのとけいは いくらですか。 Takai desu ne.　　Jaa,　　ano tokee wa　　ikura desu ka.
4	みせのひと： Mise no hito	あれは さんぜんごひゃくえんです。 Are wa　sanzengohyaku en desu.
5	メアリー： Mearii	そうですか。あれも たかいですね。 Soo desu ka.　　Are mo　takai desu ne.
6	みせのひと： Mise no hito	これは せんはっぴゃくえんですよ。 Kore wa　senhappyaku en desu yo.
7	メアリー： Mearii	じゃあ、そのとけいを ください。 Jaa,　　sono tokee o　　kudasai.

＊　　　　＊　　　　＊

A man finds a wallet on the ground.

8	しらないひと： Shiranai hito	これは だれの さいふですか。 Kore wa　dare no　saifu desu ka.
9	メアリー： Mearii	わたしの さいふです。 Watashi no　saifu desu.
10		ありがとう ございます。 Arigatoo　　gozaimasu.

II After shopping, Mary goes to a restaurant. 🔊 K02-03/04

1 みせのひと：いらっしゃいませ。メニューを どうぞ。
Mise no hito　Irasshaimase.　　Menyuu o　　doozo.

2 メアリー：　どうも。これは なんですか。
Mearii　　　Doomo.　Kore wa　nan desu ka.

3 みせのひと：どれですか。ああ、とんかつです。
Mise no hito　Dore desu ka.　Aa,　　tonkatsu desu.

4 メアリー：　とんかつ？ さかなですか。
Mearii　　　Tonkatsu?　Sakana desu ka.

5 みせのひと：いいえ、さかなじゃないです。にくです。おいしいですよ。
Mise no hito　Iie,　　sakana ja nai desu.　Niku desu.　Oishii desu yo.

6 メアリー：　じゃあ、これを おねがいします。
Mearii　　　Jaa,　　kore o　onegaishimasu.

＊　　　＊　　　＊

7 メアリー：　すみません。トイレは どこですか。
Mearii　　　Sumimasen.　Toire wa　doko desu ka.

8 みせのひと：あそこです。
Mise no hito　Asoko desu.

9 メアリー：　ありがとう ございます。
Mearii　　　Arigatoo　gozaimasu.

Ⓘ

Mary: Excuse me. How much is this?

Vendor: It is 3,000 yen.

Mary: It's expensive. Well then, how much is that watch?

Vendor: That is 3,500 yen.

Mary: I see. That is expensive, too.

Vendor: This is 1,800 yen.

Mary: Then, I'll take that watch.

＊　　＊　　＊

Stranger: Whose wallet is this?

Mary: It's my wallet. Thank you very much.

ⒾⒾ

Restaurant attendant: Welcome. Here's the menu.

Mary: Thank you. What is this?

Restaurant attendant: Which one? Oh, it is *tonkatsu* (pork cutlet).

Mary: *Tonkatsu?* Is it fish?

Restaurant attendant: No, it is not fish. It is meat. It is delicious.

Mary: Then, I'll have this.

＊　　＊　　＊

Mary: Excuse me. Where is the restroom?

Restaurant attendant: It is over there.

Mary: Thank you very much.

たんご

 K02-05 (J-E)
K02-06 (E-J)

Vocabulary

Words That Point

* これ	kore	this one
* それ	sore	that one
* あれ	are	that one (over there)
* どれ	dore	which one
この	kono	this . . .
* その	sono	that . . .
* あの	ano	that . . . (over there)
どの	dono	which . . .
ここ	koko	here
そこ	soko	there
* あそこ	asoko	over there
* どこ	doko	where
* だれ	dare	who

Food

* おいしい	oishii	delicious
* さかな	sakana	fish
* とんかつ	tonkatsu	pork cutlet
* にく	niku	meat
* メニュー	menyuu	menu
やさい	yasai	vegetable

Things

かさ	kasa	umbrella
かばん	kaban	bag
くつ	kutsu	shoes
* さいふ	saifu	wallet
ジーンズ	jiinzu	jeans
じてんしゃ	jitensha	bicycle
しんぶん	shinbun	newspaper
スマホ	sumaho	smartphone; mobile
Tシャツ	tiishatsu	T-shirt
* とけい	tokee	watch; clock
ノート	nooto	notebook

*Words that appear in the dialogue

ペン	pen	pen
ぼうし	booshi	hat; cap
ほん	hon	book

Places

ぎんこう	ginkoo	bank
コンビニ	konbini	convenience store
* トイレ	toire	toilet; restroom
としょかん	toshokan	library
ゆうびんきょく	yuubinkyoku	post office

Countries

イギリス	Igirisu	Britain
かんこく	Kankoku	Korea
ちゅうごく	Chuugoku	China

Majors

えいご	eego	English (language)
けいざい	keezai	economics
コンピューター	konpyuutaa	computer
ビジネス	bijinesu	business
れきし	rekishi	history

Family

| おかあさん | okaasan | mother |
| おとうさん | otoosan | father |

Money Matters

* いくら	ikura	how much
* ～えん	. . . en	. . . yen
* たかい	takai	expensive; high

Expressions

* いらっしゃいませ	irasshaimase	Welcome (to our store).
* (～を)おねがいします	(. . . o) onegaishimasu	. . . , please.
* (～を)ください	(. . . o) kudasai	Please give me . . .
* じゃあ	jaa	then . . . ; if that is the case, . . .
* どうぞ	doozo	Please.; Here it is.
* どうも	doomo	Thank you.

ぶんぽう Grammar

1 これ / それ / あれ / どれ

When you want to talk about "this thing," "that one," and so forth, you can use *kore*, *sore*, and *are*.

> これは いくらですか。
> Kore wa ikura desu ka.

How much is this?

> それは さんぜんえんです。
> Sore wa sanzen en desu.

That is 3,000 yen.

We have one word for "this" and two words for "that." *Kore* refers to a thing that is close to you, the speaker ("this thing here"). *Sore* is something that is close to the person you are talking to ("that thing in front of you"), and *are* refers to a thing that is neither close to the speaker nor the listener ("that one over there").

> あれは わたしの ペンです。
> Are wa watashi no pen desu.

> これは わたしの ペンです。
> Kore wa watashi no pen desu.

> それは わたしの ペンです。
> Sore wa watashi no pen desu.

There is also an expression *dore* for "which."[1]

> どれですか。
> Dore desu ka.

Which one is it (that you are talking about)?

Avoid using these *re* series words in reference to people in their earshot as in introducing people:

> ×これは ともだちの メアリーさんです。
> Kore wa tomodachi no Mearii san desu.

This is my friend Mary.[2]

2 この / その / あの / どの + Noun

In the last section, we learned that *kore*, *sore*, and *are* stand for "this thing" and "that thing." If you want to say "this book," "that watch," and so forth, you can use *kono*, *sono*, and *ano* together with a noun. In other words, the *re* series stand alone and are directly followed by *wa*, while the *no* series must be followed by a noun before it gets connected to *wa*. You can use *kono*, *sono*, and *ano* plus a noun in reference to people as well as things, unlike *kore*, *sore*, and *are*, which are sometimes considered impolite if they are used in reference to people.

このとけいは いくらですか。
Kono tokee wa   ikura desu ka.

How much is this watch?

そのとけいは さんぜんえんです。
Sono tokee wa   sanzen en desu.

That watch (in your hand) is 3,000 yen.

あのがくせいは りゅうがくせいです。
Ano gakusee wa   ryuugakusee desu.

That student over there is an international student.

If you already know that one of several students is Japanese but do not know which, you can say:

どのがくせいが[3] にほんじんですか。
Dono gakusee ga   nihonjin desu ka.

Which student is Japanese?

To summarize:

これ（は〜）	この noun（は〜）	close to the person speaking
それ（は〜）	その noun（は〜）	close to the person listening
あれ（は〜）	あの noun（は〜）	far from both people
どれ（が〜）	どの noun（が〜）	unknown

---

[1] Question words like *dore* and *nani* cannot be followed by the particle *wa*. Instead, you must use the particle *ga* and say, *Dore ga anata no pen desu ka.* (Which one is your pen?) We will turn to this issue in Lesson 8.

[2] It is okay to use the *re* series words for humans if you are referring to people that have appeared in an earlier passage, or if you are just pointing at a picture of a person.

[3] Since *dono* is a question word, just like *dore* discussed in footnote 1, we cannot use the particle *wa* with it; we must use *ga*.

3 ここ / そこ / あそこ / どこ

We will learn just one more *ko-so-a-do* set: *koko, soko, asoko,* and *doko* are words for places.

ここ	*here, near me*
そこ	*there, near you*
あそこ	*over there*
どこ	*where*

You can ask for directions by saying:

すみません。ゆうびんきょくは どこですか。　　　*Excuse me. Where is the post office?*
Sumimasen.　　Yuubinkyoku wa　　doko desu ka.

You can point toward the post office and say:

（ゆうびんきょくは） あそこです。　　　*(The post office is) right over there.*
(Yuubinkyoku wa)　　asoko desu.

We will learn how to give more specific directions in Lesson 4.

4 だれの Noun

In Lesson 1, we learned how to say things like *Mearii san no denwa bangoo* (Mary's phone number) and *Takeshi san no okaasan* (Takeshi's mother). We now learn how to ask who something belongs to. The question word for "who" is *dare,* and for "whose," we add the particle *no* and say *dare no.*

A：これは だれの かばんですか。　　　<u>*Whose* bag is this?</u>
　Kore wa　dare no　kaban desu ka.

B：それは ソラさんの かばんです。　　　*That is <u>Sora's</u> bag.*
　Sore wa　Sora san no　kaban desu.

5 Noun も

In Lesson 1, we learned how to say "Item A is this, item B is that." We now learn how to say "Item A is this, and item B is this, too." The word for "too" in Japanese is particle *mo.*

たけしさんは にほんじんです。　　　*Takeshi is a Japanese person.*
Takeshi san wa　nihonjin desu.

ゆいさん<u>も</u> にほんじんです。　　　*Yui is Japanese, <u>too.</u>*
Yui san mo　nihonjin desu.

Pay attention to where the particle is placed. In English, the word "too" can be placed after the sentence as a whole, as in the translation above. In Japanese you can only put *mo* directly after the item that is just like another that has been introduced earlier. In the example above *Yui san* gets *mo*, because it is the "likewise" item which shares the property of being a Japanese person with *Takeshi san*.[4]

A	は	X	です。	A is X.
B	も	X	です。	B *too* is X.

6 Noun じゃないです

To negate a statement of the form *X wa Y desu*, where Y is a noun, you replace *desu* with *ja nai desu*.[5]

やまださんは　がくせいじゃないです。　　*Mr. Yamada is not a student.*
Yamada san wa　　gakusee ja nai desu.

You find several stylistic variants in negative sentences. *Ja nai desu* is very colloquial. The more formal replacement for *nai desu* is *arimasen*. *Ja* is a contraction of *de wa*, which is more formal and more appropriate in the written language. Thus in addition to the above sentence, you also find:

やまださんは　がくせいじゃありません。　(more conservative speech style)
Yamada san wa　　gakusee ja arimasen.

やまださんは　がくせいではありません。　(formal, appropriate for writing)
Yamada san wa　　gakusee de wa arimasen.

---

[4] We cannot use *mo* to describe a situation like the following: Our friend, Pat, has dual citizenship; Pat is a Japanese, but at the same time, she is an American. To describe the second half of this situation, we cannot say, *Patto mo amerikajin desu*, because the sentence would mean that Pat, in addition to somebody that has been mentioned, is an American. Neither can we say, *Patto wa amerikajin mo desu*. (Japanese speakers would say, *Patto wa amerikajin demo arimasu*.)

[5] In the dialogues, there are two sentences ending with *desu* that call for special attention: *Are mo takai desu ne* (That one too is expensive), and *Oishii desu yo* (It is delicious). These sentences cannot be negated by replacing *desu* with *ja nai desu*, because *takai* and *oishii* are not nouns. *Are mo takai ja nai desu* and *oishii ja nai desu* are therefore not grammatical. Instead, one would have to say *takaku nai desu* and *oishiku nai desu*. We will learn about the conjugation pattern of adjectives in Lesson 5.

Desu and *ja nai* must always be accompanied by a noun. In answer to a question, therefore, *desu* and *ja nai* do not stand alone.

A：にほんじんですか。
Nihonjin desu ka.

Are you Japanese?

B：いいえ、にほんじんじゃないです。
Iie,　　nihonjin ja nai desu.

No, I am not Japanese.

×いいえ、じゃないです。
Iie,　　ja nai desu.

affirmative:	(X は) Y です。		X is Y.
negative:	(X は) Y	じゃないです。 じゃありません。 ではありません。	X is not Y.

7 ～ね／～よ

Statements often end with the tags *ne* or *yo*, depending on the way the speaker views the interaction with the listener. If you are seeking the listener's confirmation or agreement to what you are saying, you add *ne* ("right?") to your sentence.

リーさんの せんこうは ぶんがく ですね。
Rii san no　　senkoo wa　　bungaku desu ne.

Ms. Lee, your major is literature, right?

これは にくじゃないですね。
Kore wa　niku ja nai desu ne.

This is not meat, is it?

If you want to tell the listener that you are fully confident of what you are saying and the listener had better believe it, use *yo* ("I tell you") at the end of your sentence.

とんかつは さかなじゃないですよ。
Tonkatsu wa　　sakana ja nai desu yo.

Let me assure you. "Tonkatsu" is not fish.

スミスさんは イギリスじんですよ。
Sumisu san wa　　igirisujin desu yo.

(In case you're wondering,) Mr. Smith is British.

表現ノート
ひょう　げん

（〜を）ください ▶ *(. . . o) kudasai* is "Please give me X." You can use it to request (concrete) items in general.

（〜を）おねがいします ▶ *(. . . o) onegaishimasu* too is a request for item X. When used to ask for a concrete object, *(. . . o) onegaishimasu* sounds slightly more upscale than *(. . . o) kudasai*. It is heard often when ordering food at a restaurant ("I will have . . ."). *(. . . o) onegaishimasu* can also be used to ask for "abstract objects," such as repairs, explanations, and understanding.

（〜を）どうぞ ▶ *(. . . o) doozo* is used when an offer is made with respect to item X. In the dialogue, the restaurant attendant uses it when he is about to hand the menu to the customer.

On the pronunciation of number words ▶ Note that the words for 300, 600, 800, 3,000, and 8,000 involve sound changes. "Counters" whose first sound is *h*, like *hyaku* (hundred), generally change in sound after 3, 6, and 8. Some counters that begin with *s*, like *sen* (thousand), change in sound after 3 and 8. Refer to the table on pages 380-381.

Big numbers ▶ In addition to the digit markers for tens (*juu*), hundreds (*hyaku*), and thousands (*sen*), which are found in Western languages as well, Japanese uses the marker for tens of thousands (*man*). Thus 20,000, for example, is *niman* ($= 2 \times 10,000$), rather than *nijuusen* ($= 20 \times 1,000$). While the next unit marker in Western languages is one million, Japanese describes that number as $100 \times 10,000$, that is, *hyakuman*.

More complicated numbers can be considered the sums of smaller numbers, as in the following examples.

234,567	=	$23 \times 10,000$	にじゅうさんまん	(nijuusanman)
		$4 \times 1,000$	よんせん	(yonsen)
		5×100	ごひゃく	(gohyaku)
		6×10	ろくじゅう	(rokujuu)
		7	なな	(nana)

にほんの おかね Japanese Currency
Nihon no okane

Japan's official currency is the yen, which is pronounced *en* in Japanese. The bills and coins currently in circulation are the following:

10,000-yen bill

A portrait of Yukichi Fukuzawa (1835-1901), a philosopher and the founder of Keio University.

5,000-yen bill

A portrait of Ichiyoo Higuchi (1872-1896), a writer and poet.

2,000-yen bill

Shurei Gate, the second gate of Shuri Castle in Okinawa.

1,000-yen bill

A portrait of Hideyo Noguchi (1876-1928), a bacteriologist who devoted himself to yellow fever research.

500-yen coin

100-yen coin

50-yen coin

10-yen coin

5-yen coin

1-yen coin

All bills and coins are different sizes. For example, the bills slightly descend in length from 10,000 yen to 1,000 yen. Although credit cards and mobile payments are widespread in Japan, some small shops and restaurants may not accept them, even in major cities. Consequently, most people usually carry a certain amount of cash with them.

れんしゅう Practice

I すうじ (Numbers)

 K02-07

100	ひゃく * hyaku	1,000	せん * sen	10,000	いちまん * ichiman
200	にひゃく nihyaku	2,000	にせん nisen	20,000	にまん niman
300	さんびゃく sanbyaku	3,000	さんぜん sanzen	30,000	さんまん sanman
400	よんひゃく yonhyaku	4,000	よんせん yonsen	40,000	よんまん yonman
500	ごひゃく gohyaku	5,000	ごせん gosen	50,000	ごまん goman
600	ろっぴゃく roppyaku	6,000	ろくせん rokusen	60,000	ろくまん rokuman
700	ななひゃく nanahyaku	7,000	ななせん nanasen	70,000	ななまん nanaman
800	はっぴゃく happyaku	8,000	はっせん hassen	80,000	はちまん hachiman
900	きゅうひゃく kyuuhyaku	9,000	きゅうせん kyuusen	90,000	きゅうまん kyuuman

* Note that 10,000 is _ichiman_ (not _man_), while 10 is _juu_, 100 is _hyaku_, and 1,000 is _sen_.

A. Read the following numbers. K02-08

(a) 34	(e) 125	(i) 1,300	(m) 64,500
(b) 67	(f) 515	(j) 3,400	(n) 92,340
(c) 83	(g) 603	(k) 8,900	
(d) 99	(h) 850	(l) 35,000	

B. Look at the pictures and answer how much the things are. K02-09

(Example) Q：ペんンは　いくらですか。
Pen wa　ikura desu ka.

A：はちじゅうえんです。
Hachijuu en desu.

e.g. ペんン

￥80

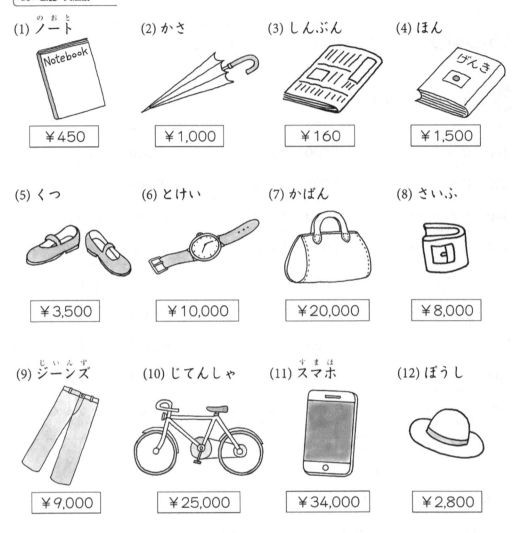

(1) ノート
¥450

(2) かさ
¥1,000

(3) しんぶん
¥160

(4) ほん
¥1,500

(5) くつ
¥3,500

(6) とけい
¥10,000

(7) かばん
¥20,000

(8) さいふ
¥8,000

(9) ジーンズ
¥9,000

(10) じてんしゃ
¥25,000

(11) スマホ
¥34,000

(12) ぼうし
¥2,800

C. Pair Work—One of you looks at picture A (p. 69) and the other looks at picture B (p. 79). Find out the price of all items. (Don't look at the other picture.)

Example) A： ノートは いくらですか。
Nooto wa　　ikura desu ka.

B： ひゃくえんです。
Hyaku en desu.

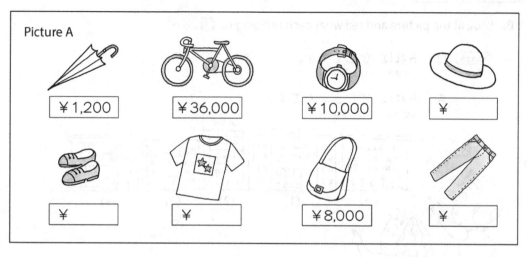

Ⅱ これは なんですか ☞Grammar 1

A. Items (1) through (6) are near you, and items (7) through (12) are near your friend. Your friend asks what these things are called in Japanese. Pay attention to これ (kore) and それ (sore). K02-10

Example 1

Friend：それは なんですか。
　　　　Sore wa　nan desu ka.

You：これは ペンです。
　　　Kore wa　pen desu.

Example 2

Friend：これは なんですか。
　　　　Kore wa　nan desu ka.

You：それは Tシャツです。
　　　Sore wa　tiishatsu desu.

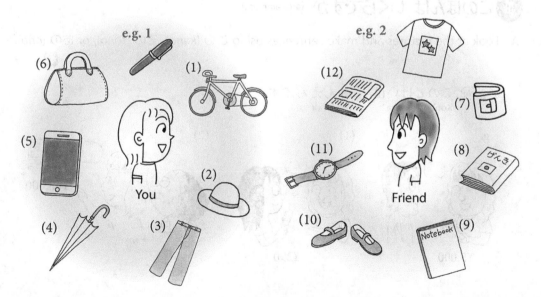

B. Look at the picture and tell what each building is. 🔊 K02-11

Example Q : あれは なんですか。
　　　　　　Are wa　　nan desu ka.

A : あれは としょかんです。
　　　　Are wa　　toshokan desu.

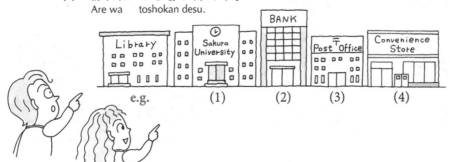

e.g.　　　(1)　　　(2)　　　(3)　　　(4)

C. Pair Work—Point out five things in the classroom and ask your partner what they are using これ (*kore*), それ (*sore*), or あれ (*are*). Refer to the picture on p. 81 for the vocabulary.

Example 1

A : あれは なんですか。
　　Are wa　　nan desu ka.

B : あれは とけいです。
　　Are wa　　tokee desu.

Example 2

A : それは なんですか。
　　Sore wa　　nan desu ka.

B : これは ペンです。
　　Kore wa　　pen desu.

Ⅲ このほんは いくらですか ☛Grammar 2

A. Look at the pictures and make sentences using この (*kono*), その (*sono*), or あの (*ano*).
🔊 K02-12

Example このとけいは ごせんえんです。
　　　　　Kono tokee wa　　gosen en desu.

e.g.　　　　　　　　(1)　　　　　　　　(2)

¥5,000　　　　　　¥290　　　　　　¥68,000

¥4,300

¥3,500

¥17,000

B. Pair Work—One of you looks at card A and the other looks at card B (p. 80). Ask and answer questions to find out the price of each item. Use この (kono), その (sono), or あの (ano) appropriately. After finding out the price of all items, decide on one item you want to buy.

Example Customer ： すみません。このほんは いくらですか。
Sumimasen.　　Kono hon wa　ikura desu ka.

Vendor ： にせんろっぴゃくえんです。
Nisen roppyaku en desu.

*　　　*　　　*

Customer ： じゃあ、そのかさを ください。
Jaa,　　　sono kasa o　　kudasai.

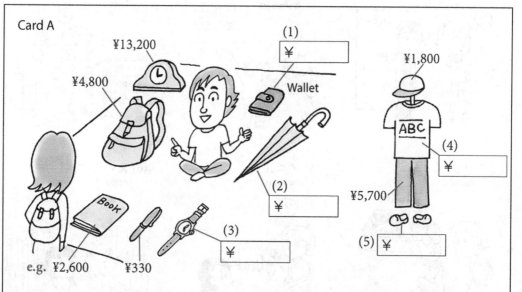

Card A

¥13,200

(1) ¥

Wallet

¥1,800

¥4,800

ABC

(4) ¥

(2) ¥

¥5,700

Book

(3) ¥

e.g. ¥2,600　　¥330

(5) ¥

Part I. You are a vendor at a flea market. Tell the customer how much each item is.
Part II. You are a customer. Ask for the prices of items (1)-(5).

C. Pair Work—Point out items your partner has and ask him/her as to how much they cost.

Example Pointing to your partner's T-shirt.

A：それは／そのＴシャツは いくらですか。
Sore wa   Sono tiishatsu wa   ikura desu ka.

B：ごひゃくえんです。
Gohyaku en desu.

Ⅳ ぎんこうは あそこです ☞Grammar 3

Look at the pictures and answer where the following are. 🔊 K02-13

Example

B：すみません。ぎんこうは どこですか。
Sumimasen.   Ginkoo wa   doko desu ka.

A：あそこです。
Asoko desu.

B：ありがとう ございます。
Arigatoo   gozaimasu.

e.g.

(1) トイレ
toire

(2) としょかん
toshokan

(3) くつ
kutsu

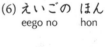

(4) やさい
yasai

(5) メニュー
menyuu

(6) えいごの ほん
eego no   hon

V これは だれの かさですか ☛Grammar 4

Pair Work—Point at each item below (picture A) and ask whose it is. Your partner will refer to picture B (p. 79) and tell you who it belongs to.

Example A：これは だれの かさですか。
Kore wa dare no kasa desu ka.

B：メアリーさんの かさです。
Mearii san no kasa desu.

Picture A

(1) 　(2) 　(3) 　(4) 　(5)

Switch roles with your partner.

(6) 　(7) 　(8) 　(9) 　(10)

VI おかあさんも にほんじんです ☛Grammar 5

Look at the pictures below and describe each. 🔊 K02-14

Example

おとうさんは にほんじんです。
Otoosan wa nihonjin desu.

おかあさんも にほんじんです。
Okaasan mo nihonjin desu.

e.g. Japanese

Father　Mother

(1) second year　(2) ¥5,800　(3) 22-years old

Mary　Masato　Takeshi　Robert

(4) 7:00

Seoul   Tokyo

(5) vegetables

(6) U. of London students

Robert   Naomi

Ⅶ メアリーさんは にほんじんじゃないです ☞Grammar 6
め あ り い

A. Look at the chart below and answer the questions. 🔊 K02-15

	Hart, Mary	きむら たけし Kimura Takeshi	Kim, Sora	Smith, Robert	やましたせんせい Yamashita sensee
Nationality	American	Japanese	Korean	British	Japanese
School	U. of Arizona	Sakura Univ.	Seoul Univ.	U. of London	Sakura Univ.
Major	Japanese	history	computer	business	(Japanese teacher)
Year	2nd year	4th year	3rd year	4th year	

Example Q：メアリーさんは にほんじんですか。
め あ り い
       Mearii san wa   nihonjin desu ka.

A：いいえ、にほんじんじゃないです。アメリカじんです。
あ め り か
     Iie,   nihonjin ja nai desu.   Amerikajin desu.

1. たけしさんは ちゅうごくじんですか。
    Takeshi san wa   chuugokujin desu ka.

2. ロバートさんは アメリカじんですか。
ろ ば あ と   あ め り か
    Robaato san wa   amerikajin desu ka.

3. やましたせんせいは かんこくじんですか。
    Yamashita sensee wa   kankokujin desu ka.

4. たけしさんの せんこうは にほんごですか。
    Takeshi san no   senkoo wa   nihongo desu ka.

5. ソラさんの せんこうは けいざいですか。
   Sora san no　　senkoo wa　　keezai desu ka.

6. たけしさんは さくらだいがくの がくせいですか。
   Takeshi san wa　Sakura daigaku no　　gakusee desu ka.

7. メアリーさんは ロンドンだいがくの がくせいですか。
   Mearii san wa　　Rondon daigaku no　　gakusee desu ka.

8. たけしさんは にねんせいですか。
   Takeshi san wa　ninensee desu ka.

9. ソラさんは いちねんせいですか。
   Sora san wa　ichinensee desu ka.

10. ロバートさんは よねんせいですか。
    Robaato san wa　yonensee desu ka.

B. Group Work—Put your belongings (textbook, note, pen, etc.) into a bag/box, and take turns picking up an item and asking who it belongs to.

Example　A：これは Bさんの ペンですか。
　　　　　　Kore wa　B san no　　pen desu ka.

　　　　　B：いいえ、わたしの ペンじゃないです。
　　　　　　Iie,　　　　watashi no　pen ja nai desu.
　　　　　　Cさんの ペンですか。
　　　　　　C san no　　pen desu ka.

　　　　　C：はい、わたしの ペンです。
　　　　　　Hai,　　watashi no　pen desu.

C. Pair Work—Ask each other yes-no questions such as year in school, major, age, belongings, etc.

Example　A：Bさんは さんねんせいですか。
　　　　　　B san wa　　sannensee desu ka.

　　　　　B：いいえ、さんねんせいじゃないです。にねんせいです。
　　　　　　Iie,　　　　sannensee ja nai desu.　　　　Ninensee desu.

Ⅷ まとめの れんしゅう (Review Exercises)

A. Role Play—One student is a store attendant. The other is a customer. Use Dialogue Ⅰ as a model.

B. Role Play—One student is a waiter/waitress. The other student goes to a restaurant. Look at the menu below and order some food or drink, using Dialogue Ⅱ as a model.
(See Culture Note in Lesson 8 [p. 208] for more information on Japanese food.)

C. Bring pictures of your friends or family and ask each other who each person is. Then, add more questions about their nationality, occupation, etc., as in the example.

L2

(Example) A：これは だれですか。
Kore wa　dare desu ka.

B：メアリーさんです。
Mearii san desu.

A：イギリスじんですか。
Igirisujin desu ka.

B：いいえ、イギリスじんじゃないです。
Iie,　　　igirisujin ja nai desu.
アメリカじんです。
Amerikajin desu.
アリゾナだいがくの がくせいです。
Arizona daigaku no　　　gakusee desu.

A：そうですか。
Soo desu ka.

D. Class Activity—Find someone who/whose . . .

name

1. is the same age _____

2. is in the same year at school _____

3. major is the same as yours _____

4. hometown (しゅっしん) is the same as yours _____
shusshin

(Example) Looking for someone who is from the same hometown as yours.

A：しゅっしんは どこですか。
Shusshin wa　　　doko desu ka.
B：ソウルです。
Souru desu.

A：そうですか。わたしもです。
Soo desu ka.　　Watashi mo desu.

→　Report to the class using 〜も.

わたしの しゅっしんは ソウルです。
Watashi no　shusshin wa　　Souru desu.
Bさんの しゅっしんも ソウルです。
B san no　　　shusshin mo　　Souru desu.

調べてみよう

Compare the Prices

There are many franchised fast food restaurants/cafes around the world such as McDonald's and Starbucks. Choose one restaurant/cafe you can find both in Japan and in your country, and compare the prices of similar items. You can visit the place (if you live in Japan) or you can check the menu on their website.

The name of the restaurant/cafe _____

Items	Price in Japan	Price in your country (convert to yen)

写真提供：日本マクドナルド（株）

Pair Work Ⅰ C. (p. 68)

Example A：ノートは いくらですか。
　　　　　　Nooto wa　ikura desu ka.

　　　　 B：ひゃくえんです。
　　　　　　Hyaku en desu.

¥100

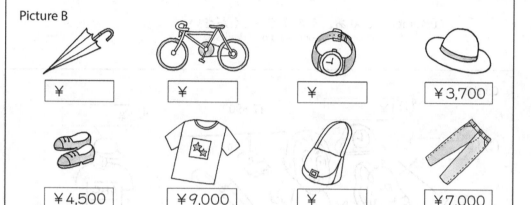

Picture B

¥　　　　　¥　　　　　¥　　　　　¥3,700

¥4,500　　　¥9,000　　　¥　　　　　¥7,000

Pair Work Ⅴ (p. 73)

Example A：これは だれの かさですか。
　　　　　　Kore wa　dare no　kasa desu ka.

　　　　 B：メアリーさんの かさです。
　　　　　　Mearii san no　　kasa desu.

Picture B

ナオミ　　　たけし　　　メアリー　　カルロス　　やましたせんせい
Naomi　　　Takeshi　　　Mearii　　　Karurosu　　Yamashita sensee

Pair Work Ⅲ B. (p. 71)

(Example) Customer ： すみません。このほんは いくらですか。
Sumimasen.　　Kono hon wa　ikura desu ka.

Vendor ： にせんろっぴゃくえんです。
Nisen roppyaku en desu.

*　　　　*　　　　*

Customer ： じゃあ、そのかさを ください。
Jaa,　　sono kasa o　　kudasai.

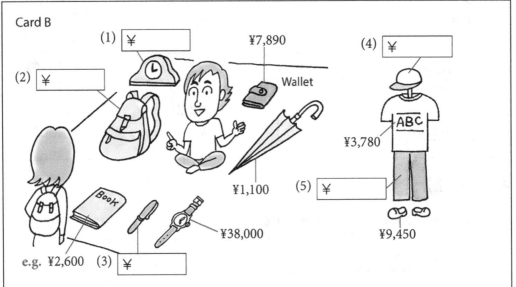

Card B

(1) ¥
(2) ¥
¥7,890
Wallet
(4) ¥
¥3,780
¥1,100
(5) ¥
¥9,450
¥38,000
Book
e.g. ¥2,600　(3) ¥

Part I. You are a customer. Ask for the prices of items (1)-(5).

Part II. You are a vendor at a flea market. Tell the customer how much each item is.

Useful Expressions

きょうしつ

I n   t h e   C l a s s r o o m

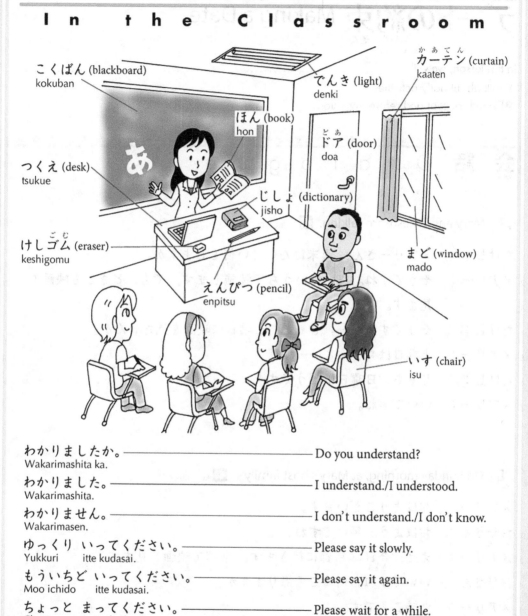

こくばん (blackboard)
kokuban

でんき (light)
denki

カーテン (curtain)
kaaten

ほん (book)
hon

ドア (door)
doa

つくえ (desk)
tsukue

じしょ (dictionary)
jisho

けしゴム (eraser)
keshigomu

まど (window)
mado

えんぴつ (pencil)
enpitsu

いす (chair)
isu

わかりましたか。———————————— Do you understand?
Wakarimashita ka.

わかりました。———————————— I understand./I understood.
Wakarimashita.

わかりません。———————————— I don't understand./I don't know.
Wakarimasen.

ゆっくり いってください。———————— Please say it slowly.
Yukkuri　itte kudasai.

もういちど いってください。————— Please say it again.
Moo ichido　itte kudasai.

ちょっと まってください。—————— Please wait for a while.
Chotto　matte kudasai.

きいてください。————————— Please listen./Please ask.
Kiite kudasai.

10ページを みてください。—————— Please look at page 10.
Juppeeji o　mite kudasai.

第3課　LESSON 3

デートの約束 Making a Date
やく　そく

In this lesson, we will..
● Talk about daily activities
● Extend, accept and refuse invitations

会話 Dialogue
かい　わ

Ⅰ　Mary and Takeshi are talking. 🔊 K03-01/02

1 たけし： 　メアリーさん、週末はたいてい何をしますか。
　　　　　　　　　　　　しゅうまつ　　　　　　　なに

2 メアリー： そうですね。たいていうちで勉強します。でも、ときどき映画を
　　　　　　　　　　　　　　　　　　　べんきょう　　　　　　　　　　　　　えいが

3　　　　　　 見ます。
　　　　　　 み

4 たけし： 　そうですか……。じゃあ、土曜日に映画を見ませんか。
　　　　　　　　　　　　　　　　　どようび　えいが　み

5 メアリー： 土曜日はちょっと……。
　　　　　　 どようび

6 たけし： 　じゃあ、日曜日はどうですか。
　　　　　　　　　　　にちようび

7 メアリー： いいですね。

Ⅱ　On Sunday morning, at Mary's host family's. 🔊 K03-03/04

1 メアリー： おはようございます。

2 お母さん： おはよう。早いですね。
　 かあ　　　　　　　はや

3 メアリー： ええ、今日は京都に行きます。京都で映画を見ます。
　　　　　　　　　きょう　きょうと　い　　　きょうと　えいが　み

4 お母さん： いいですね。何時ごろ帰りますか。
　 かあ　　　　　　　なんじ　かえ

5 メアリー： 九時ごろです。
　　　　　　 くじ

6 お母さん： 晩ご飯は？
　 かあ　　　　ばん　はん

7 メアリー： 食べません。
　　　　　　 た

8 お母さん： そうですか。じゃあ、いってらっしゃい。
　 かあ

9 メアリー： いってきます。

Ⓘ

Takeshi: Mary, what do you usually do on the weekend?

Mary: Let's see. I usually study at home. But I sometimes see movies.

Takeshi: I see. . . . Then, would you like to see a movie on Saturday?

Mary: Saturday is not a good day. (lit., Saturday is a little bit [inconvenient] . . .)

Takeshi: Then, how about Sunday?

Mary: That's fine.

会
L3

Ⅱ

Mary: Good morning.

Host mother: Good morning. You are early, aren't you?

Mary: Yes, I'm going to Kyoto today. I will see a movie in Kyoto.

Host mother: Good. Around what time will you come back?

Mary: Around nine.

Host mother: How about dinner?

Mary: I will not eat.

Host mother: I see. Well, have a nice day.

Mary: Good-bye.

単　語
たん　　ご

V o c a b u l a r y

Nouns

Entertainment and Sports

* えいが	映画	movie
おんがく	音楽	music
ざっし	雑誌	magazine
スポーツ		sports
デート		date (romantic, not calendar)
テニス		tennis
テレビ		TV

Foods and Drinks

アイスクリーム		ice cream
ハンバーガー		hamburger
おさけ	お酒	sake; alcoholic drink
おちゃ	お茶	green tea
コーヒー		coffee
みず	水	water
あさごはん	朝ご飯	breakfast
ひるごはん	昼ご飯	lunch
* ばんごはん	晩ご飯	dinner

Places

いえ	家	home; house
* うち		home; house; my place
がっこう	学校	school
カフェ		cafe

Time

あした	明日	tomorrow
* きょう	今日	today
あさ	朝	morning
こんばん	今晩	tonight
まいにち	毎日	every day
まいばん	毎晩	every night
* しゅうまつ	週末	weekend
* どようび	土曜日	Saturday

＊Words that appear in the dialogue

* にちようび	日曜日	Sunday
いつ		when
* ～ごろ		at about . . .

U-verbs

* いく	行く	to go (*destination* に/へ)
* かえる	帰る	to go back; to return (*destination* に/へ)
きく	聞く	to listen; to hear （～を）
のむ	飲む	to drink （～を）
はなす	話す	to speak; to talk (*language* を/で)
よむ	読む	to read （～を）

Ru-verbs

おきる	起きる	to get up
* たべる	食べる	to eat （～を）
ねる	寝る	to sleep; to go to sleep
* みる	見る	to see; to look at; to watch （～を）

Irregular Verbs

くる	来る	to come (*destination* に/へ)
* する		to do （～を）
* べんきょうする	勉強する	to study （～を）

Adjectives

* いい		good
* はやい	早い	early

Adverbs

あまり + negative		not much
ぜんぜん + negative	全然	not at all
* たいてい		usually
* ちょっと		a little
* ときどき	時々	sometimes
よく		often; much

Expressions

* そうですね		That's right.; Let me see.
* でも		but
* どうですか		How about . . . ?; How is . . . ?
* ええ		yes

会
L3

文法 Grammar
ぶん ぽう

1 Verb Conjugation

In this lesson, we learn about the dictionary forms[1], the present tense affirmative forms, and the present tense negative forms.

Three Groups of Verbs

We sort Japanese verbs into three groups based on their conjugation: *ru*-verbs, *u*-verbs, and irregular verbs.

(1) *Ru*-verbs

Ru-verbs are made up of a base which ends with either *e* or *i* plus the suffix *ru*. All *ru*-verbs, therefore, end with *eru* or *iru*. (So, if you see a verb that ends with *aru*, *oru*, or *uru*, you can be sure that they are not *ru*-verbs.[2])

食べる *(tabe + ru)*　　寝る *(ne + ru)*　　　起きる *(oki + ru)*　　見る *(mi + ru)*
た　　　　　　　　　　ね　　　　　　　　　お　　　　　　　　　　み

(2) *U*-verbs

U-verbs are made up of a consonant-final base plus *u* (e.g., 飲む *nom + u*). Note that 帰る ends
　　　　　　　　　　　　　　　　　　　　　　　　　　　　　　　　　　　の　　　　　　　　　かえ
with an *eru* sequence but is not a *ru*-verb as defined above. The *r* sound in 帰る comes from the
　　　かえ
base and not from the suffix.

飲む *(nom + u)*　　　　読む *(yom + u)*　　　話す *(hanas + u)*
の　　　　　　　　　　よ　　　　　　　　　はな

聞く *(kik + u)*　　　　行く *(ik + u)*　　　　帰る *(kaer + u)*
き　　　　　　　　　　い　　　　　　　　　　かえ

(3) Irregular verbs[3]

There are two "irregular verbs," する and くる. する is a very productive element. 勉強する is an
　　　　　　　　　　　　　　　　　　　　　　　　　　　　　　　　　　　　　べんきょう
example of a complex verb formed by a noun and する.

する *(suru)*　　　　　勉強する *(benkyoosuru)*　　　　　くる *(kuru)*
　　　　　　　　　　べんきょう

---

[1] Dictionary forms are used not only in dictionary entries, but also in actual contexts.

[2] The rule does not hold in the other direction. Not all verbs that end with *eru* or *iru* are *ru*-verbs. The verb 帰る
かえ
in this lesson is an example. We will learn more verbs like it in later lessons.

[3] They are not "irregular" at every turn. They just follow their own rules.

Present Tense Conjugation

Let's now turn to the present tense conjugation. With *ru*-verbs, you simply replace *ru* with *masu* (affirmative) or *masen* (negative).

Ru-verbs		
Dictionary form	Present, affirmative	Present, negative
食べる	食べます	食べません
寝る	寝ます	寝ません
起きる	起きます	起きません
見る	見ます	見ません

With *u*-verbs, you replace *u* with *imasu* and *imasen*. You can think of the change as going up and down in the same *hiragana* column (shifting between み and む in the column まみむめも, for example).

U-verbs		
Dictionary form	Present, affirmative	Present, negative
飲む	飲みます	飲みません
読む	読みます	読みません
話す	話します	話しません
聞く	聞きます	聞きません
行く	行きます	行きません

帰る is an *u*-verb, and the verb base final consonant *r* is kept in the present tense conjugation. So, instead of ×帰ます, we have:

Dictionary form: 帰る

Present, affirmative: 帰ります

Present, negative: 帰りません

With irregular verbs, the conjugation looks like the following.

Irregular verbs		
Dictionary form	Present, affirmative	Present, negative
する	します	しません
勉強する	勉強します	勉強しません
くる	きます	きません

Make sure you remember which verb belongs to which conjugation class. It is a good idea, therefore, to memorize each verb as a set: instead of memorizing just the dictionary form, try to memorize the dictionary form and the present tense affirmative, like 行く―行きます.

To recap the rules for telling which verb that ends with *hiragana* る belongs to which class, we note that if a verb ends with

- *aru* or *oru*, it is definitely an *u*-verb
- *uru*, it can either be an irregular verb or an *u*-verb
- *iru* or *eru*, it is more likely to be a *ru*-verb, but it can also be an *u*-verb.

2 Verb Types and the "Present Tense"

In this lesson we learn about a dozen verbs that describe basic human actions. These are often called "action verbs," and the "present tense" of these verbs either means (1) that a person habitually or regularly engages in these activities, or (2) that a person will, or is planning to, perform these activities in the future.[4]

Habitual actions:

私はよくテレビを見ます。 *I often watch TV.*

メアリーさんはときどき朝ご飯を食べません。 *Mary sometimes doesn't eat breakfast.*

Future actions:

私はあした京都に行きます。 *I will go to Kyoto tomorrow.*

ソラさんは今日うちに帰りません。 *Sora will not return home today.*

3 Particles

Nouns used in sentences generally must be followed by particles, which indicate the relations that the nouns bear to the verbs.[5] In this lesson, we learn four particles: を, で, に, and へ.

を (Direct object)　The particle を indicates "direct objects," the kind of things that are directly involved in, or affected by, the event. Note that this particle is pronounced "*o*."

---

[4] We will learn how to describe ongoing actions with these verbs in Lesson 7.

[5] In spoken language, particles are often "dropped." We will learn more about such cases in Lesson 15.

コーヒーを飲みます。	*I drink coffee.*
音楽を聞きます。	*I listen to music.*
テレビを見ます。	*I watch TV.*

で (Place of action)　The particle で indicates where the event described by the verb takes place.

| 図書館で本を読みます。 | *I will read books in the library.* |
| うちで昼ご飯を食べます。 | *I will eat lunch at home.* |

に　The particle に has many meanings, but here we will learn two: (1) the goal toward which things move, and (2) the time at which an event takes place.

(1) Goal of movement (for verbs like 行く, 来る and 帰る)

| 今日学校に行きません。 | *I will not go to school today.* |
| うちに帰ります。 | *I will return home.* |

(2) Time (We will discuss more about this in Section 4 below.)

| 日曜日に京都に行きます。 | *I will go to Kyoto on Sunday.* |
| 十一時に寝ます。 | *I will go to bed at eleven.* |

Approximate time references can be made by substituting ごろ or ごろに for に. Thus,

| 十一時ごろ／十一時ごろに 寝ます。 | *I will go to bed at about eleven.* |

へ (Goal of movement)　With verbs 行く, 来る and 帰る, you can replace the goal of movement に with へ. You cannot replace に for time reference with へ. Note that this particle is pronounced "*e.*"

| 今日学校へ行きません。 | *I will not go to school today.* |
| うちへ帰ります。 | *I will return home.* |

4 Time References

You need the particle に with (1) the days of the week like "on Sunday," and (2) numerical time expressions, like "at 10:45," and "in September."

日曜日に行きます。	*I will go on Sunday.*
十時四十五分に起きます。	*I get up at 10:45.*
九月に帰ります。	*I will go back in September.*

You do not use the particle に with (1) time expressions defined relative to the present moment, such as "today" and "tomorrow," (2) expressions describing regular intervals, such as "every day," and (3) the word for "when."

あした来ます。	*I will come tomorrow.*
毎晩テレビを見ます。	*I watch TV every evening.*
いつ行きますか。	*When will you go?*

You normally do not use に with (1) the parts of a day, like "in the morning" and "at night," and (2) the word for "weekend." Unlike words like あした and 毎晩 above, however, these words can be followed by に, depending on styles, emphases, and personal preferences.

朝(に)本を読みます。	*I read a book in the morning.*
週末(に)何をしますか。	*What will you do on weekends?*

5 〜ませんか

You can use ませんか (= the present tense negative verb, plus the question particle) to extend an invitation. It should be noted that its affirmative counterpart, ますか, cannot be so used. Thus a sentence like 昼ご飯を食べますか can only be construed as a question, not as an invitation.

Ａ：昼ご飯を食べませんか。	*What do you say to having lunch with me?*
Ｂ：いいですね。	*Sounds great.*
Ａ：テニスをしませんか。	*Will you play tennis with me?*
Ｂ：うーん、ちょっと。	*Um, it's slightly (inconvenient for me at this moment).*

6 Frequency Adverbs

You can add a frequency adverb such as 毎日 (every day), よく (often), and ときどき (some-times) to a sentence to describe how often you do something.

私 はときどき図書館に行きます。   *I sometimes go to a library.*

In this lesson, we also learn two adverbs which describe how *infrequent* an activity or an event is: ぜんぜん (never; not at all) and あまり (not often; not very much). These adverbs anticipate the negative at the end of the sentence. If you use ぜんぜん or あまり, in other words, you need to conclude the sentence with ません.

私 はぜんぜんテレビを見ません。   *I do not watch TV at all.*

たけしさんはあまり勉強しません。   *Takeshi does not study much.*

7 Word Order

Japanese sentences are fairly flexible in the arrangement of elements that appear in them. Gener-ally, sentences are made up of several noun-particle sequences followed by a verb or an adjective. A typical sentence, therefore, looks like the following, but several other arrangements of noun-particle sequences are also possible.

私 は	今日	図書館で	日本語を	勉強します。
topic	time	place	object	verb

I will study Japanese in the library today.

私 は	よく	七時ごろ	うちへ	帰ります。
topic	frequency	time	goal	verb

I often go back home at around seven.

8 The Topic Particle は

As we saw in Lesson 1, the particle は presents the topic of one's utterance ("As for item X, it is such that . . ."). It puts forward the item that you want to talk about. You may have noted that the topic phrases in sentences such as メアリーさんは二年生です (Mary is a sophomore), and 私 の専攻は日本語です (My major is the Japanese language), are the subjects of those sentences. A topic phrase, however, need not be the subject of a sentence. We see three sentences in the dialogue of this lesson where nonsubject phrases are made topics with the help of the particle は.

メアリーさん、<u>週末</u>はたいてい<u>何</u>をしますか。

Mary, what do you usually do on the weekend?

<u>今日</u>は<u>京都</u>に<u>行</u>きます。

I'm going to Kyoto today.

In the above two examples, は presents time expressions as the topic of each sentence. Its effects can be paraphrased like these: "Let's talk about weekends; what do you do on weekends?" "Let me say what I will do today; I will go to Kyoto."

A：<u>晩</u>ご<u>飯</u>は？   B：<u>食</u>べません。

How about dinner?   *I will not eat.*

In this example, は is used in directing the listener's attention and thereby inviting a comment or completion of a sentence. You may also note that the broached topic, <u>晩</u>ご<u>飯</u>, does not stand in subject relation to the verb, but is rather its direct object.

表現ノート
ひょう　げん

行く/来る ▶ When you move to a place where the hearer is, you say "I'm coming." in English. However in the same situation, 行きます is used in Japanese. 来る is a movement toward the place where the speaker is, while 行く is a movement in a direction away from the speaker.

ちょっと ▶ ちょっと literally means "a little," "a bit," "a small amount," as in ちょっとください (Please give me a little) and ちょっと待ってください (Please wait for a moment). It is commonly used for a polite refusal. In this case, it means "inconvenient," "impossible," and so on. Japanese people don't normally reject requests, suggestions, or invitations with いいえ (No), because it sounds too direct.

> A：土曜日に映画を見ませんか。　　*Will you see a movie on Saturday?*
> 　　どようび　えいが　み
>
> B：土曜日は、ちょっと。　　　　　*Saturday is not convenient.*
> 　　どようび　　　　　　　　　　　*(lit., Saturday is a little bit.)*

はい/ええ ▶ Both *hai* and *ee* means "yes" in response to yes-no questions. Compared to *hai*, *ee* is more conversational and relaxed. In more informal situations, *un* is used.

　Hai is also used to respond to a knock at the door or to the calling of one's name, meaning "Here," as follows. (*Ee* cannot be replaced in this case.)

> Teacher: スミスさん？　　*Mr. Smith?*
> Student: はい。　　　　　*Here.*

練習 Practice
れん しゅう

I 食べます ☞Grammar 1・2
た

Change the following verbs into 〜ます and 〜ません. Ignore the word in English for this exercise. 🔊 K03-07/08

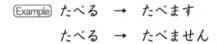

(Example) たべる　→　たべます

たべる　→　たべません

e.g. たべる

hamburger
McDonald's
5:00

(1) きく

music
home
4:30

(2) のむ

coffee
cafe
3:00

(3) はなす

おはよう
おはよう

Japanese
college
every day

(4) よむ

magazine
library
2:00

(5) みる

TV
home
tonight

(6) する

tennis
school
Saturday

(7) べんきょうする

Japanese
library
weekend

(8) いく

(9) かえる

(10) くる

(11) おきる

(12) ねる

Ⅱ 図書館で雑誌を読みます _{としょかん ざっし よ} ☛Grammar 3

A. Look at the pictures (1) to (7) on the previous page and make sentences using the cues.

(a) Add the direct objects. 🔊 K03-09

Example hamburger → ハンバーガーを食べます。_た

(b) Add the place to the above sentences. 🔊 K03-10

Example McDonald's → マクドナルドでハンバーガーを食べます。_た

B. Pair Work—Ask and answer the following questions, looking at the pictures in I. Ask more questions.

1. メアリーさんは図書館で雑誌を読みますか。_{としょかん ざっし よ}
2. メアリーさんはうちでコーヒーを飲みますか。_の
3. メアリーさんはどこでテニスをしますか。
4. メアリーさんはカフェで何を飲みますか。_{なに の}

C. Pair Work—Ask your partner questions about their daily activities using the verbs in I.

Example A：雑誌を読みますか。_{ざっし よ}
B：ええ、読みます。_よ
A：どこで読みますか。_よ
B：図書館で読みます。_{としょかん よ}

D. Pair Work—Guessing Game

(1) First, choose one item in each row. Do not show it to your partner.

e.g. ～を話します _{はな}	Chinese	Korean	English	Japanese
～を見ます _み	sports	movie	news （ニュース）	cartoon （アニメ）
～を飲みます _の	sake	green tea	water	coffee
～を読みます _よ	book	newspaper	magazine	Japanese book
～をします	date	study	telephone	tennis

(2) Ask your partner questions to find out what items they have chosen, using the verb on the left. You can ask at most two questions with each verb. If your guess is correct, you score a point.

(Example) A：中国語を話しますか。
B：いいえ、話しません。
A：英語を話しますか。
B：はい、話します。(Score!)

(3) Tabulate the score. You win the game if you have gained more points than your partner.

Ⅲ 学校に行きます ☛Grammar 3

A. Look at the pictures below and make sentences using the cues. 🔊 K03-11

(Example) go to the post office → ソラさんは郵便局に行きます。

| e.g. go to the post office | (1) go to the library | (2) come to my house |

| 1:00 | 3:00 | Sunday |

| (3) come to school | (4) return home | (5) return to the U.S. |

| 8:30 | 5:30 | tomorrow |

B. Pair Work—Ask questions, looking at the pictures in A.

(Example) A：ソラさんはどこに行きますか。

B：郵便局に行きます。
　　ゆうびんきょく　　い

会
L3

Ⅳ 何時に起きますか 🔊Grammar 4
　　なん　じ　　お

A. Look at Professor Yamashita's schedule and describe what he does when. 🔊 K03-12

(Example) 山下先生は七時半に起きます。
　　　　　やましたせんせい　しち じ はん　お

e.g.	7:30 A.M.	get up
(1)	8:00	eat breakfast
(2)	8:30	go to the university
(3)	12:00	eat lunch
(4)	4:00 P.M.	drink coffee
(5)	6:00	go home
(6)	7:30	eat dinner
(7)	11:30	go to bed

B. Answer the following questions about Professor Yamashita's schedule.

(Example) A：山下先生は何時に起きますか。
　　　　　やましたせんせい　なん じ　お
　　　　　B：七時半に起きます。
　　　　　　しち じ はん　お

C. Pair Work—Ask your partner what time they do the following things.

(Example)
A：何時に起きますか。
　　なん じ　お
B：たいてい八時ごろ起きます。
　　　　　はち じ　　お

Your partner's schedule

time	
(　　　　　)	get up
(　　　　　)	eat breakfast
(　　　　　)	go to school
(　　　　　)	eat lunch
(　　　　　)	go home
(　　　　　)	go to bed

D. Look at the pictures in Ⅰ (p. 94) and Ⅲ-A (p. 96), and add the time expressions to the sentences. 🔊 K03-13/14

(Example) (Ⅰ) 5:00 → 五時にマクドナルドでハンバーガーを食べます。
ご じ   た
(Ⅲ-A) 1:00 → ソラさんは一時に郵便局に行きます。
いち じ   ゆうびんきょく い

Ⅴ コーヒーを飲みませんか ☛Grammar 5
の

A. Make suggestions using the cues below. 🔊 K03-15

(Example) drink coffee → コーヒーを飲みませんか。
の

1. see a movie
2. come to my house
3. go to Kyoto
4. eat dinner
5. study in the library
6. talk at a cafe
7. drink tea at home
8. listen to the music

B. Pair Work—Ask your friend out for the activities in the pictures. Make sure to include the time and place of the activities as in the example below.

(Example) A：日曜日に図書館で勉強しませんか。
にちよう び   と しょかん   べんきょう
B：いいですね。／すみませんが、ちょっと……。

e.g.   (1)   (2)   (3)

(4)   (5)   (6)

C. Pair Work—Use the cues below and make suggestions to do something together. Your partner suggests an alternative.

[Example] cafe / library

→ A：カフェで勉強しませんか。
べんきょう
B：すみませんが、カフェはちょっと……。
図書館はどうですか。
としょかん
A：いいですね。

1. coffee / green tea

2. tennis / badminton (バドミントン)

3. Saturday / Sunday

4. McDonald's (マクドナルド) / Mos Burger (モスバーガー)

Ⅵ 毎日本を読みます ☞Grammar 6
まい にち ほん よ

How often do you do the following activities? Answer the questions using the expressions below.

[Example] Q：本を読みますか。
ほん よ
A：はい、よく読みます。／いいえ、あまり読みません。
よ よ

1. スポーツをしますか。

2. 雑誌を読みますか。
ざっし よ

3. コンビニに行きますか。
い

4. 映画を見ますか。
えいが み

5. コーヒーを飲みますか。
の

6. 日本の音楽を聞きますか。
に ほん おんがく き

7. 朝ご飯を食べますか。
あさ はん た

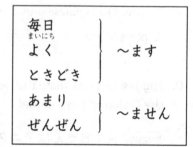

毎日 まいにち	
よく	
ときどき	〜ます
あまり	
ぜんぜん	〜ません

Ⅶ まとめの練習 (Review Exercises)
れんしゅう

A. Answer the following questions.

1. 何時に起きますか。
   なんじ　お
2. どこで勉強しますか。
   べんきょう
3. いつテレビを見ますか。
   み
4. スポーツをしますか。

5. 週末はどこに行きますか。
   しゅうまつ　　　　い
6. 朝、何を食べますか。
   あさ　なに　た
7. 今晩、何をしますか。
   こんばん　なに
8. 毎晩、何時ごろ寝ますか。
   まいばん　なんじ　　ね

B. Tell your classmates what your plans are today/tomorrow/on the weekend.

Example　今日は一時ごろ昼ご飯を食べます。
　　　　　きょう　いちじ　　ひる　はん　た
　　　　　三時に図書館で日本語を勉強します。
　　　　　さんじ　としょかん　にほんご　べんきょう
　　　　　六時ごろ家に帰ります。
　　　　　ろくじ　　いえ　かえ

C. Class Activity—Find someone who . . .

　　　　　　　　　　　　　　　　　　　　name

1. gets up at 7 o'clock　　＿＿＿＿＿＿＿＿＿＿＿＿＿＿

2. eats breakfast every day　＿＿＿＿＿＿＿＿＿＿＿＿＿＿

3. speaks Chinese　　　　　＿＿＿＿＿＿＿＿＿＿＿＿＿＿

4. watches movies at home　＿＿＿＿＿＿＿＿＿＿＿＿＿＿

5. listens to Japanese music　＿＿＿＿＿＿＿＿＿＿＿＿＿＿

6. plays tennis　　　　　　＿＿＿＿＿＿＿＿＿＿＿＿＿＿

D. Suggest to a classmate that you do something together over the weekend.
Use Dialogue I as a model.

Example　Ａ：Ｂさんはテニスをしますか。

　　　　　Ｂ：はい。

　　　　　Ａ：じゃあ、日曜日にテニスをしませんか。
　　　　　　　　　　にちようび
　　　　　Ｂ：日曜日はちょっと……。
　　　　　　　にちようび
　　　　　Ａ：そうですか。じゃあ、土曜日はどうですか。
　　　　　　　　　　　　　　　　どようび
　　　　　Ｂ：ええ、いいですね。

Culture Notes

日本の家 Japanese Houses
（に ほん いえ）

Traditionally, Japanese buildings were made of wood. Rooms were floored with 畳 (straw mats) and divided by ふすま or 障子 (two types of sliding doors).
（たたみ）（しょうじ）

Modern Japanese houses have mainly Western-style rooms, and are equipped with Western-style toilets (some with button-activated water spray feature). However, most bathrooms retain traditional characteristics—they are separated from toilets and sinks,

ふすま　　畳　　障子
　　　（たたみ）（しょうじ）

and have some space for washing one's body outside the bathtub. Usually, all family members share the same bathtub water, so it is necessary to clean one's body before getting into the bathtub.

Another traditional feature of Japanese homes is 玄関, a space inside the entrance where people remove their shoes.
（げんかん）

トイレ

お風呂 (bathroom)
（ふ ろ）

玄関
（げんかん）

写真提供（トイレ／お風呂）：(株) LIXIL

第4課

LESSON 4

初めてのデート The First Date
はじ

In this lesson, we will..

- Ask and describe where things/people are
- Talk about things that happened in the past
- Talk about habitual actions in the past

会 話 Dialogue
かい わ

I Mary goes downtown. 🔊 K04-01/02

1 メアリー： すみません。マクドナルドはどこですか。

2 知らない人： あそこにホテルがありますね。
　し　　ひと

3 　　　　　　 マクドナルドはあのホテルの前ですよ。
　　　　　　　　　　　　　　　　　　　　　　まえ

4 メアリー： ありがとうございます。

Ⅱ In the evening, at Mary's host family's house. 🔊 K04-03/04

1 メアリー： ただいま。

2 お父さん： おかえりなさい。映画はどうでしたか。
　とう　　　　　　　　　　　えいが

3 メアリー： 見ませんでした。たけしさんは来ませんでした。
　　　　　　 み　　　　　　　　　　　　　　き

4 お父さん： えっ、どうしてですか。
　とう

5 メアリー： わかりません。だから、一人で本屋
　　　　　　　　　　　　　　　　ひとり　　ほんや

6 　　　　　　 とお寺に行きました。
　　　　　　　　てら　い

7 お父さん： 人がたくさんいましたか。
　とう　　ひと

8 メアリー： はい。お寺で写真をたくさん撮り
　　　　　　　　　てら　しゃしん　　　　　　　と

9 　　　　　　 ました。

10 　　　　　　 公園にも行きました。
　　　　　　　 こうえん　い

11 お父さん： そうですか。
　とう

III Takeshi calls Mary at night. 🔊 K04-05/06

1 たけし： 　　もしもし、メアリーさん。

2 メアリー： 　あっ、たけしさん。今日来ませんでしたね。
　　　　　　　　　　　　きょう き

3 たけし： 　　行きましたよ。モスバーガーの前で一時間待ちました。
　　　　　　　い　　　　　　　　　　　　まえ　いちじかん ま

4 メアリー： 　モスバーガーじゃないですよ。マクドナルドですよ。

5 たけし： 　　マクドナルド……ごめんなさい！

Ⓘ

Mary: Excuse me. Where is McDonald's?

Stranger: There is a hotel over there. McDonald's is in front of the hotel.

Mary: Thank you very much.

Ⓘ

Mary: I'm home.

Host father: Welcome home. How was the movie?

Mary: I didn't see it. Takeshi didn't come.

Father: Oh, why?

Mary: I don't know. So, I went to a bookstore and a temple alone.

Host father: Were there a lot of people?

Mary: Yes. I took many pictures at the temple. I also went to a park.

Host father: I see.

Ⓘ

Takeshi: Hello, Mary.

Mary: Oh, Takeshi. You didn't come today, did you?

Takeshi: I went there. I waited for one hour in front of the Mos Burger place.

Mary: Not Mos Burger. McDonald's!

Takeshi: McDonald's . . . I'm sorry!

単　語
たん　ご

K04-07 (J-E)
K04-08 (E-J)

V o c a b u l a r y

Nouns

Activities

ゲーム		game
アルバイト		part-time job (more colloquially, バイト)
かいもの	買い物	shopping
クラス		class

People and Things

いぬ	犬	dog
ねこ	猫	cat
* ひと	人	person
こども	子供	child
あなた		you
いす		chair
つくえ	机	desk
* しゃしん	写真	picture; photograph
はな	花	flower
レポート		(term) paper
ごはん	ご飯	rice; meal
パン		bread

Places

* おてら	お寺	temple
* こうえん	公園	park
スーパー		supermarket
バスてい	バス停	bus stop
びょういん	病院	hospital
* ホテル		hotel
* ほんや	本屋	bookstore
まち	町	town; city
レストラン		restaurant

＊Words that appear in the dialogue

Time

きのう	昨日	yesterday
* 〜じかん	〜時間	... hours
いちじかん	一時間	one hour
せんしゅう	先週	last week
とき	時	when ...; at the time of ... （〜の）
げつようび	月曜日	Monday
かようび	火曜日	Tuesday
すいようび	水曜日	Wednesday
もくようび	木曜日	Thursday
きんようび	金曜日	Friday

U-verbs

あう	会う	to meet; to see (a person) (*person* に)
* ある		there is ... (*place* に *thing* が)
かう	買う	to buy （〜を）
かく	書く	to write (*person* に *thing* を)
* とる	撮る	to take (a picture) （〜を）
* まつ	待つ	to wait （〜を）
* わかる		to understand （〜が）

Ru-verb

* いる		(a person) is in ...; stays at ... (*place* に *person* が)

Adverbs and Other Expressions

〜ぐらい		about (approximate measurement)
* ごめんなさい		I'm sorry.
それから		and then
* だから		so; therefore
* たくさん		many; a lot
* 〜と		together with (a person); and
* どうして		why
* ひとりで	一人で	alone
* もしもし		Hello? (used on the phone)

Location Words

みぎ	右	right （〜の）
ひだり	左	left （〜の）
＊まえ	前	front （〜の）
うしろ	後ろ	back （〜の）
なか	中	inside （〜の）
うえ	上	on （〜の）
した	下	under （〜の）
ちかく	近く	near; nearby （〜の）
となり	隣	next （〜の）
あいだ	間	between （A と B の）

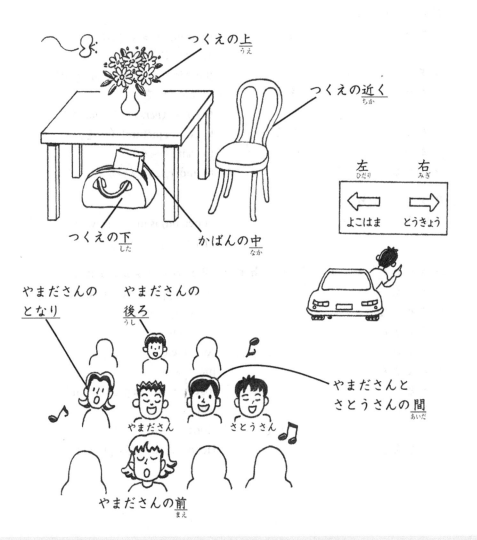

つくえの上
うえ

つくえの近く
ちか

つくえの下
した

かばんの中
なか

左
ひだり　　右
みぎ

よこはま　　とうきょう

やまださんの
となり

やまださんの
後ろ
うし

やまださんと
さとうさんの間
あいだ

やまださん

さとうさん

やまださんの前
まえ

文法 Grammar
ぶん ぽう

1 X があります / います

You can use the verbs あります (for non-living things) and います (for people and other living, moving things) when you want to say "there is/are X."

あそこにマクドナルドがあります。　　　*There's a McDonald's over there.*

The thing that you are presenting is accompanied by the particle が (unlike the verbs we have seen so far, which call for は). The place where the thing is is accompanied by the particle に (unlike the other verbs which call for で) . You usually describe the place first, and then the thing, as in the example above.[1]

You can also use あります to say that you *have* or *own* something.[2]

テレビがありません。　　　　　　　　*I don't have a TV.*

時間がありますか。　　　　　　　　　*Do you have time?*
じ かん

We also use あります when we want to say that *an event will take place.*[3]

火曜日にテストが あります。　　　　*There will be an exam on Tuesday.*
か よう び

あしたは日本語のクラスがありません。　*There will be no Japanese class tomorrow.*
に ほん ご

---

[1] ある also differs from other verbs in its colloquial substandard negative form (see footnote 1 in Lesson 3). We have ないです, instead of the expected regular formation あらないです, which is ungrammatical.

[2] Note the difference between:
　　テレビがありません (I don't have a TV), the negative version of テレビがあります, and
　　テレビじゃありません (It isn't a TV), the more conservative version of テレビじゃないです.

[3] When あります is used in the sense of an event taking place, the place description is followed by the particle で, like normal verbs and unlike the other uses of あります.
　　あした京都でお祭りがあります。　　*There will be a festival in Kyoto tomorrow.*
きょうと まつ
As we discussed in Lesson 3, some time expressions (such as 日曜日に) come with the particle に, and some others (such as あした) do not. The same rule applies to the あります sentences.
にちようび

When you want to say that there is a *person* or other living, moving thing, you need to use the verb います.[4] Thus,

あそこに留学生がいます。　　　　　　*There's an international student over there.*
　　りゅうがくせい

You can also use います to say that you *have* friends, siblings, and so forth.

日本人の友だちがいます。　　　　　　*I have a Japanese friend.*
にほんじん　とも

(place に)	thing が	あります	*There is/are . . .*
	person が	います	

2 Describing Where Things Are

We learned in Lesson 2 how to ask for, and give, the location of item X.

Ａ：マクドナルドはどこですか。　　　　*Where's McDonald's?*

Ｂ：マクドナルドは 〔 あそこ / そこ / ここ 〕 です。　*McDonald's is* 〔 *over there. / right there near you. / right here.* 〕

In this lesson, we will learn to describe the location of an item relative to another item, as in "X is in front of Y." The Japanese version looks like X は Y の前です。
まえ

（マクドナルドは）あのホテルの前です。
　　　　　　　　　　　　　　まえ

It's in front of that hotel.

---

[4] Note that the same verb "is" in English comes out differently in Japanese:
　　あそこに留学生がいます。　*There is an international student over there.*
　　りゅうがくせい
　　メアリーさんは留学生です。　*Mary is an international student.*
　　　　　　りゅうがくせい
　います and あります are strictly for descriptions of existence and location, while です is for description of an attribute of a person or a thing.

Other useful words describing locations are as follows:

location words

| X は Y の | みぎ
ひだり
まえ
うしろ
なか
うえ
した
ちかく[5]
となり[6] | です。 | X is | to the right of
to the left of
in front of
behind
inside
on/above
under/beneath
near
next to | Y. |

X は Y と Z のあいだです。　　　　X is between Y and Z.

銀行は図書館の<u>となり</u>です。
ぎんこう　としょかん
The bank is next to the library.

傘はテーブルの<u>下</u>です。
かさ　　　　　　　した
The umbrella is under the table.

レストランはスーパーと病院の<u>間</u>です。
　　　　　　　　　　　びょういん　あいだ
The restaurant is between the supermarket and the hospital.

You can use any of the above location words together with a verb to describe an event that occurs in the place. To use these phrases with verbs such as 食べる and 待つ, you will need the particle
た　　　　ま
で.

私はモスバーガーの<u>前</u>でメアリーさんを<u>待</u>ちました。
わたし　　　　　　　　まえ　　　　　　　　　　　ま
I waited for Mary in front of the Mos Burger place.

---

[5] Another word for "near" that is also commonly used is そば.

[6] Use となり to describe two people or two buildings/places that are found side by side. You can use よこ for a much wider range of things.

　　○かばんはつくえの<u>よこ</u>です。　　*The bag is by the desk.*
　　×かばんはつくえの<u>となり</u>です。　(odd)

3 Past Tense of です

The past tense versions of "XはYです" sentences are でした in the affirmative and じゃなかった です in the negative.

です	affirmative	negative
[Present]	〜です	〜じゃないです
[Past]	〜でした	〜じゃなかったです [7]

山下先生はさくら大学の学生でした。
Mr. Yamashita was a student at Sakura University.

あれは日本の映画じゃなかったです。
That was not a Japanese movie.

4 Past Tense of Verbs

The past tense forms of verbs end with ました in the affirmative and ませんでした in the negative.

Verbs	affirmative	negative
[Present]	〜ます	〜ません
[Past]	〜ました	〜ませんでした [8]

メアリーさんは九時ごろうちに帰りました。　*Mary returned home at about nine.*

私はきのう日本語を勉強しませんでした。　*I did not study Japanese yesterday.*

The various details of formation of the long forms that we learned in Lesson 3, like the *ru*-verb/ *u*-verb/irregular verb distinctions, all apply to the past tense forms as well.

---

[7] As was the case with the present tense じゃないです, you also find a more conservative variant じゃありませ んでした along with じゃなかったです. Written communications would more likely have ではありません でした, with the uncontracted form では.

[8] The colloquial substandard forms of the past tense negative verbs are なかったです, as in 帰らなかったです. We will learn how to change verbs into these forms in Lesson 9.

5 も

We learned in Lesson 2 that we use the particle も in reference to the second item which shares a common attribute with the first. You can also use も when two or more people perform the same activity.

私はきのう京都に行きました。
I went to Kyoto yesterday.

山下先生もきのう京都に行きました。
Professor Yamashita went to Kyoto yesterday, too.

Or when someone buys, sees, or eats two or more things.

メアリーさんは靴を買いました。
Mary bought shoes.

メアリーさんはかばんも買いました。
Mary bought a bag, too.

In the examples above, you are replacing は and を with も. With other particles such as に and で, you keep them and follow them up with も.

私は先週京都に行きました。
I went to Kyoto last week.

大阪にも行きました。
I went to Osaka, too.

ソラさんは土曜日に学校に来ました。
Sora came to school on Saturday.

日曜日にも学校に来ました。
She came to school on Sunday, too.

けんさんはうちで本を読みました。
Ken read a book at home.

カフェでも本を読みました。
He read a book at a cafe, too.

Just like も replacing は or を, you put も on the new item that is just like the first item introduced in the preceding sentence; in the examples above, you visited both Kyoto and Osaka, Sora came to school both on Saturday and Sunday, and so forth.

は / が / を	→	も
に / で / etc.	→	にも / でも / etc.

6 一時間
いち じ かん

The duration of an activity is expressed with a bare noun, like 一時間. Such a noun stands alone
いち じ かん
(that is, not followed by any particle).

メアリーさんはそこでたけしさんを一時間待ちました。
いち じ かん ま

Mary waited for Takeshi there for an hour.

For an approximate measurement, you can add ぐらい[9] after 〜時間.
じ かん

私はきのう日本語を三時間ぐらい勉強しました。
わたし に ほん ご さん じ かん べんきょう

I studied Japanese for about three hours yesterday.

To say one hour and a half, you can add 半 immediately after 〜時間.
はん じ かん

きのう七時間半寝ました。
しち じ かんはん ね

(I) slept for seven and a half hours last night.

If you want to say both 半 and ぐらい, ぐらい comes last, as in 一時間半ぐらい.
はん いち じ かんはん

7 たくさん

Expressions of quantity in Japanese are rather different from those in English. In Japanese, if you
want to add a quantity word like たくさん to the direct object of a sentence, you can either place
it before the noun, or after the particle を.

京都で ┌ 写真をたくさん ┐ 撮りました。   *I took many pictures in Kyoto.*
きょう と │ しゃしん │ と
└ たくさん写真を ┘
しゃしん

You can also use both these orders (quantity-noun-particle and noun-particle-quantity) in ある
and いる sentences.

┌ 野菜がたくさん ┐ あります。   *There are a lot of vegetables.*
│ や さい │
└ たくさん野菜が ┘
や さい

---

[9] As we learned in Lesson 3, we have another word for "at about a certain time," ごろ.

[10] You can use と to connect nouns only. We will learn about connecting verbs and sentences in Lesson 6.

[11] "With" as in "with chopsticks" requires another particle. See Lesson 10.

8 と

The particle と has two functions. One is to connect two nouns A and B.[10]

日本語と英語を話します。　　　　　*I speak Japanese and English.*

京都と大阪に行きました。　　　　　*I went to Kyoto and Osaka.*

The other meaning of と is "together with"; it describes *with whom* you do something.[11]

メアリーさんはソラさんと韓国に行きます。

Mary will go to Korea with Sora.

Expression Notes

表現ノート

(5)

X の前 ▶ X の前 is often used in the sense of "across (the street) from X" or "opposite X." You may also hear another word that is used in the sense of across, namely, X のむかい.

If something is behind X, or farther away from a street and cannot be directly seen because of the intervening X, in addition to calling it X の後ろ, you can also describe it as being X のうら.

えっ/あっ ▶ In the dialogues, we observe Mary's host father saying えっ, and Mary saying あっ. えっ is like the incredulous "what?" that you use when you have heard something that is hard to believe. あっ is used when you have suddenly noticed or remembered something. The small っ at the end of these little words indicates that these words, when pronounced, are very short.

Not using あなた ▶ As we learned in Lesson 1 (Expression Notes on page 45), the use of the word あなた is limited. Japanese speakers usually go without explicitly mentioning "you" in sentences.

A：今週の週末、何をしますか。　　*What are you going to do this weekend?*
B：買い物をします。　　　　　　*I am going shopping.*

If you know the name of the person you are talking to, use their name plus さん, instead of あなた. Never use あなた when you are talking to your professor or boss. Using terms of address other than their title like 先生 (teacher) and 社長 (president of a company) is considered rude in conversations with your social "superiors."

Culture Notes

日本の祝日 Japanese National Holidays
（に ほん　しゅくじつ）

As of February 2020.

1月1日 （がつついたち）	元日 （がんじつ）	New Year's Day
1月第2月曜日[1] （がつだい　げつようび）	成人の日 （せいじん　ひ）	Coming-of-Age Day (Celebrates people who turn 20 years old in that year)
2月11日 （がつ　にち）	建国記念の日 （けんこく　き ねん　ひ）	National Foundation Day
2月23日 （がつ　にち）	天皇誕生日 （てんのうたんじょう び）	Emperor's Birthday
3月20日ごろ[2] （がつ　はつか）	春分の日 （しゅんぶん　ひ）	Vernal Equinox Day
4月29日 （がつ　にち）	昭和の日 （しょう わ　ひ）	Showa Day (Birthday of Emperor Showa [1901-1989])
5月3日 （がつみっか）	憲法記念日 （けんぽう き ねん び）	Constitution Day
5月4日 （がつよっか）	みどりの日 （ひ）	Greenery Day
5月5日 （がついつか）	こどもの日 （ひ）	Children's Day
7月第3月曜日[3] （がつだい　げつよう び）	海の日 （うみ　ひ）	Marine Day
8月11日 （がつ　にち）	山の日 （やま　ひ）	Mountain Day
9月第3月曜日[3] （がつだい　げつよう び）	敬老の日 （けいろう　ひ）	Respect-for-the-Aged Day
9月23日ごろ[2] （がつ　にち）	秋分の日 （しゅうぶん　ひ）	Autumnal Equinox Day
10月第2月曜日[1] （がつだい　げつよう び）	スポーツの日 （ひ）	Health and Sports Day
11月3日 （がつみっか）	文化の日 （ぶん か　ひ）	Culture Day
11月23日 （がつ　にち）	勤労感謝の日 （きんろうかんしゃ　ひ）	Labor Thanksgiving Day

1: The second Monday　**2**: The day varies year to year　**3**: The third Monday

The period around April 29 to May 5 encompasses several holidays and is called ゴールデンウィーク (Golden Week). Some businesses close for a whole week or more during that period. (For the names of months and days, see p. 127.)

練習 Practice
れん　しゅう

I 病院があります ☛Grammar 1
びょういん

A. Look at the picture and tell what you see, using あります or います.

B. Answer the following questions.

1. あなたの町に日本のレストランがありますか。
   まち　　にほん

2. あなたの家に猫がいますか。
   いえ　ねこ

3. あなたの学校に何がありますか。
   がっこう　なに

4. あなたの学校に日本人の学生がいますか。
   がっこう　にほんじん　がくせい

5. コンビニに何がありますか。
   なに

6. この教室 (classroom) にだれがいますか。
   きょうしつ

7. 動物園 (zoo) に何がいますか。
   どうぶつえん　　　なに

8. あなたの国 (country) に何がありますか。
   くに　　　　　なに

9. あなたの家に何がありますか。
   いえ　なに

C. Look at Takeshi's schedule for the week and answer the following questions. 🔊 K04-09

	School	After School
Monday	Chinese English Computer	
Tuesday	History	Club activity
Wednesday	Chinese English Computer	
Thursday	History	Club activity
Friday	English (TEST)	Party
Saturday	NO SCHOOL	Date
Sunday	NO SCHOOL	Part-time job

club activity	サークル
party	パーティー
test	テスト

(Example) Q：月曜日に中国語のクラスがありますか。
　　　　A：はい、あります。

1. 月曜日に英語のクラスがありますか。
2. 火曜日にコンピューターのクラスがありますか。
3. 木曜日に中国語のクラスがありますか。
4. 土曜日にクラスがありますか。
5. 水曜日に何がありますか。
6. 金曜日に何がありますか。
7. 日曜日に何がありますか。

D. Pair Work—Write down your next week's schedule and ask each other what plans you have on each day of the week.

(Example) A：月曜日に何がありますか。
　　　　　B：日本語のクラスがあります。

	Your Schedule	Your Partner's Schedule
月曜日 げつよう び		
火曜日 か よう び		
水曜日 すいよう び		
木曜日 もくよう び		
金曜日 きんよう び		
土曜日 ど よう び		
日曜日 にちよう び		

会
L4

Ⅱ 図書館はどこですか ☞Grammar 2
としょかん

A. Look at the picture and tell where the following things are. 🔊 K04-10

(Example) 図書館
としょかん
→ 図書館は大学の後ろです。
としょかん　だいがく　うし
図書館はスーパーのとなりです。
としょかん

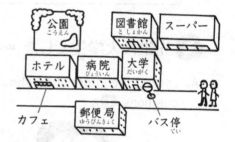

1. 郵便局　　3. バス停　　5. スーパー
ゆうびんきょく　　　　てい
2. カフェ　　4. 公園　　　6. 病院
　　　　　　こうえん　　　 びょういん

B. Pair Work—You and your partner have just moved to a new place. The room is messy. You are looking for the following things. Ask your partner where the following things are.

(Example) 本　→　A：本はどこですか。
ほん　　　　ほん
B：本はつくえの上です。
ほん　　　　うえ

1. ジーンズ　　　5. 靴
　　　　　　　　　　くつ
2. 猫　　　　　　 6. 花
ねこ　　　　　　　 はな
3. 帽子　　　　　 7. 犬
ぼうし　　　　　　 いぬ
4. 時計　　　　　 8. 傘
とけい　　　　　　 かさ

C. Pair Work—Ask and answer questions to find where the buildings are.
One student looks at map A. The other student looks at map B (p. 126). Don't look at the other's map.

(Example) A：すみません。公園はどこですか。
B：公園はホテルのとなりです。
A：ありがとうございます。
B：いいえ。

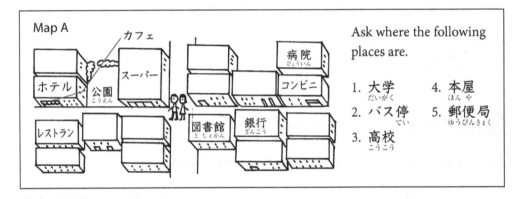

Map A

Ask where the following places are.

1. 大学
   だいがく
2. バス停
   　　てい
3. 高校
   こうこう

4. 本屋
   ほん や
5. 郵便局
   ゆうびんきょく

Ⅲ 先生は大学生でした ☞ Grammar 3
せんせい　だいがくせい

A. Look at the information about Professor Yamashita 25 years ago and answer the questions. 🔊 K04-11

Twenty-five years ago, Prof. Yamashita was
· twenty-two years old
· the fourth year at a college
· good student
· his major — Japanese history

(Example) Q：山下先生は大学生でしたか。
　　　　　　やましたせんせい　だいがくせい
A：はい、大学生でした。
　　　　　だいがくせい

Q：山下先生は十九歳でしたか。
　　やましたせんせい　じゅうきゅうさい
A：いいえ、十九歳じゃなかったです。
　　　　　　じゅうきゅうさい

1. 山下先生は子供でしたか。
   やましたせんせい　こども
2. 山下先生は一年生でしたか。
   やましたせんせい　いちねんせい
3. 山下先生はいい学生でしたか。
   やましたせんせい　　　がくせい

4. 山下先生の専攻は英語でしたか。
   やましたせんせい　せんこう　えいご
5. 山下先生の専攻は歴史でしたか。
   やましたせんせい　せんこう　れきし

B. Pair Work—Guessing Game

Ask questions and find out the prices your partner has chosen.

(1) First, choose one price in each row. Do not show it to your partner.

e.g. かばん	¥5,000	¥10,000	⟨¥15,000⟩	¥20,000
傘 かさ	¥600	¥1,000	¥1,300	¥2,000
帽子 ぼうし	¥1,600	¥2,000	¥2,400	¥3,000
Ｔシャツ ティー	¥3,500	¥4,000	¥6,500	¥8,000
時計 とけい	¥3,000	¥10,000	¥17,000	¥25,000

(2) Ask your partner questions to find out the price he/she chose. You can ask at most two questions with one item. If you have guessed correctly, you score a point.

(Example) A：そのかばんは二万円でしたか。
         B：いいえ、二万円じゃなかったです。
         A：一万五千円でしたか。
         B：はい、そうです。 (A scores a point.)

(3) Tabulate the score. You win the game if you have scored higher than your partner.

C. Pair Work—Guess what your partner had for breakfast/lunch/dinner. Choose from the items below, or add your favorites.

(Example) A：晩ご飯はピザでしたか。
         B：ええ、ピザでした。／いいえ、ピザじゃなかったです。

Ⅳ 月曜日に何をしましたか ☛Grammar 4
げつ よう び　なに

A. Change the following verbs into ～ました and ～ませんでした. 🔊 K04-12/13

Example　たべる　→　たべました
　　　　　たべる　→　たべませんでした

1. はなす　　　4. かく　　　　7. おきる　　　10. とる　　　13. きく

2. かう　　　　5. くる　　　　8. わかる　　　11. ある　　　14. かえる

3. よむ　　　　6. まつ　　　　9. する　　　　12. ねる　　　15. のむ

B. The pictures below show what Mary did last week. Tell what she did. 🔊 K04-14

Example　メアリーさんは月曜日に家でレポートを書きました。
　　　　　　　　　　げつよう び　いえ　　　　　　　か

e.g. Monday

at home

(1) Tuesday

in the library

(2) Wednesday

at school

(3) Thursday

at a cafe

(4) Friday

at her friend's house

(5) Saturday

in Kyoto

(6) Sunday

at a supermarket

C. Look at the pictures in B and answer the questions. 🔊 K04-15

(Example) Q：メアリーさんは月曜日にレポートを書きましたか。

A：はい、書きました。

Q：メアリーさんは月曜日に映画を見ましたか。

A：いいえ、見ませんでした。

1. メアリーさんは火曜日に音楽を聞きましたか。
2. メアリーさんは水曜日にテニスをしましたか。
3. メアリーさんは木曜日にたけしさんに会いましたか。
4. メアリーさんは金曜日にお寺に行きましたか。
5. メアリーさんは土曜日にレポートを書きましたか。
6. メアリーさんは日曜日に買い物をしましたか。

D. Look at the pictures in B and answer the questions. 🔊 K04-16

(Example) Q：メアリーさんは月曜日に何をしましたか。

A：家でレポートを書きました。

1. メアリーさんは水曜日に何をしましたか。
2. メアリーさんは火曜日に何をしましたか。
3. メアリーさんはいつ映画を見ましたか。
4. メアリーさんはいつ買い物をしましたか。
5. メアリーさんは金曜日にどこで晩ご飯を食べましたか。
6. メアリーさんは木曜日にどこでたけしさんに会いましたか。

E. Pair Work—Ask what your partner did on the weekend, Monday, Tuesday, etc.

(Example) A：週末、何をしましたか。

B：土曜日に友だちと晩ご飯を食べました。

それから、映画を見ました。

日曜日にたくさん勉強しました。Aさんは？

A：私は……

Ⅴ コーヒーも飲みます ☞Grammar 5
の

A. Compare sentences (a) and (b), and change sentence (b) using も. 🔊 K04-17

Example (a) ハンバーガーは二百円です。
にひゃくえん

(b) コーヒーは二百円です。　→　コーヒーも二百円です。
にひゃくえん　　　　　　　　　　にひゃくえん

1. (a) たけしさんは時計を買いました。
とけい　か

(b) たけしさんはかばんを買いました。
か

2. (a) ロバートさんは日本語を勉強します。
にほんご　べんきょう

(b) メアリーさんは日本語を勉強します。
にほんご　べんきょう

3. (a) たけしさんは土曜日にアルバイトをします。
どようび

(b) たけしさんは日曜日にアルバイトをします。
にちようび

4. (a) メアリーさんはうちで日本語を話します。
にほんご　はな

(b) メアリーさんは学校で日本語を話します。
がっこう　にほんご　はな

5. (a) あした、メアリーさんはたけしさんに会います。
あ

(b) あした、メアリーさんはソラさんに会います。
あ

6. (a) 先週、本屋に行きました。
せんしゅう　ほんや　い

(b) きのう、本屋に行きました。
ほんや　い

e.g. やまもと　たなか

student

B. Describe the pictures using も. 🔊 K04-18

Example やまもとさんは学生です。
がくせい

たなかさんも学生です。
がくせい

(1)
きむら　やまぐち

go to a hospital

(2)

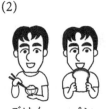

ごはん　　パン

(3)

コーヒー　おちゃ

(4)
スペインご

I speak English　Hablo español

(5) こうえん　おてら

(6) うち　としょかん

(7) どようび　にちようび

(8) かようび　もくようび

(9) とうきょう　ひろしま

会
L4

Ⅵ 一時間待ちました ☞Grammar 6
いち じ かん ま

A. Mary did a lot yesterday. Describe how many hours Mary did each activity. 🔊 K04-19

Example メアリーさんは八時間寝ました。
はち じ かん ね

e.g. 8 hours

(1) 2 hours

(2) 3 hours

(3) 1 and a half hours

(4) 1 hour

(5) 2 and a half hours

B. Pair Work—Ask your partner the following questions.

(Example) A：きのう、何時間アルバイトをしましたか。
なんじかん
B：三時間しました。
さんじかん

1. きのう、何時間勉強しましたか。
なんじかんべんきょう
2. きのう、何時間寝ましたか。
なんじかんね
3. ゲームをしますか。たいてい何時間ぐらいゲームをしますか。
なんじかん
4. インターネット (Internet) をしますか。たいてい何時間ぐらいしますか。
なんじかん

*If you want to say X minutes, see page 55.

Ⅶ まとめの練習 (Review Exercises)
れんしゅう

A. Pair Work—Using the expressions below, ask your partner how often they did the
following activities when they were a child or in high school.

(Example) A：子供の時／高校の時、よく本を読みましたか。
こども　とき　こうこう　とき　　　　ほん　よ
B：はい、よく読みました。／いいえ、あまり読みませんでした。
よ　　　　　　　　　　　　　　よ

1. 勉強する
べんきょう
2. スポーツをする
3. 映画を見る
えいが　み
4. 公園に行く
こうえん　い
5. レポートを書く
か
6. デートをする

毎日	
まいにち	
よく	～ました
ときどき	
あまり	～ませんでした
ぜんぜん	

B. Answer the following questions.

1. 毎日、何時に起きますか。
まいにち　なんじ　お
2. たいてい何時間ぐらい寝ますか。
なんじかん　ね
3. 毎日、何時間勉強しますか。
まいにち　なんじかんべんきょう
4. よくだれと昼ご飯を食べますか。
ひる　はん　た
5. 先週、スポーツをしましたか。
せんしゅう
6. きのう、どこで晩ご飯を食べましたか。
ばん　はん　た
7. 先週、写真をたくさん撮りましたか。
せんしゅう　しゃしん　と
8. きのうは何曜日でしたか。
なんようび

C. Pair Work—A and B want to play badminton together. The following is A's schedule for this week. (B's schedule is on p. 126.) Play the roles of A and B with your partner. Ask each other what the other is doing and decide on what day you will play badminton.

⟨Example⟩

A：バドミントン (badminton) を
　　しませんか。

B：いいですね。

A：月曜日はどうですか。

B：月曜日は図書館で勉強します。
　　火曜日は？

A's Schedule

University Research

Choose one Japanese university you are interested in. Find out more about the university with regard to the following. Present your findings in class. (If you want more challenge, do this in Japanese!)

1. Name of the university （大学の名前）

2. Where is it? （どこにありますか）

3. How many students are there? （学生が何人いますか）

4. How many international students are there? （留学生が何人いますか）

5. How much is the tuition? （授業料はいくらですか）

6. Other information

Pair Work Ⅱ C. (p. 118)

[Example] A：すみません。公園はどこですか。
こうえん

B：公園はホテルのとなりです。
こうえん

A：ありがとうございます。

B：いいえ。

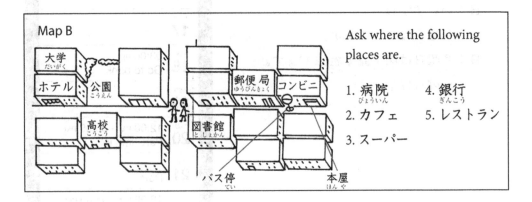

Map B

Ask where the following places are.

1. 病院　　4. 銀行
びょういん　　　ぎんこう

2. カフェ　5. レストラン

3. スーパー

Pair Work Ⅶ C. (p. 125)

[Example]

A：バドミントン (badminton) を

しませんか。

B：いいですね。

A：月曜日はどうですか。
げつようび

B：月曜日は図書館で勉強します。
げつようび　　と しょかん　　べんきょう

火曜日は？
かようび

B's Schedule

12:00 PM

< May >

| SUN 16 | MON 17 | TUE 18 | WED 19 | THU 20 | FRI 21 | SAT 22 |

SUN 16　06:00 PM　Meet Mr. Tanaka

MON 17　Study in the library

TUE 18

WED 19　Shopping in town

THU 20　Dinner at friend's house

FRI 21

SAT 22

Useful Expressions

日・週・月・年
(ひ・しゅう・つき・とし)

Days / Weeks / Months / Years

Days

日曜日 にちようび	月曜日 げつようび	火曜日 かようび	水曜日 すいようび	木曜日 もくようび	金曜日 きんようび	土曜日 どようび
		1 ついたち	2 ふつか	3 みっか	4 よっか	5 いつか	6 むいか
7 なのか	8 ようか	9 ここのか	10 とおか	11 じゅういちにち	12 じゅうににち	13 じゅうさんにち
14 じゅうよっか	15 じゅうごにち	16 じゅうろくにち	17 じゅうしちにち	18 じゅうはちにち	19 じゅうくにち	20 はつか
21 にじゅういちにち	22 にじゅうににち	23 にじゅうさんにち	24 にじゅうよっか	25 にじゅうごにち	26 にじゅうろくにち	27 にじゅうしちにち
28 にじゅうはちにち	29 にじゅうくにち	30 さんじゅうにち	31 さんじゅういちにち			

会
L4

Months

いちがつ（一月）—— January
にがつ（二月）—— February
さんがつ（三月）—— March
しがつ（四月）—— April
ごがつ（五月）—— May
ろくがつ（六月）—— June
しちがつ（七月）—— July
はちがつ（八月）—— August
くがつ（九月）—— September
じゅうがつ（十月）—— October
じゅういちがつ（十一月）— November
じゅうにがつ（十二月）—— December

Time Words

Day	Week	Month	Year
おととい the day before yesterday	にしゅうかんまえ （二週間前） two weeks ago	にかげつまえ （二か月前） two months ago	おととし the year before last
きのう（昨日） yesterday	せんしゅう（先週） last week	せんげつ（先月） last month	きょねん（去年） last year
きょう（今日） today	こんしゅう（今週） this week	こんげつ（今月） this month	ことし（今年） this year
あした（明日） tomorrow	らいしゅう（来週） next week	らいげつ（来月） next month	らいねん（来年） next year
あさって the day after tomorrow	さらいしゅう （再来週） the week after next	さらいげつ （再来月） the month after next	さらいねん （再来年） the year after next

第5課

沖縄旅行 A Trip to Okinawa
おき なわ りょ こう

In this lesson, we will..

- Talk about travel
- Describe people and things
- Make offers and invitations
- Talk about likes and dislikes

会 話 D i a l o g u e
かい わ

I Robert and Ken are vacationing in Okinawa. 🔊 K05-01/02

1 ロバート： いい天気ですね。
てん き

2 け ん： そうですね。でも、ちょっと暑いですね。
あつ

3 ロバート： ええ。わあ、きれいな海！
うみ

4 け ん： 泳ぎましょう。
およ

　　　　　　　*　　　　　*　　　　　*

5 け ん： ロバートさんはどんなスポーツが好きですか。
す

6 ロバート： サーフィンが好きです。
す

7 　　　　　　 あした一緒にやりましょうか。
いっしょ

8 け ん： でも、難しくないですか。
むずか

9 ロバート： 大丈夫ですよ。
だいじょう ぶ

II At the souvenir shop, Robert finds nice T-shirts. 🔊 K05-03/04

1 ロバート： すみません、このTシャツは、いくらですか。
ティー

2 店の人： 千八百円です。
みせ ひと　せんはっぴゃくえん

3 ロバート： あのう、Lサイズがありますか。
エル

4 店の人： はい、ありますよ。
みせ ひと

5 ロバート： じゃ、Lサイズを二枚ください。
エル　　　　に まい

III 🔊 On Monday at school. 🔊 K05-05/06

1 たけし：　　ロバートさん、旅行は楽しかったですか。

2 ロバート：　ええ。沖縄の海はすごくきれいでしたよ。

3 たけし：　　よかったですね。ぼくも海が大好きです。ホテルは高かったですか。

4 ロバート：　いいえ、あまり高くなかったです。これ、おみやげです。

5 たけし：　　ありがとう。

6 ロバート：　たけしさんのデートはどうでしたか。

7 たけし：　　……

Ⅰ

Robert: Nice weather.

Ken: Yes. But it is a little hot.

Robert: Yes. Wow, beautiful sea!

Ken: Let's swim.

　　　　*　　　*　　　*

Ken: What kind of sports do you like, Robert?

Robert: I like surfing. Shall we do it together tomorrow?

Ken: But isn't it difficult?

Robert: No.

Ⅱ

Robert: Excuse me. How much is this T-shirt?

Store attendant: It is 1,800 yen.

Robert: Um . . . Do you have a large size?

Store attendant: Yes, we do.

Robert: Then, two large ones, please.

Ⅲ

Takeshi: Robert, did you enjoy the trip?

Robert: Yes. The sea was very beautiful in Okinawa.

Takeshi: Good. I like the sea very much, too. Was the hotel expensive?

Robert: No, it wasn't so expensive. Here is a souvenir for you.

Takeshi: Thank you.

Robert: How was your date, Takeshi?

Takeshi: . . .

単　語
たん　　ご

K05-07 (J-E)
K05-08 (E-J)

V o c a b u l a r y

N o u n s

たべもの	食べ物	food
のみもの	飲み物	drink
くだもの	果物	fruit
やすみ	休み	holiday; day off; absence
* りょこう	旅行	travel
* うみ	海	sea
* サーフィン		surfing
* おみやげ	お土産	souvenir
バス		bus
* てんき	天気	weather
しゅくだい	宿題	homework
テスト		test
たんじょうび	誕生日	birthday
へや	部屋	room
* ぼく	僕	I (used by men)
* Lサイズ (エルサイズ)		size L

い - a d j e c t i v e s

あたらしい	新しい	new
ふるい	古い	old (thing—not used for people)
* あつい	暑い	hot (weather)
さむい	寒い	cold (weather—not used for things)
あつい	熱い	hot (thing)
いそがしい	忙しい	busy (people/days)
おおきい	大きい	large
ちいさい	小さい	small
おもしろい	面白い	interesting; funny
つまらない		boring
やさしい		easy (problem); kind (person)
* むずかしい	難しい	difficult
かっこいい		good-looking (conjugates like いい)
こわい	怖い	frightening

＊Words that appear in the dialogue

| * たのしい | 楽しい | fun |
| やすい | 安い | inexpensive; cheap (thing) |

な-adjectives

* すき (な)	好き	fond of; to like （〜が）
きらい (な)	嫌い	disgusted with; to dislike （〜が）
* だいすき (な)	大好き	very fond of; to love （〜が）
だいきらい (な)	大嫌い	to hate （〜が）
* きれい (な)		beautiful; clean
げんき (な)	元気	healthy; energetic
しずか (な)	静か	quiet
にぎやか (な)		lively
ひま (な)	暇	not busy; free (time)

U-verbs

* およぐ	泳ぐ	to swim
きく	聞く	to ask (*person* に)
のる	乗る	to ride; to board （〜に）
* やる		to do; to perform （〜を）

Ru-verb

| でかける | 出かける | to go out |

Adverbs and Other Expressions

* いっしょに	一緒に	together
* すごく		extremely
* だいじょうぶ	大丈夫	It's okay.; Not to worry.; Everything is under control.
とても		very
* どんな		what kind of . . .
* 〜まい	〜枚	[counter for flat objects]

文法 Grammar
ぶん ぽう

1 Adjectives (Present Tense)

There are two types of adjectives in Japanese: "い-adjectives" and "な-adjectives." They conjugate for tense (present and past), polarity (affirmative and negative), and so forth, just as verbs do. The two types of adjectives follow different conjugation patterns.

You just add です to both い-adjectives and な-adjectives for affirmative present tense sentences. In negative sentences, you replace the last い of an い-adjective with くない. な-adjectives are just like nouns and you only need to change です to じゃないです.

[Present]	affirmative	negative
い-adjectives e.g. さむい	さむい<u>です</u> *It is cold.*	さむ<u>くないです</u> (or さむ<u>くありません</u>) *It is not cold.*
な-adjectives e.g. 元気 (な) げん き	元気です げん き *She is healthy.*	元気<u>じゃないです</u> げん き (or 元気<u>じゃありません</u>) げん き *She is not healthy.*

A：その本はおもしろいですか。 　　　*Is that book interesting?*
　　ほん

B：いいえ、あまりおもしろくないです。 　*No, it is not very interesting.*

A：今日、ひまですか。 　　　　　　　　*Are you free today?*
　　きょう

B：いいえ、ひまじゃないです。 　　　　*No, I'm not.*

With both い- and な-adjectives, you find two negative forms: ないです and ありません. The ないです pattern is more colloquial, and ありません is more conservative and more appropriate in the written language. Just like negation with nouns (see Lesson 2), じゃ in the negative version can also be replaced with では in more formal situations. Don't apply the noun/な-adjective pattern to い-adjectives. It is wrong to say ×さむいじゃないです, for example.

Unlike verbs, adjectives conjugate fairly uniformly. The only irregularity worth noticing at this stage is the behavior of the adjective いい (good). The first syllable of いい is changed to よ in all forms except the dictionary form.[1] Compound adjectives like かっこいい that are built with いい follow this syllable change[2] and we say かっこ<u>よ</u>くないです.

[Present] (irregular)

	affirmative	negative
いい	いいです	<u>よ</u>くないです
		(or <u>よ</u>くありません)

If you want to say things like "very hot," and "a little hot," you can add "degree adverbs" like すごく (extremely), とても (very) and ちょっと (a little; slightly) before adjectives.

沖縄の海は<u>とても</u>きれいです。　　　*The sea is very beautiful in Okinawa.*
おきなわ　うみ

この部屋は<u>ちょっと</u>暑いです。　　　*This room is a little hot.*
　へ や　　　　　　　あつ

2 Adjectives (Past Tense)

With い-adjectives, you change the last い to かったです in the affirmative. In the negative, you only need to change the present tense くない to くなかったです. な-adjectives are again just like nouns. Don't confuse the two patterns. It is wrong to say × さむいでした, for example.

[Past]

	affirmative	negative
い-adjectives		
e.g. さむい	さむ<u>かったです</u>	さむ<u>くなかったです</u>
		(or さむ<u>くありませんでした</u>)
	It was cold.	*It was not cold.*
な-adjectives		
e.g. 元気（な）	元気<u>でした</u>	元気<u>じゃなかったです</u>
げん き	げん き	げん き
		(or 元気<u>じゃありませんでした</u>)
		げん き
	She was healthy.	*She was not healthy.*

---

[1] There actually are alternative forms, よい and よいです, but they are much less frequently used than いい and いいです in the spoken language.

[2] Despite its appearance when it is written in *hiragana*, かわいい (cute), which we will learn in Lesson 7, is not made up of いい, and therefore does not go through this い to よ change, and we say かわ<u>いく</u>ないです.

Ａ：テストは難しかったですか。   *Was the exam difficult?*

Ｂ：いいえ、ぜんぜん難しくなかったです。   *No, it was not difficult at all.*

Ａ：その町はにぎやかでしたか。   *Was the town lively?*

Ｂ：いいえ、にぎやかじゃなかったです。   *No, it was not livery.*

The い-adjective いい (good) is again irregular. Its first syllable is changed to よ.

[Past] (irregular)	affirmative	negative
いい	<u>よ</u>かったです	<u>よ</u>くなかったです
		(or <u>よ</u>くありませんでした)

3 Adjectives (Noun Modification)

You can use い- and な- adjectives to modify nouns. Place the dictionary form of an い-adjective before the noun you want to modify. With な-adjectives, you see な, which was missing before です, return.

い-adjectives:	おもしろい映画	*an interesting movie*
な-adjectives:	きれいな写真	*a beautiful picture*

きのう、おもしろい映画を見ました。   *I saw an interesting movie yesterday.*

山下先生はこわい先生です。   *Professor Yamashita is a scary teacher.*

京都できれいな写真を撮りました。   *I took a beautiful picture in Kyoto.*

ここはとてもにぎやかな町です。   *This is a very vibrant city.*

4 好き（な）/ きらい（な）

Some Japanese adjectives are like verbs in English, and they take a subject and an object. 好き（な）(to be fond of; to like), and きらい（な）(to be disgusted with; to dislike) are examples. If you like something or somebody, for example, 私は will be the subject and the object of your affection will be Y が.[3]

$$
X \text{ は } Y \text{ が}^4 \left\{ \begin{array}{l} 好き \\ きらい \end{array} \right\} \text{ です。} \qquad X \left\{ \begin{array}{l} likes \\ dislikes \end{array} \right\} Y.
$$

ロバートさんは日本語のクラスが好きです。　Robert likes his Japanese classes.

山下先生は魚がきらいです。　Professor Yamashita dislikes fish.

If you like or dislike something (or somebody) very much, you can use the intensified forms of 好きです and きらいです, namely, 大好きです (like very much) and 大きらいです (hate), which are more often used than the degree modifier とても in combination with 好きです and きらいです.

たけしさんはコーヒーが大好きです。　Takeshi likes coffee a lot.

ソラさんはなっとうが大きらいです。　Sora hates natto (Japanese fermented soybeans).

If you want to be neutral and say that you neither like nor dislike something, you can say:

好きでもきらいでもないです。　I neither like nor dislike (it).

You can use 好きな and きらいな as modifiers of nouns. For example, you can say things like:

これは私の好きな本です。　This is my favorite book.

---

[3] In the expression of romantic or familial affection, the complex particle のことが can replace が. Thus,
たけしさんはメアリーさんのことが好きです。　＝メアリーさんが好きです。
Takeshi is in love with Mary.

[4] In contexts where you are contrasting two or more items, the particle は is used instead of が. Thus,
私は野菜は好きですが、肉はきらいです。　I like vegetables, but I don't like meat.

5 〜ましょう / 〜ましょうか

Take a long form of a verb and replace the ます ending with ましょう or ましょうか and you will get the Japanese expression for "let's . . . ," which you can use to suggest a plan of action.

一緒に図書館で勉強しましょう。
Let's study in the library together.

あそこでコーヒーを飲みましょうか。
Shall we drink coffee over there?

6 Counting

When we count items in Japanese, we use different number words for different kinds of items; the words used for counting people are different from the words used for counting books, for example. Number words often come *after*, rather than *before*, the items counted in a sentence.

	item	number		
リーさんは	Ｔシャツを	三枚	買いました。	*Lee bought three T-shirts.*

The number word, 三枚, is made up of the numeral 三 and the "counter" 枚. This counter is used for sheets of paper and other flat objects. There will be other counters in later lessons—for people, for books, for stick-like objects, and so forth. You can find what counter to use for what kind of items, and how the sound of number words changes in combination with counters in the table on pages 380-381.

表現ノート
ひょう げん

忙しい/にぎやか（な） ▶ 忙しい is used when we describe people and is not used
for places. When you want to say that Tokyo is busy, you should use にぎやか（な）.

たけしさんは忙しいです。	*Takeshi is busy.*
東京はにぎやかです。	*Tokyo is busy/lively.*

Note that the sentence below is also acceptable, since the subject "I" is omitted in
the sentence.

日曜日は忙しいです。	*I am busy on Sunday.*
＝日曜日は（私は）忙しいです。	

そうですね/そうですか ▶ Use そうですね when you agree with what you just
heard. You share the same opinion about Ken in this example.

A：けんさんはとてもいい人です。	*Ken is a very nice person.*
B：そうですね。	*That's right / I agree. / Uh-huh.*

You can also use そうですね with the last ね prolonged, as a hesitation marker,
trying to buy time to think further.

A：一緒に映画に行きませんか。	*Let's go to the cinema.*
B：そうですねえ。	*Well, let me see . . .*

Use そうですか with the falling intonation, when what you just heard is new to
you. In the example below, you probably do not know Ken.

A：けんさんはとてもいい人です。	*Ken is a very nice person.*
B：そうですか。	*I see. / Oh, he is, huh?*

If you say そうですか with the rising intonation, you will be indicating that you
are not completely sure with what you just heard.

A：今日は水曜日ですよ。	*Today is Wednesday.*
B：そうですか？火曜日じゃないですか？	*Is it really? Isn't this Tuesday?*

練習 Practice
れん しゅう

I 高いです ☛Grammar 1
たか

A. Change the following adjectives into the affirmative. 🔊 K05-09

Example たかい   →   たかいです

　　　　 げんきな →   げんきです

e.g. たかい	げんきな	(1) やすい	(2) あたらしい	(3) ふるい

(4) あつい	(5) さむい	(6) おおきい	(7) ちいさい	(8) たのしい

(9) おもしろい	(10) つまらない	(11) むずかしい	(12) やさしい

 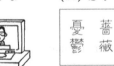

(13) こわい	(14) いい	(15) かっこいい	(16) いそがしい

(17) ひまな	(18) きれいな	(19) しずかな	(20) にぎやかな

 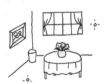  

B. Change the above adjectives into the negative. 🔊 K05-10

(Example) たかい　　→　たかくないです

　　　　　げんきな　→　げんきじゃないです

C. Answer the following questions.

(Example) Q：日本語のクラスは難しいですか。

　　　　　A：ええ、難しいです。／いいえ、難しくないです。

1. 今日はひまですか。
2. 先生はやさしいですか。
3. 学校は大きいですか。
4. 部屋はきれいですか。

5. 日本の食べ物はおいしいですか。
6. クラスはおもしろいですか。
7. 宿題は難しいですか。
8. あなたの町は静かですか。

D. Pair Work—Make affirmative and negative sentences with your partner.

(Example) きれいな

　→　友だちの部屋はきれいです。
　　　でも、私の部屋はきれいじゃないです。

1. おもしろい
2. いい

3. こわい
4. おいしい

5. 高い
6. かっこいい

7. 元気な
8. ひまな

E. Pair Work—Make your own sentences on the topics below using adjectives, and tell your partner.

(Example) テストは難しくないです。やさしいです。

1. 私は
2. 私の町は
3. 私のとなりの人は

4. 私の部屋は
5. 東京は
6. ハワイ (Hawaii) は

Ⅱ 高かったです ☛Grammar 2
<small>たか</small>

A. Change the following adjectives into the past affirmative. 🔊 K05-11

(Example) たかい　　→　たかかったです

げんきな　→　げんきでした

1. やすい	4. おもしろい	7. たのしい	10. にぎやかな
2. あつい	5. つまらない	8. いい	11. きれいな
3. さむい	6. いそがしい	9. しずかな	12. ひまな

B. Change the following adjectives into the past negative. 🔊 K05-12

(Example) やすい　→　やすくなかったです

ひまな　→　ひまじゃなかったです

1. たかい	4. つまらない	7. いそがしい	10. しずかな
2. たのしい	5. おおきい	8. かっこいい	11. きれいな
3. やさしい	6. いい	9. にぎやかな	12. げんきな

C. This is what Robert wrote down about the trip to Okinawa. Look at the memo and make sentences. 🔊 K05-13

(Example) 沖縄は暑かったです。
<small>おきなわ　あつ</small>

e.g. Okinawa—hot
1. food—not expensive
2. food—delicious
3. hotel—not big
4. hotel—new
5. restaurant—not quiet
6. sea—beautiful
7. surfing—fun

D. Pair Work—Practice a dialogue with your partner, substituting the underlined parts.
A and B are talking about A's vacation.

(Example)

went to Okinawa ── very hot

→　A：休みに沖縄に行きました。
<ruby>休<rt>やす</rt></ruby>　<ruby>沖縄<rt>おきなわ</rt></ruby>　<ruby>行<rt>い</rt></ruby>

　　B：そうですか。どうでしたか。

　　A：とても暑かったです。
<ruby>暑<rt>あつ</rt></ruby>

1. saw a movie　　　　　　── scary

2. stayed home（うちにいる）── very boring

3. went to a party　　　　── not fun

4. went to a restaurant　── not delicious

5. (your own)

会
L5

Ⅲ　<ruby>高<rt>たか</rt></ruby>い<ruby>時計<rt>とけい</rt></ruby>ですね　☛Grammar 3

A. Look at the pictures and make comments on them.　🔊 K05-14

(Example)　<ruby>時計<rt>とけい</rt></ruby>　→　<ruby>高<rt>たか</rt></ruby>い<ruby>時計<rt>とけい</rt></ruby>ですね。

e.g.

¥100,000

(1) ホテル

(2) テレビ

(3) <ruby>宿題<rt>しゅくだい</rt></ruby>

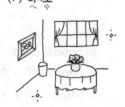

(4) <ruby>人<rt>ひと</rt></ruby>

(5) <ruby>人<rt>ひと</rt></ruby>

(6) <ruby>町<rt>まち</rt></ruby>

(7) <ruby>部屋<rt>へや</rt></ruby>

B. Answer the questions using the given cues. 🔊 K05-15

(Example)　Q：メアリーさんはどんな人ですか。

　　　　　A：やさしい人です。

e.g. メアリー　　　(1) ナオミ　　　　(2) ロバート　　　(3) ウデイ

　　kind　　　　　beautiful　　　　　funny　　　　energetic

C. Pair Work—Let's talk about towns, people, schools, etc.

(Example)　お母さん　→　A：お母さんはどんな人ですか。

　　　　　　　　　　　　B：おもしろい人です。

　　　　　　　　　　　　A：そうですか。

1. お母さん／お父さん　　　　　4. (name of a school)
2. (name of a teacher) 先生　　　5. (name of a town)
3. (name of a friend) さん

Ⅳ 魚が好きですか　☛Grammar 4

A. Pair Work—Choose the items from the following categories and ask your partners whether they like them.

(Example)　A：魚が好きですか。

　　　　　　B：はい、好きです／大好きです。

　　　　　　　いいえ、あまり好きじゃないです／きらいです／大きらいです。

1. Foods: meat／なっとう (fermented beans)／アイスクリーム
2. Sports: サッカー (soccer)／スキー (skiing)／ゴルフ (golf)
3. Music: ロック (rock)／ジャズ (jazz)／クラシック (classical music)
4. School work: test／Japanese class／homework
5. Drinks: sake／green tea／coffee

　　　　Note: If you neither like it nor dislike it, you can use 好きでもきらいでもないです.

B. Answer the following questions.

1. どんなスポーツが好きですか。
2. どんな食べ物が好きですか。
3. どんな飲み物が好きですか。
4. どんな果物が好きですか。
5. どんな映画が好きですか。
6. どんな音楽が好きですか。

Ⅴ 映画を見ましょう ☞Grammar 5

A. Change the following into ましょう sentences. 🔊 K05-16

Example テニスをする → テニスをしましょう。

1. いっしょに帰る
2. 先生に聞く
3. 映画を見る
4. おみやげを買う
5. 出かける

6. 待つ
7. 泳ぐ
8. 写真を撮る
9. バスに乗る
10. 六時に会う

B. Pair Work—Make follow-up suggestions using ましょうか.

Example 寒いですね。
→ Ａ：寒いですね。お茶を飲みましょうか。
Ｂ：そうしましょう。

1. 暑いですね。
2. 十二時ですね。
3. この宿題は難しいですね。
4. あしたは先生の誕生日ですよ。
5. あのレストランはおいしいですよ。
6. あしたはテストがありますね。

Ⅵ まとめの練習 (Review Exercises)
れんしゅう

A. Role Play—Ask what kind of activities your partner likes and ask to do them together. Use the last half of Dialogue I as a model.

(Example)　A：どんな音楽が好きですか。
　　　　　　　　おんがく　す
　　　　　　B：Jポップ (J-pop) が好きです。
　　　　　　　　ジェー　　　　　　す
　　　　　　A：私も好きです。一緒にコンサート (concert) に行きましょうか。
　　　　　　　　わたし　す　　　　いっしょ　　　　　　　　　　　い
　　　　　　　　(Continue the conversation)

B. Role Play—Using Dialogue Ⅱ as a model, buy some T-shirts.

Sサイズ (size S)
エス
Mサイズ (size M)
エム
Lサイズ (size L)
エル
LLサイズ／XLサイズ (size XL)
エルエル　　　　　エックスエル

C. Class Activity—Show and Tell
Bring pictures you took on a trip. Explain to your class where you went, what you did, how it was, etc. Afterwards, other students will ask in detail about the trip.

(Example questions)

どこに行きましたか。
　　　　い
天気はどうでしたか。
てんき
だれと行きましたか。
　　　　い
ホテルはいくらでしたか。

Culture Notes

日本の祭り Japanese Festivals
（にほん　まつり）

There are many festivals in Japan. Some are famous, while others are known only to the locals. Some are very traditional, while others are rather new. Here are some examples of well-known festivals. Where do you want to visit?

札幌　雪祭り
（さっぽろ　ゆきまつ）

The Sapporo Snow Festival is held for a week in early February. It features large snow sculptures constructed in a park on the main avenue.

京都　祇園祭
（きょうと　ぎおんまつり）

The Kyoto Gion Festival is held in July. On the 17th and the 24th, beautifully decorated floats parade on the main streets in Kyoto.

青森　ねぶた祭り
（あおもり　まつ）

The Aomori Nebuta Festival is held August 2–7. Huge colorful lanterns are pulled through the streets, accompanied by people dancing and playing flutes and drums.

徳島　阿波踊り
（とくしま　あわおど）

The Tokushima Awa Dance Festival is held August 12–15. Groups of people form lines and dance around the center of town.

仙台　七夕祭り
（せんだい　たなばたまつ）

The Sendai Tanabata Festival is held August 6–8, and is famous for its large, elaborate decorations made with colorful Japanese paper.

写真提供：（一財）徳島県観光協会

第6課

L E S S O N 6

ロバートさんの一日 A Day in Robert's Life
いち にち

In this lesson, we will..

- Make requests
- Ask for and give permission
- Talk about rules and regulations
- Offer help
- Give reasons for doing/not doing something

会 話 D i a l o g u e
かい わ

Ⅰ In class. 🔊 K06-01/02

1 山下先生： ロバートさん、次のページを読んでください。
  やましたせんせい   つぎ   よ

2 ロバート： ……

3 山下先生： ロバートさん、起きてください。クラスで寝てはいけませんよ。
  やましたせんせい   お   ね

4 ロバート： 先生、教科書を忘れました。
           せんせい きょうかしょ わす

5 山下先生： 教科書を持ってきてくださいね。毎日使いますから。
  やましたせんせい きょうかしょ も   まいにちつか

6 ロバート： はい、すみません。

Ⅱ After class. 🔊 K06-03/04

1 ソ ラ： ロバートさん、今日は大変でしたね。
                 きょう たいへん

2 ロバート： ええ。後でソラさんのノートを借りてもいいですか。
              あと   か

3 ソ ラ： いいですよ。

4 ロバート： ありがとう。すぐ返します。
                      かえ

5 ソ ラ： ロバートさん、あしたテストがありますよ。

6 ロバート： えっ。本当ですか。
              ほんとう

7 ソ ラ： ええ。ロバートさん、金曜日に休みましたからね。
                       きんようび やす

8 ロバート： じゃあ、今日は家に帰って、勉強します。
                きょう いえ かえ   べんきょう

Ⅲ On the bus. 🔊 K06-05/06

1 おばあさん：　あの、すみません。このバスはさくら病院へ行きますか。

2 ロバート：　　ええ、行きますよ。……あの、どうぞ座ってください。

3 おばあさん：　いいえ、けっこうです。すぐ降りますから。

4 ロバート：　　そうですか。じゃあ、荷物を持ちましょうか。

5 おばあさん：　あ、どうもすみません。

会
L6

Ⅰ

Prof. Yamashita: Robert, please read the next page.

Robert: . . .

Prof. Yamashita: Robert, please wake up. You cannot sleep in the class.

Robert: Mr. Yamashita, I forgot to bring the textbook.

Prof. Yamashita: Please bring your textbook with you. We use it every day.

Robert: I understand. I'm sorry.

Ⅱ

Sora: Robert, you had a hard time today.

Robert: Yes. May I borrow your notebook later, Sora?

Sora: Yes.

Robert: Thank you. I'll return it soon.

Sora: Robert, we will have a test tomorrow.

Robert: Really?

Sora: Yes. You were absent from the class last Friday. (That's why you didn't know about it.)

Robert: Well then, I'll go home and study today.

Ⅲ

Old woman: Excuse me. Does this bus go to Sakura Hospital?

Robert: Yes, it does. . . . Well, take this seat, please.

Old woman: No, thank you. I'll get off soon.

Robert: Is that so? Then, shall I hold your bag for you?

Old woman: Thank you.

単 語
たん　ご

K06-07 (J-E)
K06-08 (E-J)

V o c a b u l a r y

N o u n s

かんじ	漢字	kanji; Chinese character
* きょうかしょ	教科書	textbook
* ページ		page
* つぎ	次	next
おかね	お金	money
* にもつ	荷物	baggage
パソコン		personal computer
シャワー		shower
エアコン		air conditioner
でんき	電気	electricity; light
まど	窓	window
でんしゃ	電車	train
くに	国	country; place of origin
こんしゅう	今週	this week
らいしゅう	来週	next week
らいねん	来年	next year
よる	夜	night

な - a d j e c t i v e

* たいへん (な)	大変	tough (situation)

U - v e r b s

あそぶ	遊ぶ	to play; to spend time pleasantly
いそぐ	急ぐ	to hurry
* かえす	返す	to return (a thing) (*person* に *thing* を)
けす	消す	to turn off; to erase（〜を）
しぬ	死ぬ	to die
* すわる	座る	to sit down（*seat* に）
たつ	立つ	to stand up
たばこをすう	たばこを吸う	to smoke
* つかう	使う	to use（〜を）
てつだう	手伝う	to help（*person/task* を）

* Words that appear in the dialogue

はいる	入る	to enter （～に）
* もつ	持つ	to carry; to hold （～を）
* やすむ	休む	(1) to be absent (from . . .) （～を）
		(2) to rest

Ru-verbs

あける	開ける	to open (something) （～を）
しめる	閉める	to close (something) （～を）
おしえる	教える	to teach; to instruct
		(person に thing を)
* わすれる	忘れる	to forget; to leave behind （～を）
* おりる	降りる	to get off （～を）
* かりる	借りる	to borrow （person に thing を）
シャワーをあびる	シャワーを 浴びる	to take a shower
つける		to turn on （～を）

Irregular Verbs

でんわする	電話する	to call （～に）
つれてくる	連れてくる	to bring (a person) （～を）
* もってくる	持ってくる	to bring (a thing) （～を）

Adverbs and Other Expressions

* あとで	後で	later on
* すぐ		right away
ゆっくり		slowly; leisurely; unhurriedly
* けっこうです	結構です	That would be fine.; That wouldn't be necessary.
* ほんとうですか	本当ですか	Really?

会
L6

文法 ぶん ぽう G r a m m a r

1 Te-form

Te-forms are a *very* important part of Japanese grammar. In this lesson, we will learn, among their various uses, to use them in:

- making requests (". . . , please.")
- forming a sentence that describes two events or activities. ("I did this and did that.")
- giving and asking for permission ("You may . . . / May I . . . ?")
- stating that something is forbidden ("You must not . . .")

The conjugation paradigm of *te*-forms is complex, as we need to learn separate rules for *ru-*, *u-*, and irregular verbs. Furthermore, the rule for *u*-verbs is divided into five sub-rules.

Ru-verbs	る	→	て	食べる	→	食べて
U-verbs with final	う つ る¹	→	って	会う 待つ とる	→ → →	会って 待って とって
	む ぶ ぬ	→	んで	読む 遊ぶ 死ぬ	→ → →	読んで 遊んで 死んで
	く	→	いて (Exception)	書く 行く	→ →	書いて 行って
	ぐ	→	いで	泳ぐ	→	泳いで
	す	→	して	話す	→	話して
Irregular verbs	する くる			する くる	→ →	して きて

---

¹ As we discussed in Grammar 1 of Lesson 3, some verbs that end with the *hiragana* る are *ru*-verbs and some others are *u*-verbs. Review the discussion on how the vowel before the final る syllable determines which verb belongs to which class. In this book we learn the following *u*-verbs that end with *iru* or *eru*: 帰る (return), 入る (enter), 知る (know), いる (need), 切る (cut), and 走る (run).

Note that *te*-forms and stems (the forms you find before ます) of an *u*-verb are totally different from each other, while they look similar in *ru*-verbs (食べて and 食べます). Be careful not to come up with improper forms such as ×会いて (compare 会います) and ×読みて (compare 読みます) in *u*-verbs. You may want to memorize each verb as a set, as in 書く―書きます―書いて. Refer to the verb conjugation table at the end of this volume (p. 382).

2 〜てください

Use a verbal *te*-form together with ください to make a polite request to another person "please do . . . for me."[2]

教科書を読んでください。

Please read the textbook.

すみません。ちょっと教えてください。

Excuse me. Please teach me a little. (= Tell me, I need your advice.)

3 Describing Two Activities

You can use a *te*-form to combine two or more verbs, as in describing a sequence of events or actions ("I did this and then I did that"). In other words, the *te*-form does the work of "and" with verbs. (Note that two verbs cannot be joined by と, which only connects nouns.) The tense of the verb at the end of each sentence determines when these events take place.

図書館に行って、本を借ります。

I will go to the library and check out some books.

今日は、六時に起きて、勉強しました。

Today I got up at six and studied.

食堂に行って、昼ご飯を食べましょう。

Let's go to the cafeteria and have lunch.

The *te*-form of a verb can also be used to connect a verb more "loosely" with the rest of a sentence. In the first example below, the verb in the *te*-form describes the manner in which the action described by the second verb is performed. In the second example, the *te*-form describes the situation for which the apology is made.

---

[2] If you are talking to a very close friend or a member of your family, a *te*-form, by itself, can be used as a request.
　　窓を開けて。　　*Open the window, will you?*

バスに乗って、会社に行きます。

I go to work by bus. (I take a bus to work.)

教科書を忘れて、すみません。

I am sorry for not bringing in the textbook. (I left the book at home, and I am sorry.)

4 〜てもいいです

A verbal *te*-form plus もいいです means "you may do . . . ," which describes an activity that is permitted.[3] To ask for permission, you can turn it into a question sentence, 〜てもいいですか. If somebody asks for permission and if you want to grant it, you can either repeat the whole verb *te*-form plus もいいです construction, or just say いいです. て needs to be a part of a verb and cannot stand alone. So you cannot just say × てもいいです or × もいいです. The polite and graceful way to grant permission is to say どうぞ.

教科書を見てもいいですよ。	*You may use the textbook.*
Ａ：トイレに行ってもいいですか。	*May I go to the bathroom?*
Ｂ：はい、いいですよ。／どうぞ。	*You may. / Please.*

5 〜てはいけません

A verbal *te*-form plus はいけません means "you must not do . . . ," a strong prohibition statement, as in rules and regulations.

ここで写真を撮ってはいけません。	*You must not take pictures here.*

If somebody asks you for permission but you want to deny it, you can use てはいけません, but the sentence may sound too harsh unless you are in a place of authority. We will learn a softer way to say "please don't" in Lesson 8.

---

[3] In casual speech, you can drop も and say 食べていいです as well as 食べてもいいです. In contrast, は in the construction てはいけません, which is discussed in the next section, cannot be dropped.

6 〜から

A sentence that ends with から (because) explains the reason or the cause of a situation, a proposal, and so forth.

> (situation)。(explanation) から。[4]

私は今晩勉強します。あしたテストがありますから。
I will study this evening. (Because) we will have an exam tomorrow.

バスに乗りましょう。タクシーは高いですから。
Let's go by bus. (Because) taxis are expensive.

7 〜ましょうか (Offering Assistance)

In Lesson 5 we learned ましょうか meaning "Let's . . ." ましょうか is also used in the sense of "let me do . . . ," in offering assistance. If you see somebody having a hard time opening the lid of a bottle, for example, you can offer help by saying:

（私が）やりましょうか。　　　　　　　*I'll do it.*

Or to a person who is carrying a heavy bag:

荷物を持ちましょうか。　　　　　　*Shall I carry your bag?*

---

[4] The explanation clause may also precede the situation clause. Thus the first example above can also be paraphrased as:

あしたテストがありますから、私は今晩勉強します。

We will discuss this further in Lesson 9.

日本の教育制度 (1) Japan's Educational System (1)
にほん　きょういくせいど

Most children in Japan attend kindergartens or nursery schools before entering elementary school. Compulsory education comprises six years of elementary school and three years of junior high school. Although not compulsory, over 95% of junior high students go on to high school for three years. About half of high school graduates attend a university or junior college. Admission to high schools and universities is usually based on an entrance exam.

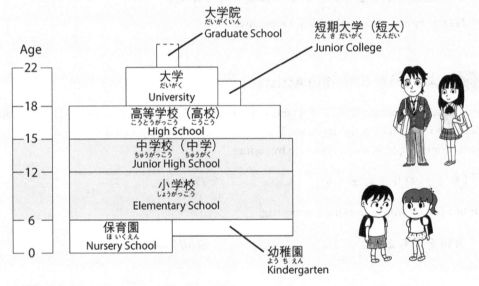

The Japanese school year starts in April and ends in March, with a long vacation in summer and two shorter breaks in winter and spring.

[Typical Japanese School Calendar (Elementary to High School)]

School year begins											School year ends
April	May	June	July	Aug.	Sep.	Oct.	Nov.	Dec.	Jan.	Feb.	Mar.

夏休み
なつやす
Summer Vacation

冬休み
ふゆやす
Winter Vacation

春休み
はるやす
Spring Vacation

[Sample timetable for a 4th year student studying at a public elementary school]

		Monday	Tuesday	Wednesday	Thursday	Friday
	8:20-8:35	Morning Activities (Reading, Studying, etc.)				
1	8:45-9:30	Japanese	Mathematics	Japanese	Arts/Crafts	Integrated Studies
2	9:40-10:25	Music	Japanese	Social Studies	Arts/Crafts	Mathematics
3	10:50-11:35	Mathematics	Science	Mathematics	Science	Music
4	11:45-12:30	Social Studies	Physical Education	Moral Education	Japanese	English
		Lunch, Lunch Break and Cleaning				
5	1:55-2:40	Physical Education	Social Studies	Calligraphy	Mathematics	Japanese
6	2:50-3:35		Integrated Studies	Science	Club Activities	Social Studies

会
L6

Expression Notes

表現ノート
ひょう げん

どうも ▶ どうも is normally used with ありがとう, as in どうもありがとう (Thank you very much), or with すみません, as in どうもすみません (I am very sorry/Thank you very much). When used alone, it is an abbreviation of どうもありがとう or どうもすみません. Therefore, when you want to show your gratitude or regret, you can just say どうも instead of saying a long sentence. どうも functions in many ways, depending on the situation. Some people use どうも as "hello" or "good-bye."

お ▶ Many words that begin with お can also be used without it. お in such words simply adds smoothness and nuance of social refinement, without changing the meaning of the words.

e.g. お酒 お金 お風呂 お祭り (festival)
　　　さけ 　かね 　ふ ろ 　まつ

練習 P r a c t i c e
れん しゅう

I *Te*-form ☞Grammar 1

A. Change the following verbs into *te*-forms. 🔊 K06-09

(Example) おきる → おきて

1. たべる	4. かく	7. あそぶ	10. いそぐ	13. しぬ
2. かう	5. くる	8. とる	11. いく	14. はなす
3. よむ	6. まつ	9. する	12. ねる	15. かえる

B. Let's sing a *te*-form song! (Battle Hymn of the Republic) 🔊 K06-10

♪1.　　あう　あって　まつ　まって　とる　とって
　　　　よむ　よんで　あそぶ　あそんで　しぬ　しんで
　　　　かく　かいて　けす　けして　いそぐ　いそいで
　　　　みんな　*u*-verb　*te*-form

♪2.　　うつる　って　むぶぬ　んで　く　いて　ぐ　いで
　　　　(repeat twice)
　　　　す　して　*u*-verb　*te*-form

II 窓を開けてください ☞Grammar 2
まど あ

A. Make polite requests. 🔊 K06-11

(Example) 日本語を話してください。
に ほん ご　 はな

e.g.　Please speak Japanese.
1. Please stand up.
2. Please listen.
3. Please read the book.
4. Please look at page 35.
5. Please bring the textbook.

6. Please teach me kanji.
7. Please return my book.
8. Please speak slowly.
9. Please come with me.
10. Please call me tomorrow.
11. Please bring your friend.

B. What are they saying in the following situations?

Example 窓を開けてください。
まど　あ

会
L6

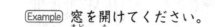

e.g.   (1)   (2)   (3)

(4)   (5)   (6)   (7)

C. Pair Work—Make your own request, such as "Please stand up" and "Please take a picture," and ask your partner to act it out.

Example A：コーヒーを飲んでください。   →   B pretends to drink coffee.
の

Ⅲ 朝起きて、コーヒーを飲みます ☞Grammar 3
あさ お　　　　　　　　　　　　　の

A. Look at the pictures below and combine the pictures using *te*-forms. 🔊 K06-12

(Example) 朝起きて、コーヒーを飲みます。
あさ お　　　　　　　　　　　　　　の

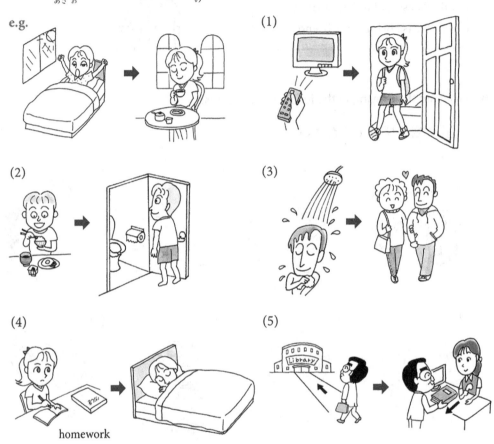

e.g.

(1)

(2)

(3)

(4)

homework

(5)

Library

B. Change the following into *te*-forms and make complete the sentences.

(Example) 朝起きる → 朝起きて、新聞を読みます。
あさ お　　　　　　　　　　あさ お　　　　　しんぶん　　　よ

1. 友だちのうちに行く
とも　　　　　　　　　い

2. うちに帰る
かえ

3. 電車を降りる
でんしゃ　　　お

4. 友だちに会う
とも　　　　あ

5. 自転車を借りる
じ てんしゃ　　　か

6. 大学に行く
だいがく　　　い

C. Pair Work—Make questions using the following cues. When you answer, use ～て.

(Example) あしたの夜_{よる}

→　A：あしたの夜_{よる}、何_{なに}をしますか。

　　B：図書館_{としょかん}で勉強_{べんきょう}して、家_{いえ}に帰_{かえ}ります。

1. 今日_{きょう}の夜_{よる}
2. あしたの朝_{あさ}
3. きのうの朝_{あさ}

4. きのうの夜_{よる}
5. 今週_{こんしゅう}の週末_{しゅうまつ}
6. 先週_{せんしゅう}の週末_{しゅうまつ}

Ⅳ 写真_{しゃしん}を撮_とってもいいですか 🖙Grammar 4

A. Look at the pictures below, and ask if it is okay to do those things. 🔊 K06-13

(Example) 写真_{しゃしん}を撮_とってもいいですか。

[At a temple]

[At a Japanese home]

B. Pair Work—Play the roles of people in the pictures in A, and make dialogues.

(Example) A：写真_{しゃしん}を撮_とってもいいですか。

　　B：ええ、いいですよ。どうぞ。／

　　すみません。ちょっと……。

C. Make short conversations in the following situations using ～てもいいですか.

[With your teacher]

1. You are in class. You realize you need to go to the bathroom as soon as possible.

2. You are in class. You feel sick and want to return home.

3. You have forgotten to do the homework. You are sure you can bring it in tomorrow.

4. You want to ask your teacher something, but you cannot phrase it in Japanese.

[With a friend]

5. You missed the class yesterday. You want to borrow your friend's notebook.

6. You and your friend are in a dark room, and you feel somewhat uncomfortable.

7. You are invited to your friend's party, and you want to bring your friend.

Ⅴ 食べてはいけません ☞Grammar 5

A. You are the teacher of a rowdy class. Ban the following disruptive activities. 🔊 K06-14

Example 食べてはいけません。

B. Pair Work—Ask your partner if it is all right to do the following things.

Example 図書館で電話する
　　　→　A：図書館で電話してもいいですか。
　　　　　B：はい、電話してもいいです。／
　　　　　　　いいえ、電話してはいけません。

1. 図書館で話す
2. 図書館で昼ご飯を食べる
3. 図書館でコーヒーを飲む
4. 図書館でパソコンを使う

5. あなたの国で十八歳の人は
　　たばこを吸う
6. あなたの国で十八歳の人は
　　お酒を飲む

C. Tell the class what can and can't be done at school and at the place you live.

Example 学校でたばこを吸ってはいけません。
　　　　ホストファミリーのうちで朝シャワーを浴びてもいいです。
　　　　(host family)

Ⅵ 勉強します。あしたテストがありますから。　　☛Grammar 6

A. Add reasons to the following sentences.

Example 勉強します。　→　勉強します。あしたテストがありますから。

1. 先週は大変でした。
2. あの映画を見ません。
3. よくあのレストランに行きます。
4. きのうクラスを休みました。
5. (name of a friend) が大好きです。
6. 友だちに教科書を借りました。

B. Pair Work—Ask each other why you think the following.

Example 昼ご飯を食べません。
　　　→　A：私は昼ご飯を食べません。
　　　　　B：どうしてですか。
　　　　　A：あまりお金がありませんから。Bさんは？
　　　　　B：私も昼ご飯を食べません。クラスがありますから。

1. 今週は大変です。
   こんしゅう　たいへん
2. (name of a place) が好きです。
   　　　　　　　　　　　　す
3. 週末、(name of a movie) を見ます。
   しゅうまつ　　　　　　　　　　み
4. (name of a celebrity) がきらいです。

5. お金がぜんぜんありません。
   　かね
6. 来年は日本語を勉強しません。
   らいねん　にほんご　べんきょう
7. 来週、(name of a place) に行きます。
   らいしゅう　　　　　　　　　　い
8. 花を買います。
   はな　か

Ⅶ テレビを消しましょうか 👉Grammar 7
　　　　　　　け

A. Pair Work—Propose to do the following things, using ましょうか. 🔊 K06-15

Example A：テレビを消しましょうか。
　　　　　　　　　　け
　　　　　B：すみません。お願いします。／いいえ、大丈夫です。
　　　　　　　　　　　　ねが　　　　　　　　　　　　　だいじょうぶ

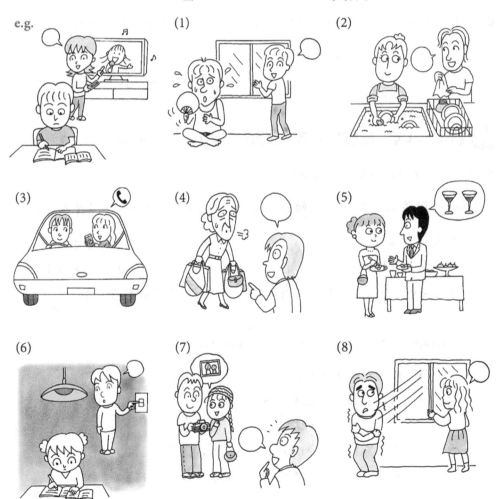

B. Pair Work—Make a conversation in the following situations.

(Example) You and your partner are in a room. Your partner looks hot.

→ A：窓を開けましょうか。

B：ありがとう。お願いします。

1. You and your partner are in a room. Your partner looks cold.

2. Your partner has trouble with Japanese homework.

3. You are talking with a Japanese (= your partner) in English, but he doesn't seem to understand English.

4. You come into a room. The room is dark and your partner is studying there.

5. Your partner forgot to bring glasses and cannot read the menu on the wall of a restaurant.

Ⅷ まとめの練習 (Review Exercises)

A. Role Play—Play the roles of A and B with your partner.

(Example)

Example-A	Example-B
You are short of money and want to borrow some money from your friend.	You don't have money to lend to your friend because you went on a trip last week.

A：あのう、お金を借りてもいいですか。

B：どうしてですか。

A：あしたは友だちの誕生日ですから。

B：でも、私もお金がありません。先週、旅行に行きましたから。

(1)

1-A	1-B
You have a date tomorrow and want to borrow a car（くるま）from your friend.	You just bought a car（くるま）and don't want anyone to use it.

(2)

2-A	2-B
You lost your Japanese textbook, but you need to study for a test tomorrow.	You have a big test in Japanese and need your textbook to prepare for the test.

(3)

3-A	3-B
You are now in your friend's house. You see a cake （ケーキ） that looks very delicious. You love cakes.	You just baked a cake （ケーキ） for your mother's birthday. Your friend is in your house now.

B. Answer the following questions.

1. 今晩、何をしますか。 (Answer with "〜て、〜。")
2. あなたの寮 (dormitory)／シェアハウス (shared house) で何をしてはいけませんか。
3. 電車の中でたばこを吸ってもいいですか。
4. 大学に何を持ってきますか。
5. よく電車に乗りますか。
6. 先週、宿題を忘れましたか。
7. 子供の時、どこで遊びましたか。
8. 子供の時、よくお母さんを手伝いましたか。
9. 図書館でよく本を借りますか。
10. よくクラスを休みますか。

Useful Expressions

道を聞く／教える
みち　　き　　　おし

D i r e c t i o n s

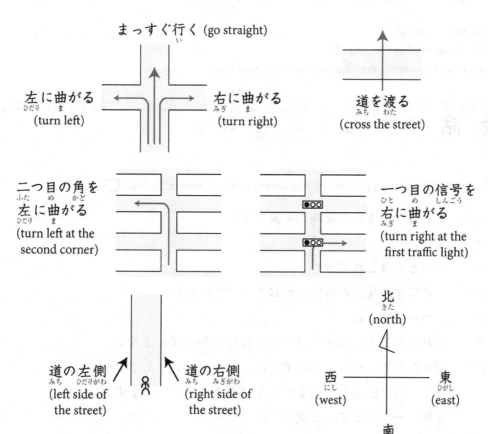

まっすぐ行く (go straight)
い

左に曲がる
ひだり　ま
(turn left)

右に曲がる
みぎ　ま
(turn right)

道を渡る
みち　わた
(cross the street)

二つ目の角を
ふた　め　かど
左に曲がる
ひだり　ま
(turn left at the
second corner)

一つ目の信号を
ひと　め　しんごう
右に曲がる
みぎ　ま
(turn right at the
first traffic light)

北
きた
(north)

道の左側
みち　ひだりがわ
(left side of
the street)

道の右側
みち　みぎがわ
(right side of
the street)

西
にし
(west)

東
ひがし
(east)

南
みなみ
(south)

＊　　　＊　　　＊

A：すみません。郵便局はどこですか。
　　　　　ゆうびんきょく
　Excuse me, where is a post office?

B：まっすぐ行って、三つ目の角を右に曲がって
　　　　　い　　　　みっ　め　かど　みぎ　ま
　　ください。郵便局は右側にありますよ。
　　　　　　ゆうびんきょく　みぎがわ
　Go straight and turn right at the third corner.
　The post office is on the right.

A：どうもありがとうございます。

第7課 LESSON 7

家族の写真 Family Picture
かぞく　しゃしん

In this lesson, we will...

● Talk about families and friends
● Describe how people are dressed and how they look

会 話 Dialogue
かい　わ

Ⅰ Sora is showing a picture of her family to her roommate, Yui. 🔊 K07-01/02

1 ゆい： これはソラさんの家族の写真ですか。
　　　　　　　　　　　　かぞく　しゃしん

2 ソラ： ええ。

3 ゆい： ソラさんはどれですか。

4 ソラ： これです。高校の時はめがねをかけていました。
　　　　　　　　　こうこう　とき

5 ゆい： かわいいですね。

6 ソラ： これは父です。ニューヨークの会社で働いています。
　　　　　　　　ちち　　　　　　　　　　　　かいしゃ　はたら

7 ゆい： 背が高くて、かっこいいですね。これはお姉さんですか。
　　　　　せ　たか　　　　　　　　　　　　　　　　ねえ

8 ソラ： ええ。姉は結婚しています。今ソウルに住んでいます。
　　　　　　　あね　けっこん　　　　　いま　　　　す

9 　　　　子供が一人います。三歳です。
　　　　　こども　ひとり　　　　さんさい

10 ゆい： そうですか。あっ、猫がいますね。
　　　　　　　　　　　　　ねこ

11 　　　　ちょっと太っていますね。
　　　　　　　　ふと

12 ソラ： ええ、よく食べますから。
　　　　　　　　た

Ⅱ Yui's phone rings. 🔊 K07-03/04

1 ロバート： もしもし、ゆいさん、今何をしていますか。

2 ゆ い： 別に何もしていません。今、ソラさんの写真を見ています。

3 ロバート： そうですか。きのうおいしいコーヒーを買いました。

4 よかったら飲みに来ませんか。

5 ゆ い： いいですね。ソラさんも一緒に行ってもいいですか。

6 ロバート： もちろん。

7 ゆ い： じゃあ、すぐ行きます。

Ⓘ

Yui: Is this your family picture, Sora?

Sora: Yes.

Yui: Which is you?

Sora: This. I was wearing glasses when I was in high school.

Yui: You are cute.

Sora: This is my father. He works at a company in New York.

Yui: He is tall and good-looking. Is this your older sister?

Sora: Yes. My sister is married. She lives in Seoul now. She has one child. He is three years old.

Yui: I see. Oh, there is a cat. He is a little fat.

Sora: Yes, because he eats a lot.

Ⓤ

Robert: Hello, Yui, what are you doing now?

Yui: I'm not doing anything especially. I am looking at Sora's pictures.

Robert: I see. I bought some delicious coffee yesterday. Won't you come to drink it, if you like?

Yui: That sounds good. Is it all right if Sora comes with me?

Robert: Of course.

Yui: We'll come right now.

単語
たん　ご

K07-05 (J-E)
K07-06 (E-J)

V o c a b u l a r y

N o u n s

* かぞく	家族	family
おじいさん		grandfather; old man
おばあさん		grandmother; old woman
おにいさん	お兄さん	older brother
* おねえさん	お姉さん	older sister
* ちち	父	(my) father
はは	母	(my) mother
あに	兄	(my) older brother
* あね	姉	(my) older sister
いもうと	妹	younger sister
おとうと	弟	younger brother
きょうだい	兄弟	brothers and sisters
おとこのひと	男の人	man
おんなのひと	女の人	woman
* かいしゃ	会社	company
しょくどう	食堂	cafeteria; dining commons
デパート		department store
かみ	髪	hair
くち	口	mouth
め	目	eye
* めがね	眼鏡	glasses
うた	歌	song
サークル		club activity
くるま	車	car

い - a d j e c t i v e s

ながい	長い	long
みじかい	短い	short (length)
はやい	速い	fast
* せがたかい	背が高い	tall (stature)
せがひくい	背が低い	short (stature)
あたまがいい	頭がいい	bright; smart; clever (conjugates like いい)
* かわいい		cute

＊Words that appear in the dialogue

な -adjectives

しんせつ（な）	親切	kind
べんり（な）	便利	convenient

U-verbs

うたう	歌う	to sing （〜を）
かぶる		to put on (a hat) （〜を）
はく		to put on (items below your waist) （〜を）
しる	知る	to get to know （〜を）
しっています	知っています	I know
しりません	知りません	I do not know
＊すむ	住む	to live （〜にすんでいます）
＊はたらく	働く	to work
＊ふとる	太る	to gain weight
ふとっています	太っています	to be on the heavy side; overweight

Ru-verbs

＊（めがねを）かける		to put on (glasses)
きる	着る	to put on (clothes above your waist) （〜を）
やせる		to lose weight
やせています		to be thin

Irregular Verb

＊けっこんする	結婚する	to get married （〜と）

Adverbs and Other Expressions

〜が		. . . , but
＊なにも＋negative	何も	not . . . anything
〜にん	〜人	[counter for people]
＊ひとり	一人	one person
ふたり	二人	two people
＊べつに＋negative	別に	nothing in particular
＊もちろん		of course
＊よかったら		if you like

会
L7

文 法 G r a m m a r
ぶん ぽう

1 〜ている (Action in Progress)

In this lesson, we will learn to use verb *te*-forms together with the helping verb いる. To understand what such a sentence means, we will need to understand the semantics of Japanese verbs. Japanese verbs can be classified into the following three types.

    (1) verbs that describe *activities* that last for some time (e.g., 食べる, 読む)
    (2) verbs that describe *changes* that are more or less instantaneous (e.g., 死ぬ, 起きる)[1]
    (3) verbs that describe continuous *states* (e.g., ある, いる)

You can use verbs in the first group, such as 食べる and 読む, in their *te*-form with the helping verb いる to describe *actions in progress*.[2] We will discuss the verbs of the second type in the following section. The third type which describes states does not go with ている.

| Activity verbs ている = action in progress |

ソラさんは今勉強しています。	*Sora is studying right now.*
たけしさんは英語の本を読んでいます。	*Takeshi is reading a book in English.*
今、何をしていますか。	*What are you doing right now?*

You can also use a 〜ています sentence to describe what a person does by occupation or by habit. The first example below therefore has two possible interpretations: you are actually teaching English right at this moment, or you are an English-language teacher (but are not necessarily in class right now.) The second example means that Mary is in the habit of studying Japanese (but of course she does not spend 24 hours a day doing so).

---

[1] Among the verbs we have learned so far, verbs such as 起きる, 行く, 帰る, 来る, わかる, 出かける, 乗る, 座る, 死ぬ, 消す, 忘れる, 借りる, 降りる, 持ってくる, 連れてくる, 結婚する, 太る, やせる, 着る are change verbs. In most cases you can determine whether a verb is in the activity class or a change class by checking if the verb allows for a phrase describing duration, such as 一時間. Compare, for example,

    ○私はきのう一時間本を読みました。   *I read a book for an hour yesterday.*
    ×私は一時間死にました。   (Ungrammatical, much as the English translation
                                 "I died for an hour," which is also odd.)

読む thus is an activity verb, and 死ぬ is a change verb.

[2] The distinction between いる and ある that we learned in Lesson 4 does not apply to this helping verb 〜ている: you can use 〜ている both for living things and for inanimate objects.

私は英語を教えています。
<ruby>私<rt>わたし</rt></ruby> <ruby>英語<rt>えいご</rt></ruby> <ruby>教<rt>おし</rt></ruby>

I teach English. / I am teaching English (right now).

メアリーさんは毎日日本語を勉強しています。
<ruby>毎日<rt>まいにち</rt></ruby> <ruby>日本語<rt>にほんご</rt></ruby> <ruby>勉強<rt>べんきょう</rt></ruby>

Mary studies Japanese every day.

The helping verb いる conjugates as a *ru*-verb. Thus we have long forms as in the following.

e.g. 食べ<ruby>た<rt></rt></ruby>ている	affirmative	negative
[Present]	食べています *He is eating.*	食べていません *He is not eating.*
[Past]	食べていました *He was eating.*	食べていませんでした *He was not eating.*

2 ～ている (Result of a Change)

Verbs in the second group discussed in the previous section describe changes from one state to another. If you get married, or 結婚する, for example, your status changes from being single to being married. With these verbs, ている describes *the result of a change.*[3] A change took place in the past, and its significance still remains until the present moment.

> Change verbs ている ＝ result of a change

山下先生は結婚しています。
<ruby>山下先生<rt>やましたせんせい</rt></ruby> <ruby>結婚<rt>けっこん</rt></ruby>

Professor Yamashita is married.[4]
(= state resulting from getting married)

ゆいさんは窓の近くに座っています。
<ruby>窓<rt>まど</rt></ruby> <ruby>近<rt>ちか</rt></ruby> <ruby>座<rt>すわ</rt></ruby>

Yui is seated near the window.
(= state resulting from seating herself there)

Here are some more examples of verbs that are commonly used in the ～ている framework.

持つ → 持っている　　　ソラさんはお金をたくさん持っています。
<ruby>も<rt></rt></ruby>　　<ruby>も<rt></rt></ruby>　　　　　　　　　<ruby>金<rt>かね</rt></ruby>　　　　　　<ruby>も<rt></rt></ruby>
(has)

Sora has a lot of money.

---

[3] In Lesson 9, we will observe that this *result of a change* reading is actually not restricted to change verbs but can be associated with activity verbs in certain contexts.

[4] Note that the sentence does *not* mean Professor Yamashita *is getting married*.

知る _し	→	知っている⁵ _し (knows)	山下先生は母を知っています。 _{やましたせんせい はは し} *Professor Yamashita knows my mother.*
太る _{ふと}	→	太っている _{ふと} (is overweight)	トムさんはちょっと太っています。 _{ふと} *Tom is a little overweight.*
やせる	→	やせている (is thin)	私の弟はとてもやせています。 _{わたし おとうと} *My younger brother is very thin.*
着る _き	→	着ている _き (wears)	メアリーさんはTシャツを着ています。 _{ティー き} *Mary is wearing/wears a T-shirt.*
起きる _お	→	起きている _お (is awake)	お父さんは起きています。 _{とう お} *Dad is up and awake.*
住む _す	→	住んでいる _す (lives in)	家族は東京に住んでいます。 _{かぞく とうきょう す} *My family lives in Tokyo.*

Note that verbs like 行く and 来る belong to the change class. Thus 行っている and 来ている indicate the result of prior movements, *not* movements that are currently in progress. You may want to be careful with what the following sentences mean.

中国に行っています。　*Somebody has gone to/is in China.* (Not: *She is going to China.*)
_{ちゅうごく い}

うちに来ています。　　*Somebody has come over to visit.* (Not: *Somebody is coming over.*)
_き

You can simply use the present tense and say メアリーさんは来ます, for example, if you want to say that Mary is coming, because the present tense in Japanese refers both to the present and to the future.

3 メアリーさんは髪が長いです
_{かみ なが}

To describe somebody who has long hair, one could say:

トムさんの髪は長いです。　　*Tom's hair is long.*
_{かみ なが}

But in fact it would be far more natural in Japanese to say:

トムさんは髪が長いです。　　*Tom has long hair. (= As for Tom, he has long hair.)*
_{かみ なが}

---

5 The negation of 知っています is 知りません, without the ている formation.
_し _し

This applies not only to discussion of the length of one's hair, but to descriptions of a person's physical attributes in general. See the Parts of the Body section at the end of this lesson for the name of body parts.

$$
\text{Aさんは} \left\{ \begin{array}{c} 目 \\ \text{め} \\ 耳 \\ \text{みみ} \\ 手 \\ \text{て} \\ 足 \\ \text{あし} \\ \vdots \end{array} \right\} \text{が} \left\{ \begin{array}{c} 大きい \\ \text{おお} \\ 小さい \\ \text{ちい} \\ かわいい \\ \vdots \end{array} \right\} \qquad \textit{Person A has a body part which is . . .}
$$

In idiomatic collocations, we also have:

背が高い *is tall*   背が低い *is short*   頭がいい *is bright/smart*
せ　たか　　　　　　　　　　せ　ひく　　　　　　　　　　あたま

会
L7

4 Adjective/Noun *Te*-forms for Joining Sentences

In the last lesson, we discussed the use of verbal *te*-forms to join sentences. い- and な-adjectives and です after nouns also have *te*-forms, which can be used to combine two elements to form longer sentences.

The *te*-form of an い-adjective is formed by substituting くて for the final い. The *te*-form of a な-adjective and a noun＋です sequence is formed by adding で to the base or the noun.

い-adjectives:	安い やす	→	安くて やす
(irregular)	いい	→	よくて
な-adjectives:	元気（な） げんき	→	元気で げんき
noun ＋です：	日本人です に ほんじん	→	日本人で に ほんじん

あの店の食べ物は安くて、おいしいです。
みせ　　た　もの　やす
The food at that restaurant is <u>inexpensive</u> <u>and</u> delicious.

ホテルはきれいで、よかったです。
The hotel was <u>clean, and</u> we were happy.

山下先生は日本人で、五十歳ぐらいです。
やましたせんせい　に ほんじん　　ご じゅっさい
Professor Yamashita is <u>a Japanese and</u> he is about fifty years old.

As with the *te*-form conjunction of verbs in Lesson 6, you can use the *te*-form of conjunction of adjectives in sentences describing the past and the present. The last adjective determines the overall tense of each of these sentences.

5 Verb Stem ＋ に行く

If a person moves to another place in order to do something, we can describe their movement and its purpose this way:

$$
\text{destination of movement} \left\{ \begin{array}{c} に \\ へ \end{array} \right\} \quad \boxed{\begin{array}{c} \text{the purpose of movement} \\ \text{(verb stem)} \end{array}} \quad に \left\{ \begin{array}{c} 行く \\ 来る \\ 帰る \end{array} \right\}
$$

The purpose of movement is a phrase consisting of a verb, its object, and so forth.[6] Verbs describing the purpose of a movement must be in their stem forms. Stems are the part you get by removing ます from the verbs' present tense long forms.

stems:　　食べる　→　食べ（ます）　　読む　→　読み（ます）　etc.

デパートに かばんを買い に行きました。

I went to a department store to buy a bag.

メアリーさんは日本に 日本語を勉強し に来ました。

Mary has come to Japan to study Japanese.

6 Counting People

The "counter" for people is 人, but "one person" and "two people" are irregular: 一人 and 二人.

1　ひとり（一人）
2　ふたり（二人）
3　さんにん（三人）
4　よにん（四人）
5　ごにん（五人）
6　ろくにん（六人）
7　しちにん／ななにん（七人）
8　はちにん（八人）
9　きゅうにん（九人）
10　じゅうにん（十人）

何人いますか。

To count people in a class, for example, you can add 〜人 after the noun and the particle が, and
say:

---

person が　Ｘ人　います

私のクラスに（は）インドネシア人の学生が一人います。
There is one Indonesian student in our class.

The place expressions are often followed by には instead of に in this type of sentence.

Expression Notes

表現ノート

8

遊ぶ ▶ 遊ぶ means "to play," "to spend time pleasantly," or "to pay a social call."

子供の時、よく友だちと遊びました。　　*When I was a child, I often*
　　　　　　　　　　　　　　　　　　　　played with friends.

先週の週末は東京に遊びに行きました。　*I went to Tokyo to have fun*
　　　　　　　　　　　　　　　　　　　　last weekend.

私のうちに遊びに来てください。　　　　*Please come and see us.*

Note that "to play" as used below requires different words.

Sports:	to play tennis	テニスを<u>する</u>
Games:	to play games	ゲームを<u>する</u>
	to play cards	トランプを<u>する</u>
Music instruments:	to play the guitar	ギターを<u>弾く</u>

知る/わかる ▶ If you don't know the answer to a question but should have
thought about it, you should say わかりません instead of 知りません (see Lesson 4 Dialogue 2, for example). 知りません in such a context would sound rude,
implying that your ignorance on that matter is none of the inquirer's business.

---

[6] You can also use some nouns like 買い物 (shopping) for the purpose phrase, as in
デパートに買い物に行きました。　*I went to a department store for shopping.*

練習 Practice

I テレビを見ています ☞Grammar 1

A. Look at the pictures below and answer the questions. 🔊 K07-07

> (Example) Q：メアリーさんは何をしていますか。
>
> A：テレビを見ています。

e.g.　(1)　(2)　(3)

(4)　(5)　(6)　(7)

(8)　(9)　(10)　(11)

B. Pair Work—What were you doing at the following times yesterday? Be as specific as possible (where, with whom, and so on).

> (Example) 2 P.M.　→　A：午後二時ごろ何をしていましたか。
>
> B：友だちと部屋で勉強していました。

1. 6 A.M.　　　3. 10 A.M.　　　5. 6 P.M.　　　7. 11 P.M.

2. 8 A.M.　　　4. 12:30 P.M.　　6. 8 P.M.

C. Class Activity—Let's play charades. The teacher gives a sentence card to each student. One of the students mimes the sentence. All other students guess what the person is doing and raise their hands when they recognize the action. The person that gets the most points is the winner.

Example 田中さんは海で泳いでいます。
たなか　　うみ　およ

Ⅱ ニューヨークに住んでいます ☞Grammar 2
す

A. This is Sora's family. Answer the following questions. 🔊 K07-08

Example Q：お父さんはどこに住んでいますか。
とう　　　　　す
A：ニューヨークに住んでいます。
す

1. お姉さんはどこに住んでいますか。
ねえ　　　　　　す
2. 弟さんはアメリカに住んでいますか。
おとうと　　　　　　　　す
3. お母さんは何をしていますか。
かあ　　なに
4. お姉さんは何をしていますか。
ねえ　　なに
5. お姉さんは結婚していますか。
ねえ　　けっこん

6. 弟さんは結婚していますか。
おとうと　　けっこん
7. お父さんは何歳ですか。
とう　　なんさい
8. 弟さんは何歳ですか。
おとうと　なんさい
9. お父さんは韓国で働いて
とう　　かんこく　はたら
いますか。

Father	lives in N.Y.	works at a company	48 years old
Mother		high school teacher	45 years old
Sister	lives in Seoul	works at a hospital; married	24 years old
Brother	lives in London	student; not married	18 years old

B. Pair Work—Ask about your partner's family and fill in the blanks below.

	何歳ですか なんさい	何をしていますか なに	どこに住んでいますか す	結婚していますか けっこん
お父さん とう				
お母さん かあ				
お兄さん にい				
お姉さん ねえ				
弟さん おとうと				
妹さん いもうと				

Ⅲ この人は目が大きいです ☞Grammar 2・3

A. Describe the physical characteristics of the following people. 🔊 K07-09

(Example) この人は目が大きいです。

e.g. (1) (2) (3)

(4)  (5) (6)  (7)

B. Look at the picture below and answer the questions. 🔊 K07-10

(Example) Q：女の人はやせていますか。

A：はい、やせています。

1. 女の人は太っていますか。
2. 女の人はＴシャツを着ていますか。
3. 男の人は何を着ていますか。
4. 女の人はジーンズをはいていますか。
5. 男の人はめがねをかけていますか。
6. 男の人は傘を持っていますか。
7. 女の人は背が高いですか。
8. 男の人は背が低いですか。
9. 女の人は髪が長いですか。
10. 男の人は目が小さいですか。

女の人　　男の人

C. Look at the picture below and describe each person.

Example
水野さんは帽子をかぶっています。

川村
かわむら
小川
おがわ
水野
みずの
山中
やまなか
中山
なかやま

D. Class Activity—One student describes another student without mentioning the name. The rest of the class guesses who the student is.

Example 髪が短いです。Ｔシャツを着ています。ジーンズをはいていません。
かみ みじか ティー き

Ⅳ ゆいさんはかわいくて、やさしいです ☞Grammar 4

A. Mary has been enjoying her life in Japan. She talks about her friends and life in Japan. Make sentences using two adjectives like the example. K07-11

Example ゆいさんはかわいくて、やさしいです。

e.g. ゆい	(1) ロバート	(2) ナオミ	(3) ソラ
かわいい やさしい	背が高い せ たか かっこいい	目が大きい め おお きれいな	頭がいい あたま 親切な しんせつ

(4) 山下先生 やましたせんせい	(5) 日本語のクラス に ほん ご	(6) 宿題 しゅくだい	(7) 食堂 しょくどう
元気な げん き おもしろい	にぎやかな 楽しい たの	難しい むずか 大変な たいへん	安い やす おいしい

B. Describe the following items using two or more adjectives.

(Example) my older brother

→ 兄はかっこよくて、やさしいです。
　　あに

　兄はかっこいいですが、こわいです。
　あに

1. my hometown
2. my country
3. my Japanese class

4. one of my family members
5. Japanese people
6. people of my country

C. Naomi and her friends went on a trip to Tokyo last month. Make sentences describing the city using two adjectives. 🔊 K07-12

(Example) 東京 — big & lively
　　とうきょう

→ 東京は大きくて、にぎやかでした。
　とうきょう　　おお

Tokyo

1. 新幹線 (Bullet Train)　　— fast & convenient
　しんかんせん
2. ホテル　　　　　　　　— old & not clean
3. ホテルの人　　　　　　— kind & good
4. レストラン　　　　　　— expensive & not delicious
5. 神社 (shrine)　　　　　— quiet & beautiful
　じんじゃ
6. 東京スカイツリー (Tokyo Skytree) — tall & scary
　とうきょう

D. Pair Work—Answer the following questions using two or more adjectives.

(Example) 家に犬がいますか。／どんな犬ですか。
　　　　いえ　いぬ　　　　　　　　いぬ

→ A：家に犬がいますか。
　　いえ　いぬ

　B：はい。

　A：どんな犬ですか。
　　　　　いぬ

　B：小さくて、かわいいです。
　　ちい

　A：そうですか。

1. どこに住んでいますか。／どんな町ですか。

2. パソコンを持っていますか。／どんなパソコンですか。

3. 好きな人がいますか。／どんな人ですか。

4. 週末何をしましたか。／どうでしたか。

5. 休みにどこに旅行に行きましたか。／どんな町でしたか。

Ⅴ 京都に写真を撮りに行きます ☞Grammar 5

A. Sora is going to the following places to do the things below. Make sentences like the example. 🔊 K07-13

Example 京都 ― 写真を撮る

→ ソラさんは京都に写真を撮りに行きます。

1. 図書館 ― 本を返す
2. 食堂 ― 昼ご飯を食べる
3. 大阪 ― 友だちに会う
4. 友だちのうち ― 勉強する
5. 町 ― 遊ぶ
6. デパート ― 靴を買う
7. 高校 ― 英語を教える
8. カフェ ― コーヒーを飲む

B. For what purpose would you go to the following places?

1. コンビニに＿＿＿＿＿＿＿＿＿＿＿＿に行きます。

2. 東京に＿＿＿＿＿＿＿＿＿＿＿＿に行きました。

3. 図書館に＿＿＿＿＿＿＿＿＿＿＿＿に行きます。

4. 家に＿＿＿＿＿＿＿＿＿＿＿＿に帰ります。

5. 大学に＿＿＿＿＿＿＿＿＿＿＿＿に来ました。

C. Pair Work—Look at the pictures below and practice the dialogue with your partner.

(Example) A：ナオミさんは友だちのうちに何をしに行きますか。

B：遊びに行きます。

e.g. to play (have fun)

friend's house

ナオミ

(1) to borrow

library

ウデイ

(2)

cafe

カルロス

(3) to buy souvenir

department store

ヤスミン

(4)

home

メアリー

(5)

temple

ようこ

Ⅵ 日本人が何人いますか ☞Grammar 6

A. Look at the picture below and count the people. 🔊 K07-14

(Example) A：日本人が何人いますか。

B：四人います。

1. 男の人が何人いますか。
2. 女の人が何人いますか。
3. アメリカ人が何人いますか。
4. 学生が何人いますか。

B. Pair Work—Ask your partner the following questions.

(Example) A：この部屋に学生が何人いますか。
　　　　　　へや　　　がくせい　　なんにん
　　　　　B：二十人います。
　　　　　　にじゅうにん

1. この部屋に日本人が何人いますか。
　　　　へや　にほんじん　なんにん
2. この部屋に＿＿＿＿＿＿人が何人いますか。
　　　　へや　　　　　　　　　じん　なんにん
　　　　　　　　　　(nationality)
3. あなたの学校に日本語の先生が何人いますか。
　　　　　　がっこう　にほんご　せんせい　なんにん
4. 日本人の友だちが何人いますか。
　　にほんじん　とも　　なんにん
5. 兄弟がいますか。何人いますか。
　　きょうだい　　　　なんにん

Ⅶ まとめの練習
　　　　れんしゅう

A. Answer the following questions.

1. どこに住んでいますか。
　　　　す
2. 結婚していますか。
　　けっこん
3. 自転車／車を持っていますか。
　　じてんしゃ　くるま　も
4. 日本の歌を知っていますか。
　　にほん　うた　し
5. サークルに入っていますか。
　　　　　　はい
6. 日本語の先生は今日何を着ていますか／はいていますか。
　　にほんご　せんせい　きょうなに　き
7. お父さん／お母さんはどこで働いていますか。
　　とう　　　かあ　　　　　はたら
8. おじいさん／おばあさんはどこに住んでいますか。
　　　　　　　　　　　　　　　　　す
9. 子供の時、自転車を持っていましたか。
　　こども　とき　じてんしゃ　も
10. 高校の時、日本語を知っていましたか。
　　こうこう　とき　にほんご　し

B. Class Activity—Show a picture of your family to the class and describe it.

Culture Notes

家族の呼び方 Kinship Terms
かぞく　よ　かた

	1. Referring to other families	2. Referring to yours		3. Addressing yours
		A. formal	B. informal	
Father	お父さん とう	父 ちち	お父さん とう	お父さん／パパ とう
Mother	お母さん かあ	母 はは	お母さん かあ	お母さん／ママ かあ
Older brother	お兄さん にい	兄 あに	お兄さん にい	お兄ちゃん にい
Older sister	お姉さん ねえ	姉 あね	お姉さん ねえ	お姉ちゃん ねえ
Younger brother	弟さん おとうと	弟 おとうと		——
Younger sister	妹さん いもうと	妹 いもうと		——
Husband	ご主人 しゅじん	主人／夫 しゅじん おっと	だんな／うちの人, etc. ひと	お父さん とう
Wife	奥さん おく	家内／妻 かない つま	奥さん／嫁さん, etc. おく よめ	お母さん かあ
Grandfather	おじいさん	祖父 そふ	おじいさん	おじいちゃん
Grandmother	おばあさん	祖母 そぼ	おばあさん	おばあちゃん
Child	お子さん こ	うちの子 こ		——

There are many other kinship terms in addition to those listed in the table above. Equal or younger members of your family can be addressed by their given name instead of the kinship term. As the table indicates, the term used for a particular type of family member varies according to the following situations:

1. Speaking about somebody else's family
2-A. Speaking about your own family in a formal situation, such as a job interview
2-B. Speaking about your own family in a casual situation
3. Speaking to your family

A：田中さんのお父さんは何歳ですか。　*How old is your father, Mr. Tanaka?*
たなか　とう　なんさい
B：[formal]　　父は五十歳です。　*My father is 50 years old.*
ちち　ごじゅっさい
[informal]　お父さんは五十歳です。
とう　ごじゅっさい

You can also address members of your family with the terms that the youngest member would use. For example, a wife can call her husband お父さん or パパ, and a mother can call
とう
her oldest son お兄ちゃん.
にい

Mother: お兄ちゃん、お父さんが待っていますよ。
にい　とう　ま
Son (literally, *older brother*), *your father is waiting.*

体 の 部 分
Parts of the Body

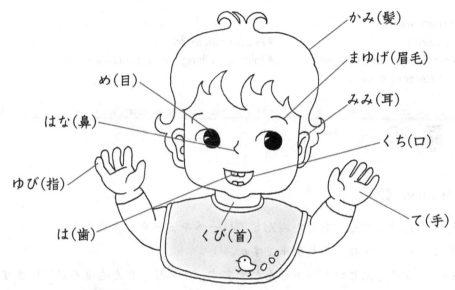

かみ（髪）

まゆげ（眉毛）

め（目）

みみ（耳）

はな（鼻）

くち（口）

ゆび（指）

は（歯）

くび（首）

て（手）

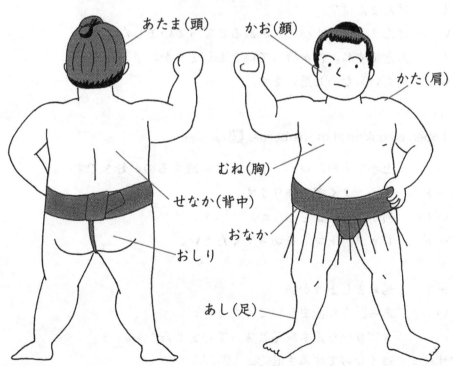

あたま（頭）

かお（顔）

かた（肩）

むね（胸）

せなか（背中）

おなか

おしり

あし（足）

第8課 | LESSON 8

バーベキュー Barbecue

In this lesson, we will..
- Talk casually
- Express thoughts and opinions
- Report someone's speech
- Request not to do
- Talk about things we like/dislike to do

会話 Dialogue
(かい)(わ)

I At school. 🔊 K08-01/02

1 ゆ い： たけしさん、あしたみんなでバーベキューをしませんか。

2 たけし： いいですね。だれが来ますか。

3 ゆ い： ソラさんとロバートさんが来ます。メアリーさんも来ると思います。

4 たけし： けんさんは？

5 ゆ い： けんさんはアルバイトがあると言っていました。

6 たけし： 残念ですね。何か持っていきましょうか。

7 ゆ い： 何もいらないと思います。

II Robert is cooking at the barbecue. 🔊 K08-03/04

1 ゆ い： 上手ですね。ロバートさんは料理するのが好きですか。

2 ロバート： ええ、よく家で作ります。

3 ゆ い： 何か手伝いましょうか。

4 ロバート： じゃあ、トマトを切ってください。

　　　　　　　　*　　　　　　*　　　　　　*

5 ロバート： 始めましょうか。

6 ゆ い： あっ、まだ飲まないでください。

7 　　　　　 メアリーさんも来ると言っていましたから。

8 メアリー： 遅くなってすみません。

9 みんな： じゃあ、乾杯！

(I)

Yui: Takeshi, would you like to have a barbecue party tomorrow?

Takeshi: That's nice. Who will come?

Yui: Sora and Robert will come. I think Mary will come, too.

Takeshi: How about Ken?

Yui: Ken said he had a part-time job.

Takeshi: Too bad. Shall I bring something?

Yui: I think nothing is needed.

(II)

Yui: You are good (at cooking). Do you like cooking, Robert?

Robert: Yes, I often cook at home.

Yui: Shall I help you with something?

Robert: Well then, cut the tomatoes, please.

        *   *   *

Robert: Shall we start?

Yui: Oh, don't drink yet. Mary said that she would come.

Mary: I'm sorry for being late.

Everyone: Well then . . . Cheers!

会
L8

単語
たん ご

🔊 K08-05 (J-E)
K08-06 (E-J)

■■
V o c a b u l a r y

N o u n s

はれ	晴れ	sunny weather
あめ	雨	rain
くもり	曇り	cloudy weather
ゆき	雪	snow
てんきよほう	天気予報	weather forecast
きおん	気温	temperature
		(weather—not used for things)
なつ	夏	summer
ふゆ	冬	winter
けさ	今朝	this morning
あさって		the day after tomorrow
まいしゅう	毎週	every week
こんげつ	今月	this month
らいげつ	来月	next month
かいしゃいん	会社員	office worker
しごと	仕事	job; work; occupation
カメラ		camera
カラオケ		karaoke
ところ	所	place
* トマト		tomato
はし		chopsticks
パーティー		party
* バーベキュー		barbecue
ホームステイ		homestay; living with a local family
おふろ	お風呂	bath
スペイン		Spain
* なにか	何か	something

な - a d j e c t i v e s

* じょうず（な）	上手	skillful; good at . . . （〜が）
へた（な）	下手	clumsy; poor at . . . （〜が）
ゆうめい（な）	有名	famous

＊Words that appear in the dialogue

U-verbs

あらう	洗う	to wash（〜を）
* いう	言う	to say
* いる		to need（〜が）
* おそくなる	遅くなる	to be late
おふろにはいる	お風呂に入る	to take a bath
* おもう	思う	to think
* きる	切る	to cut（〜を）
* つくる	作る	to make（〜を）
（あめ／ゆきが）ふる	（雨／雪が）降る	(rain/snow) falls
* もっていく	持っていく	to take (a thing)（〜を）

Ru-verbs

| すてる | 捨てる | to throw away（〜を） |
| * はじめる | 始める | to begin（〜を） |

Irregular Verbs

うんてんする	運転する	to drive（〜を）
せんたくする	洗濯する	to do laundry（〜を）
そうじする	掃除する	to clean（〜を）
* りょうりする	料理する	to cook

Adverbs and Other Expressions

うん		uh-huh; yes
ううん		uh-uh; no
いつも		always
おそく	遅く	(do something) late
* かんぱい	乾杯	Cheers! (a toast)
* みんなで		all (of the people) together
* ざんねん（ですね）	残念（ですね）	That's too bad.
* まだ＋ negative		not . . . yet
〜について		about . . . ; concerning . . .
〜ど	〜度	. . . degrees (temperature)
どう		how

会
L8

文法 G r a m m a r

1 Short Forms

In this and the next lesson, we will learn a new paradigm of conjugation, which we will call "short forms."[1] Compare the long forms, which we already know, and the short forms:

Present, affirmative

	long forms	short forms	
· verbs:	読みます	読む	(= Dictionary form)
· い-adjectives:	かわいいです	かわいい	(Drop です.)
· な-adjectives:	静かです	静かだ	(Replace です with だ.)
· noun + です:	学生です	学生だ	(Replace です with だ.)

Present, negative

	long forms	short forms	
· verbs:	読みません	読まない	→ More on this below.
· い-adjectives:	かわいくないです	かわいくない	(Drop です.)
(exception) いい:	よくないです	よくない	
· な-adjectives:	静かじゃないです	静かじゃない	(Drop です.)
· noun + です:	学生じゃないです	学生じゃない	(Drop です.)

Let's look at the verbs in the negative in detail. *Ru-*, *u-*, and irregular verbs conjugate differently.

Verb short forms (present, negative)

· *ru*-verbs: Drop the final る and add ない.

  食べる → 食べない

· *u*-verbs: Drop the last -*u* and add -*anai*. Verbs that have う, however, get わ instead of あ.

  書く → 書かない   会う → 会わない

· irregular verbs: The vowels change.

  する → しない   くる → こない

· exception: The verb ある is totally replaced by the adjective ない.

  ある → ない

---

[1] Various names have been given to this paradigm. They include "plain forms," "informal forms," and "direct style." Long forms, on the other hand, are often called "polite forms," "formal forms," and "distal style."

Think of the *u*-verb conjugation as moving up and down in the *hiragana* chart. Let's take 書く for example. The dictionary form 書く is the combination of the verb base in the kanji 書 and the bottom *hiragana* of that row, く. 書きます is the combination of 書, き, and the ます ending on the right. 書かない is 書, か and ない.

	書 か	話 はな	待 ま	死 し	読 よ	作 つく	泳 およ	呼 よ	買 か	
negative	か	さ	た	な	ま	ら	が	ば	わ ²	〜ない
stem	き	し	ち	に	み	り	ぎ	び	い	〜ます
affirmative	く	す	つ	ぬ	む	る	ぐ	ぶ	う	= Dictionary form

2 Short Forms in Informal Speech

Close friends or family members speak with each other using short forms at the end of sentences as a sign of intimacy. The use of long forms, in contrast, tends to imply the speaker's intention to "keep a proper distance" from the listener. Short forms, then, are like talking on a first-name basis, while long forms are like using "Mr." and "Ms."

会
L8

(Between friends) A：今日、学校に行く？ (Short form)
きょう がっこう い
Are you going to school today?

B：ううん、行かない。
い
No, I'm not.

(To a stranger) A：すみません、この電車は新宿に行きますか。 (Long form)
でんしゃ しんじゅく い
Excuse me, does this train go to Shinjuku?

B：いいえ、行きませんよ。
い
No, it doesn't.

It may not be easy to decide when it is appropriate to switch to short forms. First of all, Japanese speakers are often very conscious of seniority. A year's difference in age may in many cases totally preclude the possibility of establishing a truly "equal" relationship. Second, license to use short forms is not mutual; senior partners may feel perfectly justified in using short forms while expecting their junior partners to continue addressing them with long forms. Thus, if somebody who is older, say, your Japanese language professor, talks to you using short forms, they would be greatly surprised if you were to do the same.

---

² Note that we have 買わない, with わ instead of あ, because the bases of *u*-verbs ending with the *hiragana* う
か
actually end with the consonant *w*, which remains silent in 買う and 買います, but resurfaces in 買わない.
か か か

Professor:	この漢字、わかる？ <ruby>漢字<rt>かん じ</rt></ruby>	Do you know this kanji?
Student:	はい、わかります。	Yes, I do.
	（×うん、わかる。）	

(Long form preferred, because you are talking to somebody who is older.)

In the casual conversations, you drop the question particle か, and use the rising intonation to ask a question.[4]

どんな<ruby>音楽<rt>おんがく</rt></ruby>を<ruby>聞<rt>き</rt></ruby>く？　　（×どんな<ruby>音楽<rt>おんがく</rt></ruby>を<ruby>聞<rt>き</rt></ruby>く<u>か</u>？）
What kind of music do you listen to?

Also, in the spoken language, you usually drop the sentence-final だ after a な-adjective or a noun. (You keep the last だ in the written language, however.)

A：<ruby>元気<rt>げん き</rt></ruby>？	Are you good?
B：うん、<ruby>元気<rt>げん き</rt></ruby>。	Yes, I am.
（Rather than: <ruby>元気<rt>げん き</rt></ruby><u>だ</u>。）	

You keep だ when you follow it up with ね or よ.

メアリーさんは<ruby>二年生<rt>に ねんせい</rt></ruby>だよ。　　*Mary is a sophomore.*
（Rather than: メアリーさんは<ruby>二年生<rt>に ねんせい</rt></ruby><u>だ</u>。）

はい and いいえ are usually replaced by the less formal うん and ううん.

| A：よくスポーツをする？ | Do you often play sports? |
| B：うん、する。／ううん、しない。 | Yes, I do. / No, I don't. |

③ Short Forms in Quoted Speech: ～と<ruby>思<rt>おも</rt></ruby>います

To describe what you think, you use the short form, plus と<ruby>思<rt>おも</rt></ruby>います (I think that . . .). と is a quotation particle, which does the job of both the English word "that" in indirect quotation and of quotation marks (" ") in direct quotation.

（<ruby>私<rt>わたし</rt></ruby>は）たけしさんはメアリーさんが<ruby>好<rt>す</rt></ruby>きだと<ruby>思<rt>おも</rt></ruby>います。
I think Takeshi likes Mary.

---

[3] Particles are more often dropped in casual speech than in careful, polite speech or writing.
[4] We usually write the question mark at the end of such a sentence, because we cannot rely on the intonation.

To say that you *don't think* something is the case, it is more common in Japanese to say it like 〜な
いと思います (*I think* that something is *not* the case) than 〜と思いません (*I don't think*).
Therefore:

（私は）メアリーさんはたけしさんが好きじゃないと思います。

I don't think Mary likes Takeshi. (= I think Mary doesn't like Takeshi.)

4 Short Forms in Quoted Speech: 〜と言っていました

To quote a person's utterances, you use the short form plus と言っていました[5] (They said "...").
Note that the present tense in Yasmin's original utterance is preserved in Mary's report.

ヤスミンさんは、あした試験があると言っていました。

Yasmin said that there would be an exam tomorrow.

山下先生は結婚していないと言っていました。

Professor Yamashita said that he is not married.

あした試験が
あります。

ヤスミンさんは
あした試験があると
言っていました。

---

[5] The action in progress expression in と言っていました indicates that you were there when somebody said
that, as in "I heard them saying..." If you were not there when the utterance was made, as in "(the long dead)
Napoleon said...," と言いました sounds more appropriate.

5 〜ないでください

To request that someone refrain from doing something, one can use a negative verbal short form plus でください.

ここで写真を撮らないでください。
Please don't take pictures here.

> verb (short, negative) + でください   *Please don't . . .*

ないでください often is a better answer than てはいけません to a てもいいですか question.

A：この部屋に入ってもいいですか。
May I enter this room?

B：入らないでください。   Compare: 入ってはいけません。
Please don't.   (Implies that you are in a position of authority.)

6 Verb のが好きです/上手です

A verb short form + の turns a verb into a noun describing an action. Thus in combination with が好きです／きらいです, for example, you can describe what you like/dislike doing.

（私は）日本語を勉強するのが好きです。
I like studying the Japanese language.

（私は）部屋を掃除するのがきらいです。
I don't like cleaning my room.

"To be good/bad at doing something" is 〜が上手です (is good at . . .) and 〜が下手です (is bad at . . .).[6]

ロバートさんは料理を作るのが上手です。
Robert is good at cooking meals.

たけしさんは英語を話すのが下手です。
Takeshi is not a good speaker of English.

---

[6] To describe one's skills or lack thereof, we also often use a different set of expressions, namely, 〜がとくいです (is comfortable with . . .) and 〜がにがてです (is uncomfortable with . . .).

　私は日本語を話すのがとくいです。   *I am good at/comfortable with speaking Japanese.*

| person は activity (verb) のが $\left\{ \begin{array}{c} 好き \\ きらい \\ 上手 \\ 下手 \end{array} \right\}$ です。 | likes doing . . .
 doesn't like doing . . .
 is good at doing . . .
 is poor at doing . . . |

It is a common mistake to use the *te*-form of a verb in such contexts, misled by the association between 〜ている and the verb in the *-ing* form in English.

× たけしさんは英語を話してが下手です。

7 The Subject Particle が

Consider what ロバートさんは沖縄に行きました means. This sentence of course is about Robert and describes what he did. It is likely to be uttered when the topic of Robert has already been breached. Grammatically speaking, (1) the noun ロバート stands as the subject in relation to the verb 行く (he was the person who performed the going), and (2) the noun is, per the function of the particle は, presented as the topic of the sentence (*as for* Robert, he went to Okinawa).

What if we both know that somebody went to Okinawa recently, and *I* know that it was Robert, but *you* don't? I will say:

ロバートさんが沖縄に行きました。 *ROBERT went to Okinawa.*

This sentence means that *Robert* went to Okinawa, which in English would be uttered with an extra emphasis on the name Robert, which is the new piece of information in this sentence.

Question words like だれ and 何 in the subject of a sentence are followed by が rather than は.

だれが沖縄に行きましたか。 Compare: × だれは沖縄に行きましたか。
Who went to Okinawa?

As we learned in Lesson 2, a question word that is the subject of a sentence is never followed by the particle は, but always by the particle が (p. 61). As we have seen, a noun that will provide the answer to such a question is also followed by the particle が.

A：どのクラスがおもしろいですか。
   Which class is (the most) interesting?
B：日本語のクラスがおもしろいです。
   Japanese class is.

Ａ：（このクラスで）だれがめがねをかけていますか。

Who wears glasses (in this class)?

Ｂ：山下先生がめがねをかけています。
やましたせんせい

Professor Yamashita does.

8 何か and 何も
なに　　　　　　なに

The word for "something" is 何か, and the word for "anything" in negative sentences is 何も.
なに　　　　　　　　　　　　　　　　　　　　　　　　　　　　　　　　　　　　　なに

"Some" and "any" in		
· positive statements:	何か なに	*something*
· questions:	何か なに	*anything?*
· negative statements:	何も + negative なに	*not . . . anything*

When 何か and 何も are used in places where the particles は, が, and を are expected, they are
なに　　　　なに
often used on their own, without the help of particles. We will learn in Lesson 10 what to do in
cases where particles other than these are expected.

猫が何か持ってきました。
ねこ　なに　　も

The cat has brought something.

猫は何か食べましたか。
ねこ　なに　た

Did the cat eat anything?

いいえ、猫は何も食べませんでした。
ねこ　なに　た

No, the cat did not eat anything.

表現ノート
ひょう げん

～する ▶ Most irregular verbs are compounds of nouns and the verb する. Here, if you have learned an irregular verb, you have also learned a noun.

verbs	nouns	
勉強する べんきょう to study	勉強 べんきょう study	e.g. 日本語の勉強は楽しいです。 に ほん ご べんきょう たの *Japanese language study is fun.*
料理する りょう り to cook	料理 りょう り cooking	e.g. ロバートさんの料理はおいしいです。 りょう り *Robert's cooking is good.*

Some of these nouns can be used as the "object" of the verb する.

私は日本語の勉強をしました。　　　　　*I studied Japanese.*
わたし に ほん ご べんきょう

Compare: 私は日本語を勉強しました。
わたし に ほん ご べんきょう

たけしさんは部屋の掃除をしました。　　*Takeshi cleaned his room.*
へ や そうじ

Compare: たけしさんは部屋を掃除しました。
へ や そうじ

You can use both these nouns and their する verbs in sentences with 好きです
す
and きらいです, for example. You need to add の to the verbs, as we discussed in Grammar 6. Pay attention to the particles before these words, too.

日本語の勉強が好きです。／日本語を勉強するのが好きです。
に ほん ご べんきょう す に ほん ご べんきょう す
I like studying Japanese.

遅い/遅く ▶ Although both 遅い and 遅く mean "late," they have different usages,
おそ おそ おそ おそ
since 遅い is an adjective and 遅く is an adverb. 遅い modifies nouns or works as
おそ おそ おそ
a predicate, and 遅く modifies verbs.
おそ

A：きのう一時に寝ました。　　　*I went to bed at one o'clock yesterday.*
いち じ ね

B：遅いですね。　　　　　　　　*It's late.*
おそ

週末には、十時ごろ起きて、遅い朝ご飯を食べます。
しゅうまつ じゅう じ お おそ あさ はん た
On weekends, I get up around 10:00 and eat late breakfast.

きのう、遅く寝ました。　　　　*I went to bed late yesterday.*
おそ ね

You can also apply this rule to 早い/早く.
はや はや

練習 Practice
れん しゅう

Ⅰ Short Forms ☞Grammar 1

A. Change the affirmatives into negatives. 🔊 K08-07

(Example) かく → かかない

1. みる	5. はく	9. あらう	13. おもう
2. あける	6. はじめる	10. くる	14. もっていく
3. すむ	7. つくる	11. わすれる	15. はいる
4. かける	8. せんたくする	12. ある	16. かえる

B. Change the affirmatives into negatives. 🔊 K08-08

(Example) たかい → たかくない
げんきだ → げんきじゃない
がくせいだ → がくせいじゃない

1. ゆうめいだ	4. かわいい	7. やすい	10. いい
2. あめだ	5. みじかい	8. きれいだ	11. かっこいい
3. いそがしい	6. しんせつだ	9. たいへんだ	12. すきだ

Ⅱ Informal Speech ☞Grammar 2

A. Answer the following questions in informal speech, first in the affirmative, then in the negative. 🔊 K08-09/10

(Example) Q：よく魚を食べる？
さかな た
A：うん、食べる。／ううん、食べない。
た た

1. 今日、勉強する？
きょう べんきょう
2. 今日、友だちに会う？
きょう とも あ
3. よくお茶を飲む？
ちゃ の

4. よく電車に乗る？
でんしゃ の
5. 毎日、日本語を話す？
まいにち にほんご はな
6. 毎日、お風呂に入る？
まいにち ふ ろ はい

7. あした、大学に来る？
   だいがく く

8. 今日、宿題がある？
   きょう しゅくだい

9. 自転車を持っている？
   じてんしゃ も

10. 来週、カラオケに行く？
    らいしゅう い

11. 毎週、部屋を掃除する？
    まいしゅう へや そうじ

12. 毎日、洗濯する？
    まいにち せんたく

B. Answer the following questions in informal speech, first in the affirmative, then in the negative. 🔊 K08-11/12

(Example) Q：元気？
         げんき

         A：うん、元気。／ううん、元気じゃない。
           げんき げんき

1. ひま？

2. 忙しい？
   いそが

3. この教科書はいい？
   きょうかしょ

4. 先生はこわい？
   せんせい

5. 料理が上手？
   りょうり じょうず

6. お風呂が好き？
   ふろ す

7. スポーツがきらい？

8. 今日は休み？
   きょう やす

9. 日本語のクラスはおもしろい？
   にほんご

10. 日本語のクラスは難しい？
    にほんご むずか

Ⅲ 日本人だと思います ☛Grammar 3
   にほんじん おも

A. Make a guess about Mary, using 〜と思います. 🔊 K08-13
                                        おも

(Example) good at Japanese

   → メアリーさんは日本語が上手だと思います。
             にほんご じょうず おも

1. likes Takeshi

2. busy

3. a good student

4. not tall

5. not quiet

6. not a first-year student

7. often cooks

8. drives a car

9. doesn't smoke

10. not married

11. speaks Japanese every day

12. doesn't go home late at night

13. doesn't drink coffee much

14. often goes to see movies

B. Make a guess about Professor Yamashita and the place below and answer the following questions.

Example Q：山下先生はいい先生ですか。
A：はい、いい先生だと思います。／
いいえ、いい先生じゃないと思います。

A

Picture A

1. ひまですか。
2. 頭がいいですか。
3. 背が高いですか。
4. こわいですか。
5. 仕事が好きですか。
6. 結婚していますか。
7. お金をたくさん持っていますか。
8. よくスポーツをしますか。
9. スペイン語を話しますか。

Picture B

1. ここは日本ですか。
2. 有名な所ですか。
3. 暑いですか。
4. 冬は寒いですか。
5. 人がたくさん住んでいますか。
6. 夏によく雨が降りますか。

B

C. Discuss the following topics in pairs or groups.

Example university cafeteria

→ A：大学の食堂についてどう思いますか。
B：安くて、おいしいと思います。私はよく食べに行きます。
Aさんはどう思いますか。
A：私は……。

1. this town
2. this class
3. Japanese language
4. Mary and Takeshi
5. (your school/university)
6. (your own topic)

Ⅳ ナオミさんは忙しいと言っていました ☞Grammar 4
いそが い

A. Report what the following people said, using 〜と言っていました. 🔊 K08-14
い

(Example) Q：ナオミさんは何と言っていましたか。
なん い

A：今月は忙しいと言っていました。
こんげつ いそが い

ナオミ

e.g. 今月は忙しいです。
こんげつ いそが

1. 来月もひまじゃないです。
らいげつ
2. あしたは買い物をします。
か もの
3. 毎日漢字を勉強しています。
まいにちかん じ べんきょう

ロバート

4. ホームステイをしています。
5. お父さんは親切です。
とう しんせつ
6. お母さんは料理が上手です。
かあ りょうり じょうず
7. お兄さんは会社員です。
にい かいしゃいん
8. 家族は英語を話しません。
か ぞく えい ご はな

天気予報
てん き よ ほう

9. あしたは晴れです。
は
10. あしたは寒くないです。
さむ
11. あしたの気温は八度です。
き おん はち ど
12. あさっては曇りです。
くも
13. ときどき雪が降ります。
ゆき ふ

会
L8

B. Pair Work—Ask your partner the following questions. Take notes and report to the class later, using 〜と言っていました.
い

1. 週末は何をしますか。
しゅうまつ なに
2. この町はどうですか。
まち
3. 友だち／家族はどんな人ですか。
とも か ぞく ひと
4. どんな人が好きですか。
ひと す

Ⅴ 写真を見ないでください ☞Grammar 5
しゃしん　み

A. What would these people say when they want someone . . . 🔊 K08-15

(Example) not to look at the photo → 写真を見ないでください。
しゃしん　み

1. not to call
2. not to come to my house
3. not to go
4. not to smoke
5. not to throw away the magazine

6. not to speak English
7. not to sleep in class
8. not to forget your homework
9. not to be late
10. not to start the test yet
11. not to use smartphones

B. Ask a person in the same room if they mind you doing the following things.

(Example) 窓を開ける
まど　あ
→　A：窓を開けてもいいですか。
まど　あ
B：すみません。開けないでください。寒いですから。／
あ　　　　　　　　　　さむ
いいですよ。どうぞ。

1. たばこを吸う
す
2. テレビをつける
3. 写真を撮る
しゃしん　と

4. エアコンを消す
け
5. パソコンを使う
つか
6. (your own request)

Ⅵ 勉強するのが好きです 👉Grammar 6
べんきょう　　　　　す

A. Tell what Mary is good/poor at, using 上手です or 下手です. 🔊 K08-16
じょうず　　　　へた

(Example) tennis (good)

→ メアリーさんはテニスが上手です。
じょうず

swimming (poor)

→ メアリーさんは泳ぐのが下手です。
およ　　　へた

1. Spanish (good)
2. cooking (poor)
3. making sushi (poor)
4. eating <u>with chopsticks</u> (good)
　　　（はし で）
5. taking pictures (good)
6. driving a car (poor)
7. speaking Japanese (good)
8. writing <u>love letters</u> (good)
　　（ラブレター）

会
L8

B. Pair Work—Ask if your partner likes to do the following activities.

(Example) studying

→ A：勉強するのが好きですか。
べんきょう　　　す
B：はい、好きです／大好きです。
す　　　だいす
いいえ、あまり好きじゃないです／
す
きらいです／大きらいです。
だい

1. eating
2. sleeping
3. singing
4. doing shopping
5. playing sports
6. studying Japanese
7. doing cleaning
8. doing laundry
9. cooking
10. taking a bath
11. driving a car
12. washing a car

Note: If you neither like it nor dislike it, you can use 好きでもきらいでもないです。
す

C. Class Activity—Talk with each of your classmates, using the following questions as a starter and expand the conversation.

1. 何をするのが好きですか。
なに　　　　す
2. 何をするのがきらいですか。
なに

Ⅶ だれがイギリス人ですか ☛Grammar 7

A. Use the table below and answer the questions. 🔊 K08-17

(Example) Q：だれがイギリス人ですか。

A：ロバートさんがイギリス人です。

1. だれが韓国人ですか。

2. だれが料理をするのが上手ですか。

3. だれがいつも食堂で食べますか。

4. だれがデートをしましたか。

5. だれが犬が好きですか。

Robert	British	is good at cooking	cooks often	went to Okinawa last weekend	doesn't like cats
Mary	American	is good at tennis	does not cook	had a date last weekend	likes dogs
Sora	Korean	is good at singing	cooks sometimes	went to Tokyo last weekend	likes cats
Takeshi	Japanese	is good at swimming	always eats at cafeteria	had a date last weekend	doesn't like cats

B. Pair Work—Use the table above and ask your partner questions with だれが.

Ⅷ 何もしませんでした ☛Grammar 8

A. You went to a party but did nothing there. Make sentences using the cues. 🔊 K08-18

(Example) パーティーに行きましたが、(eat)

→ パーティーに行きましたが、何も食べませんでした。

1. パーティーに行きましたが、(drink)

2. カラオケがありましたが、(sing)

3. テレビがありましたが、(watch)

4. カメラを持っていましたが、(take)

5. ゆみさんに会いましたが、(talk)

6. パーティーに行きましたが、(do)

B. Answer the following questions.

(Example) Q：きのうの晩ご飯は何か作りましたか。

A：はい、パスタ (pasta) を作りました。／

いいえ、何も作りませんでした。

1. けさ、何か食べましたか。
2. きのう、何か買いましたか。
3. パーティーに何か持っていきますか。

4. 今、何かいりますか。
5. 週末、何かしますか。

Ⅸ まとめの練習

A. Pair Work—A and B are making plans for a one-day trip with two other friends, C and D. A knows C's schedule and B knows D's schedule. Play the roles of A and B. Discuss your and your friends' schedules using 〜と言っていました, and find out which days all four of you are available. (B's schedule is on the next page.)

会
L8

(Example) A：十六日はひまですか。

B：いいえ、買い物に行きます。十八日は、どうですか。

A：私は、何もしません。でも、Cさんは映画を見に行くと言っていました。

B：そうですか。じゃあ……

Student A

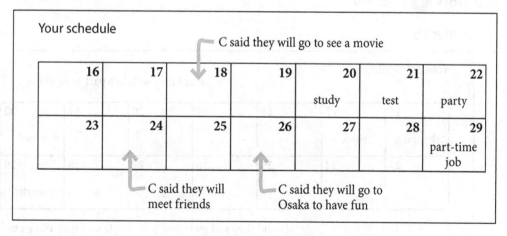

B. Pair Work/Group Work—You are planning a party. Decide on the following points and fill in the chart. Use Dialogue Ⅰ as a model.

いつですか	
どこでしますか	
どんなパーティーですか	
何を持っていきますか	
だれが来ますか	

C. Class Activity—Find someone who . . .

1. likes to study Japanese _____

2. hates to do cleaning _____

3. likes to sing _____

4. is poor at driving _____

5. whose mother is good at cooking _____

6. (your own question)

_____ _____

Then, report to the class:

_____さんは_____と言っていました。

Pair Work Ⅸ A. (p. 205)

Student B

Your schedule

D said they will do a part-time job

16	17	18	19	20	21	22
shopping	work					tennis
23	24	25	26	27	28	29
						work

D said they will go to eat dinner

D said they will go to Kyoto to see temples

調べてみよう
しら

Japanese Cooking Party

Plan a Japanese-themed cooking party.

1. Each member of the group will choose a Japanese dish, and prepare a list of the ingredients and a simple recipe for the dish. (See the example below.)

2. Compare the lists in your group and discuss what your group will cook.

3. Share your group's ingredients list and recipe with the rest of the class.

4. Cook and enjoy!

Example カレーライス

Ingredients

ごはん (cooked rice)　じゃがいも (potatoes)　にんじん (carrots)

玉ねぎ (onions)　肉 (meat)　カレールー (Japanese curry roux)
たま　　　　　　にく

Recipe (You don't have to write the recipe in Japanese)

1. Cut meat and vegetables and stir-fry.

2. Add water and bring to boil. Reduce heat, cover and simmer until ingredients are tender.

3. Add curry roux. Simmer, stirring constantly.

4. Serve hot over cooked rice.

会
L8

日本の食べ物 Foods in Japan
にほん　　　た　　もの

A traditional Japanese meal consists of a bowl of white rice
(ご飯), a couple of dishes (おかず), and soup (often みそ汁),
はん　　　　　　　　　　　　　　　　　　　　　　　　　　　　　しる
and is called 定食 (set menu) in cafeterias. However, many
ていしょく
Japanese don't eat traditional food or rice-based dishes for
every meal. A great variety of food is served in restaurants
and even at home because Japan has adopted and adapt-
ed many foreign dishes over time.

ご飯　おかず　みそ汁
はん　　　　　　　　しる

Common dishes in Japan

カレーライス	おにぎり	ラーメン	うどん	パスタ
Curry with rice	Rice balls	Ramen noodles	*Udon* noodles	Pasta

| ぎょうざ | 牛丼 | ハンバーグ | さしみ | お好み焼き |
	ぎゅうどん			この　や
Dumplings	Beef rice bowl	Hamburger steak	Raw seafood	Savory pancake

What did Yui and Professor Yamashita eat for breakfast today?

ゆい（20歳）
はたち

山下先生（47歳）
やましたせんせい　　さい

トースト／スープ／ヨーグルト
Toast, soup, and yogurt

ご飯／焼き魚／たまご／みそ汁
はん　や　ざかな　　　　　　しる
Rice, broiled fish, egg, and *miso* soup

Useful Expressions

スーパーで

At the Supermarket

Expressions

アボカドはありますか。————————Do you have avocado?

この中にお酒が入っていますか。———Is there alcohol in this?
<small>なか</small> <small>さけ</small> <small>はい</small>

これはハラルフードですか。————Is this halal?

ピーナッツアレルギーがあります。———I have an allergy to peanuts.

袋をお願いします。————————Can I have a bag?
<small>ふくろ</small> <small>ねが</small>

Vocabulary

果物：
<small>くだもの</small>

野菜：
<small>やさい</small>

いちご
(strawberry)

すいか
(watermelon)

にんじん
(carrot)

たまねぎ
(onion)

みかん
(mandarin orange)

じゃがいも
(potato)

なす
(eggplant)

りんご
(apple)

もも
(peach)

ぶどう
(grape)

きゅうり
(cucumber)

キャベツ
(cabbage)

肉：
<small>にく</small>

牛肉 (beef)
<small>ぎゅうにく</small>

豚肉 (pork)
<small>ぶたにく</small>

鶏肉 (chicken)
<small>とりにく</small>

第9課　LESSON 9

かぶき Kabuki

In this lesson, we will...

- Talk casually about the things that happened in the past
- Express thoughts and opinions about past events
- Report someone's speech　　● Order food in a restaurant or shop　　● Give reasons

---

会 話 D i a l o g u e

I Mary and Takeshi are talking. 🔊 K09-01/02

1 たけし：　　メアリーさんはかぶきが好きですか。

2 メアリー：　かぶきですか。あまり知りません。

3 　　　　　　でも、ロバートさんはおもしろかったと言っていました。

4 たけし：　　かぶきのチケットを二枚もらったから、見に行きませんか。

5 メアリー：　ええ、ぜひ。いつですか。

6 たけし：　　来週の木曜日です。十二時から四時までです。

II During intermission at a Kabuki theater. 🔊 K09-03/04

1 メアリー：　きれいでしたね。

2 たけし：　　出ている人はみんな男の人ですよ。

3 メアリー：　本当ですか。

4 たけし：　　ええ。ところで、もう昼ご飯を食べましたか。

5 メアリー：　いいえ、まだ食べていません。

6 たけし：　　じゃあ、買いに行きましょう。

Ⅲ At a concession stand. K09-05/06

1 たけし： すみません。お弁当を二つください。
　 　　　　　　　　　べんとう　ふた

2 店の人： はい。
　 みせ ひと

3 たけし： それから、お茶を一つとコーヒーを一つ。
　 　　　　　　　　お茶　ひと　　　　　　　　　　　ひと

4 店の人： 二千八百円です。どうもありがとうございました。
　 みせ ひと　 に せんはっぴゃくえん

Ⓘ

Takeshi: Mary, do you like Kabuki?

Mary: Kabuki? I don't know it well. But Robert said it was interesting.

Takeshi: I got two tickets for Kabuki, so would you like to go to see it?

Mary: Sure. When is it?

Takeshi: On Thursday next week. From twelve noon to four.

Ⓘ

Mary: It was beautiful.

Takeshi: The people who appear are all men.

Mary: Really?

Takeshi: Yes. By the way, did you already eat lunch?

Mary: No, I haven't eaten yet.

Takeshi: Then, shall we go to buy lunch?

Ⓘ

Takeshi: Excuse me. Two box lunches, please.

Vendor: Here you are.

Takeshi: And then, one tea and one coffee.

Vendor: That is 2,800 yen. Thank you very much.

会
L9

単語

<ruby>単<rt>たん</rt></ruby>　<ruby>語<rt>ご</rt></ruby>

K09-07 (J-E)
K09-08 (E-J)

V o c a b u l a r y

N o u n s

たんご	単語	word; vocabulary
さくぶん	作文	essay; composition
しけん	試験	exam
てがみ	手紙	letter
メール		e-mail
ギター		guitar
ピアノ		piano
コンサート		concert
* チケット		ticket
* かぶき	歌舞伎	Kabuki; traditional Japanese theatrical art
スキー		ski
* おべんとう	お弁当	boxed lunch
ピザ		pizza
びょうき	病気	illness; sickness
くすり	薬	medicine
いいこ	いい子	good child
いろ	色	color
こんど	今度	near future
せんげつ	先月	last month
きょねん	去年	last year

い - a d j e c t i v e s

あおい	青い	blue
あかい	赤い	red
くろい	黒い	black
しろい	白い	white
さびしい	寂しい	lonely
わかい	若い	young

な - a d j e c t i v e

いじわる（な）	意地悪	mean-spirited

＊Words that appear in the dialogue

U-verbs

おどる	踊る	to dance
おわる	終わる	(something) ends （〜が）
くすりをのむ	薬を飲む	to take medicine
にんきがある	人気がある	to be popular
はじまる	始まる	(something) begins （〜が）
ひく	弾く	to play (a string instrument or piano) （〜を）
* もらう		to get (from somebody) (*person* に *thing* を)

Ru-verbs

おぼえる	覚える	to memorize （〜を）
* でる	出る	(1) to appear; to attend （〜に）
		(2) to exit （〜を）

Irregular Verbs

| うんどうする | 運動する | to exercise |
| さんぽする | 散歩する | to take a walk |

Adverbs and Other Expressions

そう		(I think) so
* 〜から		from ...
* 〜まで		to (a place/a time)
* ぜひ	是非	by all means
* ところで		by the way
* みんな		all
* もう		already

Numbers (used to count small items)

* ひとつ	一つ	one
* ふたつ	二つ	two
みっつ	三つ	three
よっつ	四つ	four
いつつ	五つ	five
むっつ	六つ	six
ななつ	七つ	seven
やっつ	八つ	eight
ここのつ	九つ	nine
とお	十	ten

会 L9

文法 G r a m m a r

1 Past Tense Short Forms

Here we will learn the past tense paradigm of short forms. With four parts of speech and two polarities, there are eight forms in the chart, but you need to learn only three rules.

(1) Verbs: Replace the *te*-form endings て and で with た and だ.
(2) い-adjectives: Replace the last い with かった. You may also think of this in terms of "dropping です from the long form."
(3) な-adjectives and nouns: Replace the long form でした ending with だった.
Negation: ない conjugates as an い-adjective. Therefore, for all categories, you can replace the last ない with なかった.

Past, affirmative

compare with:

- verbs:　　　　　食べ<u>た</u>　　　　　食べ<u>て</u>
　　　　　　　　　読ん<u>だ</u>　　　　　読ん<u>で</u>
- い-adjectives:　かわい<u>かった</u>　　かわいい／かわい<u>かったです</u>
- な-adjectives:　静か<u>だった</u>　　　静か<u>でした</u>
- noun + です：　学生<u>だった</u>　　　学生<u>でした</u>

Past, negative

- verbs:　　　　　読ま<u>なかった</u>　　読ま<u>ない</u>
- い-adjectives:　かわいく<u>なかった</u>　かわいく<u>ない</u>
- な-adjectives:　静かじゃ<u>なかった</u>　静かじゃ<u>ない</u>
- noun + です：　学生じゃ<u>なかった</u>　学生じゃ<u>ない</u>

---

2 Past Tense Short Forms in Informal Speech

Short form predicates in the past tense can be used in the same way as the present tense forms, which we discussed in Lesson 8. Note that the question particle か is dropped in informal speech.

A：けさ、朝ご飯を食べた？　　　　　　*Did you have breakfast this morning?*
B：うん、食べた。／ううん、食べなかった。　*Yes, I did. / No, I didn't.*

Unlike だ in the present tense, だった is not dropped in informal speech.

A：先週は忙しかった？ *Were you busy last week?*
せんしゅう いそが

B：ううん、忙しくなかった。ひまだった。 *No, I wasn't. I had free time.*
いそが

3 Past Tense Short Forms in Quoted Speech: ～と思います
おも

As in the present tense, you use the short form in the past tense with ～と思います (I think) to
おも
report what you think took place in the past.

A：あ、私のとんかつがない！ *Hey, my pork cutlet is gone!*
わたし

B：トムさんが食べたと思います。 *I think Tom ate it.*
た おも

去年の冬はあまり寒くなかったと思います。
きょねん ふゆ さむ おも
I don't think last winter was very cold. (= I think last winter was not very cold.)

4 Past Tense Short Forms in Quoted Speech: ～と言っていました
い

If you heard somebody utter a sentence in the past tense, you can report it with the short form
past tense with ～と言っていました。
い

ヤスミンさんは、昼ご飯を食べなかったと言っていました。
ひる はん た い
Yasmin said that she didn't have lunch.

Note that Japanese does not have the "sequence of tense" rule, and the tense of the original utterance is preserved when it is reported. If you are reporting somebody's utterance in which the present tense is used, you must also use the present tense inside the quote. Thus, if your friend Yasmin said 今、晩ご飯を食べています, using the present tense, your report will have 晩ご飯を食べている in the present tense, rather than 晩ご飯を食べていた in the past tense.

ヤスミンさんは晩ご飯を食べていると言っていました。

Yasmin said that she <u>was</u> having dinner.

5 Qualifying Nouns with Verbs and Adjectives

The following table shows various forms of noun modification. The phrases in the left qualify the noun 人 (person) to their right. Example 1 is a straightforward adjectival modification. Example 2 contains a phrase describing a person's attribute (Lesson 7), and Example 3 has a な-adjective with a grammatical object (Lesson 5). Example 4 has a verb in the short form (Lesson 8).

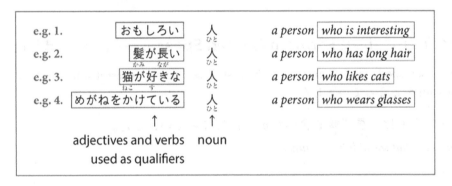

e.g. 1.	おもしろい	人	*a person*	*who is interesting*
e.g. 2.	髪が長い	人	*a person*	*who has long hair*
e.g. 3.	猫が好きな	人	*a person*	*who likes cats*
e.g. 4.	めがねをかけている	人	*a person*	*who wears glasses*

adjectives and verbs   noun
used as qualifiers

Here we focus on a verb + ている, which is very frequently used as noun modifiers, describing people on the basis of their current actions and states.[1]

Ａ：ゆいさんはどの人ですか。　　　　*Which one is Yui?*

Ｂ：あそこで本を読んでいる人です。　　*Yui is the one who is reading a book over there.*

あそこで写真を撮っている学生はロバートさんです。
The student taking pictures over there is Robert.

---

[1] Short forms other than ている can also be used for noun modification, as in 毎日運動する人 (a person who exercises every day) and たばこをすわない人 (a person who does not smoke). We will explore a wider range of verb forms used in noun modification in Lesson 15.

6 もう〜ました and まだ〜ていません

You can use the affirmative past tense of a verb 〜ました both (i) to talk about an event that happened at a certain time in the past (きのう *yesterday*, for example), just like *did* in English, and also (ii) to talk about a past event that still has an effect at present, just like *have done* in English (used with adverbs like もう *already*, for example).

(i) きのう宿題をしました。   *I did the homework yesterday.*

(ii) もう宿題をしました。   *I have already done the homework.*

With the negative, the past is used only to talk about a finished time period like きのう, but てい る is used if your intention is to talk about how things stand now ("not yet").

(i) きのう宿題をしませんでした。   *I did not do the homework yesterday.*

(ii) まだ宿題をしていません。   *I have not done the homework yet.*

もう〜ました	*have already . . .*
まだ〜ていません	*have not . . . yet*

会
L9

7 Explanation から、Situation

We learned in Lesson 6 that から added to a sentence means "because."

朝ご飯を食べませんでした。忙しかったですから。
I didn't have breakfast. (Because) I was busy.

You can put these two sentences into one, by moving the "explanation＋から" sequence to the beginning of a sentence for which the explanation is offered. The resulting order of elements resembles that of a "therefore" sentence more closely than that of a "because" sentence in English.

explanation	から、	situation	。

= situation , *because* explanation .

= explanation ; *therefore,* situation .

あした試験があるから、今晩勉強します。

I will study this evening, because we will have an exam tomorrow.

(= We will have an exam tomorrow; therefore, I will study this evening.)

寒かったから、出かけませんでした。

We didn't go out, because it was cold.

(= It was cold; therefore, we didn't go out.)

Before the conjunction から, you find both the long and short forms. Thus the から clauses in the above examples can be rewritten as あした試験がありますから and 寒かったですから.[2] The long form before から is more polite, and is frequently found in request and suggestion sentences.

かぶきのチケットがありますから、一緒に見に行きましょう。

Let's go to see Kabuki. I have tickets.

---

[2] The long form before から is inappropriate when the entire sentence ends in a short form, however. Thus it is inappropriate to say: ✕寒かったですから、出かけなかった。

練習 P r a c t i c e
れん しゅう

Ⅰ Past Tense Short Forms ☛Grammar 1

A. Verbs

(a) Change the following verbs into the past affirmative. 🔊 K09-09

Example かく → かいた

1. はなす
2. しぬ
3. のむ
4. かける

5. いく
6. あそぶ
7. つくる
8. でる

9. あらう
10. くる
11. ひく
12. まつ

13. いそぐ
14. もらう
15. おどる
16. せんたくする

(b) Change the following verbs into the past negative. 🔊 K09-10

Example かく → かかなかった

1. みる
2. すてる
3. しる
4. かける

5. はく
6. はじまる
7. つくる
8. かえる

9. あらう
10. くる
11. いう
12. やすむ

13. おぼえる
14. うたう
15. せんたくする
16. うんどうする

B. Adjectives and Nouns

(a) Change the following into the past affirmative. 🔊 K09-11

Example たかい → たかかった
げんきな → げんきだった
がくせい → がくせいだった

1. ゆうめいな
2. あめ
3. あかい

4. かわいい
5. みじかい
6. しんせつな

7. やすい
8. きれいな
9. いいてんき

10. かっこいい
11. さびしい
12. びょうき

(b) Change the following into the past negative. 🔊 K09-12

Example たかい　　→　たかくなかった

げんきな　→　げんきじゃなかった

がくせい　→　がくせいじゃなかった

1. いじわるな　　4. かわいい　　　7. あおい　　　10. かっこいい

2. びょうき　　　5. ながい　　　　8. しずかな　　11. おもしろい

3. わかい　　　　6. べんりな　　　9. いいてんき　12. さびしい

IIInｆormal Speech ☛Grammar 2

A. Using the cues below, make questions about yesterday in informal speech. How do you answer those questions? 🔊 K09-13

Example テレビを見る

→　Q：きのうテレビを見た？

A：うん、見た。／ううん、見なかった。

1. ピザを食べる
2. 散歩する
3. 図書館で本を借りる
4. うちを掃除する
5. うちで料理する
6. 友だちに会う
7. 単語を覚える

8. 学校に来る
9. 家族に電話する
10. パソコンを使う
11. 手紙をもらう
12. 遊びに行く
13. 運動する
14. メールを書く

B. Make questions about childhood in informal speech. How do you answer those questions? 🔊 K09-14

Example 元気

→　Q：子供の時、元気だった？

A：うん、元気だった。／ううん、元気じゃなかった。

1. かわいい   7. 楽_{たの}しい

2. 髪_{かみ}が長_{なが}い   8. スポーツが好_すき

3. 背_せが高_{たか}い   9. 宿題_{しゅくだい}がきらい

4. 勉強_{べんきょう}が好_すき   10. 頭_{あたま}がいい

5. スキーが上手_{じょうず}   11. 先生_{せんせい}はやさしい

6. さびしい   12. いじわる

C. Pair Work—Ask each other what you did yesterday, last weekend, etc., and how it was. Use informal speech.

Example   A：先週_{せんしゅう}の週末_{しゅうまつ}何_{なに}をした？

         B：お寺_{てら}に行_いった。

         A：どうだった？

         B：きれいだったよ。

Ⅲ 元気_{げんき}だったと思_{おも}います   ☞Grammar 3   会 L9

A. Make a guess about what the following people were like when they were in high school.

Example   元気_{げんき}でしたか。   🔊 K09-15

     →   Q：メアリーさんは高校_{こうこう}の時_{とき}、元気_{げんき}でしたか。

          A：はい、元気_{げんき}だったと思_{おも}います。／

              いいえ、元気_{げんき}じゃなかったと思_{おも}います。

(a) メアリーさんについて

   1. かわいかったですか。   4. よく勉強_{べんきょう}しましたか。

   2. 日本語_{にほんご}が上手_{じょうず}でしたか。   5. 日本_{にほん}に住_すんでいましたか。

   3. 人気_{にんき}がありましたか。

(b) 山下先生_{やましたせんせい}について

   1. 背_せが高_{たか}かったですか。   4. 踊_{おど}るのが上手_{じょうず}でしたか。

   2. よくデートをしましたか。   5. かっこよかったですか。

   3. よくギターを弾_ひきましたか。

B. Pair Work—Talk about the childhood of someone you and your partner know, using the following expressions.

(Example) 頭がいい
あたま

→　A：ロバートさんは子供の時、頭がよかったと思います。
こども　とき　あたま　　　おも

　　　B：私もそう思います。
わたし　　　おも

1. かわいい　　　　　4. 運動するのが好き　　　7. ピアノを弾くのが上手
　　　　　　　　　　　　うんどう　　　　す　　　　　　　　　　　ひ　　　　じょうず

2. 元気　　　　　　　5. よく遊ぶ　　　　　　　8. 髪が長い／短い
げんき　　　　　　　　　　　あそ　　　　　　　　　　かみ　なが　　みじか

3. いい子　　　　　　6. 背が高い／低い　　　　9. たくさん本を読む
　　こ　　　　　　　　せ　たか　　ひく　　　　　　　　ほん　よ

Ⅳ　ヤスミンさんは、病気だったと言っていました　☞Grammar 4
びょうき　　　い

A. Report what the following people said, using ～と言っていました. 🔊 K09-16
い

(Example)　お父さんは、若い時、マイケル・ジャクソンが好きだったと言ってい
とう　　　わか　とき　　　　　　　　　　　　　　　す　　　　　　　い
ました。

e.g. 若い時、マイケル・ジャクソンが好きでした。
わか　とき　　　　　　　　　　　　す

1. 友だちとよく踊りに行きました。
とも　　　　おど　い

2. 踊るのがあまり上手じゃなかったです。
おど　　　　　　　じょうず

3. マイケルの歌をたくさん覚えました。
うた　　　　　　おぼ

4. 先月、かぶきを見に行きました。
せんげつ　　　　み　い

5. かぶきは十二時に始まって、四時に終わりました。
じゅうにじ　はじ　　　　よじ　お

6. かぶきは長かったです。
なが

7. かぶきはおもしろかったです。

8. 先週、大学に行きませんでした。
せんしゅう　だいがく　い

9. 病気でした。
びょうき

10. 薬を飲んで、寝ていました。
くすり　の　　　ね

B. Pair Work—Ask your partner the following questions. Take notes and report to the class later, using 〜と言_いっていました.

1. 先週_{せんしゅう}、何_{なに}をしましたか。どうでしたか。

2. 子供_{こども}の時_{とき}、どんな子供_{こども}でしたか。よく何_{なに}をしましたか。

3. 夏休_{なつやす}み／冬休_{ふゆやす}みにどこへ行_いきましたか。どうでしたか。

4. 高校_{こうこう}の時_{とき}、よく何_{なに}をしましたか。

Ⅴ めがねをかけている人_{ひと}です ☞Grammar 5

A. Look at the picture below and answer the questions.

〔Example〕 中村_{なかむら}さん → Q：中村_{なかむら}さんはどの人_{ひと}ですか。

A：黒_{くろ}いＴシャツを着_きている人_{ひと}です。

お弁当_{べんとう}を食_たべている人_{ひと}です。

1. 田中_{たなか}さん   3. 野村_{のむら}さん   5. 大川_{おおかわ}さん

2. 山口_{やまぐち}さん   4. 森_{もり}さん   6. 鈴木_{すずき}さん

会
L9

森_{もり} 大川_{おおかわ} 鈴木_{すずき}

野村_{のむら}

田中_{たなか} 中村_{なかむら} 山口_{やまぐち}

B. Pair Work—One of you looks at picture A below and the other looks at picture B (p. 227). Ask each other questions and identify all the people in the picture.

(Example) みさき → A：みさきさんはどの人ですか。

　　　　　　　　　 B：テレビを見ている人です。

Picture A

えり

つばさ

みさき

じゅん

ひな

Ask which of the people are the following:

1. しょう
2. あい
3. ゆうと
4. りん

C. Class Activity—Describe your classmates.

The class is divided into two groups, A and B. Each member of group A acts out something and freezes in the middle of doing so. Members of group B answer the teacher's questions, using 〜ている人です. Take turns when finished.

(Example) Teacher： マイクさんはどの人ですか。

　　　　　 Student： 車を運転している人です。

Ⅵ まだ食べていません ☞Grammar 6

A. You have two to-do lists. ☑ are things you have done, and ☐ are things you haven't. Answer the following questions using もう〜ました or まだ〜ていません. 🔊 K09-17

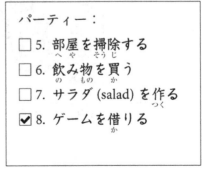

今週のクラス：
☑☐ e.g. 新しい漢字を覚える
☑ 1. 宿題をする
☐ 2. 新しい単語を覚える
☐ 3. 作文を書く
☐ 4. 試験の勉強をする

パーティー：
☐ 5. 部屋を掃除する
☐ 6. 飲み物を買う
☐ 7. サラダ (salad) を作る
☑ 8. ゲームを借りる

Example　A：もう新しい漢字を覚えましたか。
　　　　 B：☑ → はい、もう覚えました。
　　　　　　 □ → いいえ、まだ覚えていません。

B. Pair Work—Ask if your partner has done . . . yet. If the answer is no, ask your partner out, as in the example (1). If yes, ask your partner how it was, as in (2).

Example　the name of a newly released movie　→　『ワンピース』を見る

(1) A：もう『ワンピース』を見ましたか。
　　 B：いいえ、まだ見ていません。Aさんは？
　　 A：私もまだ見ていません。よかったら、一緒に見ませんか。
　　 B：ええ、いいですね。

(2) A：もう『ワンピース』を見ましたか。
　　 B：ええ、もう見ました。
　　 A：そうですか。どうでしたか。
　　 B：すごくおもしろかったですよ。

会
L9

1. the name of a newly released movie　　＿＿＿＿＿＿＿＿＿＿＿＿を見る
2. the name of a new game　　　　　　　＿＿＿＿＿＿＿＿＿＿＿＿をする
3. the name of a new restaurant/shop/place　＿＿＿＿＿＿＿＿＿＿＿＿に行く

Ⅶ 天気がいいから、遊びに行きます ☞Grammar 7

A. Match up the phrases to make sense.

1. 料理するのがきらいだから　　　　　　　・　　・今はひまです。
2. 試験が終わったから　　　　　　　　　　・　　・行きませんか。
3. 旅行に行ったから　　　　　　　　　　　・　　・お弁当を買います。
4. コンサートのチケットを二枚もらったから・　　・急ぎましょう。
5. 天気がよくなかったから　　　　　　　　・　　・遊びに行きませんでした。
6. クラスが始まるから　　　　　　　　　　・　　・お金がありません。

B. Complete the following sentences adding reasons.

1. _____から、お金がぜんぜんありません。
   <ruby>金<rt>かね</rt></ruby>

2. _____から、日本語を勉強しています。
   <ruby>日本語<rt>にほんご</rt></ruby>　<ruby>勉強<rt>べんきょう</rt></ruby>

3. _____から、先週の週末は忙しかったです。
   <ruby>先週<rt>せんしゅう</rt></ruby>　<ruby>週末<rt>しゅうまつ</rt></ruby>　<ruby>忙<rt>いそが</rt></ruby>

4. _____から、きのう学校を休みました。
   <ruby>学校<rt>がっこう</rt></ruby>　<ruby>休<rt>やす</rt></ruby>

5. _____から、花を買いました。
   <ruby>花<rt>はな</rt></ruby>　<ruby>買<rt>か</rt></ruby>

6. _____から、_____。

Ⅷ まとめの<ruby>練習<rt>れんしゅう</rt></ruby>

A. Role Play—One of you is working at a fast-food restaurant. The other is a customer. Using Dialogue Ⅲ as a model, order some food and drinks from the menu below. Be sure to say how many you want.

B. Answer the following questions.

1. ピアノを弾きますか。

2. ギターを弾くのが上手ですか。

3. 踊るのが好きですか。

4. 病気の時、よく薬を飲みますか。

5. よく散歩しますか。

6. 去年の誕生日に何かもらいましたか。だれに何をもらいましたか。

7. 今日、クラスは何時に始まりましたか。何時に終わりますか。

8. 子供の時、よく友だちと遊びましたか。

9. 何色のTシャツを持っていますか。

10. 白い帽子を持っていますか。

11. 今度の試験は難しいと思いますか。

12. あなたの国では、どんなスポーツが人気がありますか。

会
L9

Pair Work Ⅴ B. (p. 224)

Example みさき → A：みさきさんはどの人ですか。

B：テレビを見ている人です。

Picture B

Ask which of the people are the following:

1. つばさ
2. じゅん
3. ひな
4. えり

Culture Notes

日本の伝統文化 Japanese Traditional Culture
にほん　でんとうぶんか

歌舞伎
か ぶ き
Kabuki

文楽
ぶんらく
Puppet theater

箏
こと
Traditional string instrument

能
のう
Masked musical

狂言
きょうげん
Traditional comic theater

落語
らくご
Humorous storytelling

相撲
すもう
Sumo wrestling

柔道
じゅうどう
Judo

剣道
けんどう
Japanese fencing

お茶（茶道）
ちゃ　さどう
Tea ceremony

生け花（華道）
い　ばな　かどう
Flower arrangement

書道
しょどう
Calligraphy

Useful Expressions

色
(いろ)

C o l o r s

There are two kinds of words for colors.

Group 1: い-adjectives

黒い (くろ) —————— black		白い (しろ) —————— white	
赤い (あか) —————— red		青い (あお) —————— blue	
黄色い (きいろ) —————— yellow		茶色い (ちゃいろ) —————— brown	

These words become nouns without the い.

赤いかばん (あか)　　　　　　　　　　　　*red bag*

赤がいちばん好きです。(あか)(す)　　　*I like red the best.*

Group 2: Nouns

緑／グリーン (みどり) ———— green		紫 (むらさき) —————— purple	
紺色 (こんいろ) —————— navy blue		灰色／グレー (はいいろ) ———— gray	
水色 (みずいろ) —————— light blue		金色／ゴールド (きんいろ) ———— gold	
銀色／シルバー (ぎんいろ) —— silver		ピンク —————— pink	
オレンジ —————— orange		ベージュ —————— beige	

These words need の in order to make noun phrases.

緑／グリーンのセーター (みどり)　　　*green sweater*

Here are some words related to colors.

顔が青いですね。(かお)(あお)　　　　　*You look pale.*

白黒の写真 (しろくろ)(しゃしん)　　　　*black and white picture*

青信号 (あおしんごう)　　　　　　　　　*green light*

第10課　L E S S O N　10

冬休みの予定 Winter Vacation Plans
ふゆ やす　　　　よ てい

In this lesson, we will...

- Compare things and people
- Talk about future plans
- Describe changes in states
- Talk about means of transportation and the time required
- Ask about tours and make reservations

会話 D i a l o g u e
かい わ

I Winter vacation is approaching. 🔊 K10-01/02

1 メアリー：　寒くなりましたね。
　　　　　　さむ

2 たけし：　　ええ。メアリーさん、冬休みはどうしますか。
　　　　　　　　　　　　　　　　ふゆやす

3 メアリー：　北海道か九州に行くつもりですが、まだ決めていません。
　　　　　　ほっかいどう きゅうしゅう い　　　　　　　　き

4 たけし：　　いいですね。

5 メアリー：　北海道と九州とどっちのほうがいいと思いますか。
　　　　　　ほっかいどう きゅうしゅう　　　　　　　　　　おも

6 たけし：　　冬は北海道のほうがおもしろいと思います。ぼくの友だちは
　　　　　　ふゆ ほっかいどう　　　　　　　　　おも　　　　　　　とも

7　　　　　　食べ物もおいしいと言っていましたよ。
　　　　　　た もの　　　　　　　い

8 メアリー：　そうですか。ところで、たけしさんはどこかに行きますか。
　　　　　　　　　　　　　　　　　　　　　　　　　　　い

9 たけし：　　お金がないから、どこにも行きません。
　　　　　　かね　　　　　　　　　　い

10 メアリー：　そうですか。じゃあ、たけしさんにおみやげを買ってきますよ。
　　　　　　　　　　　　　　　　　　　　　　　　　　　か

11 たけし：　　わあ、ありがとう。

II At the hotel front desk. 🔊 K10-03/04

1 メアリー：　　すみません。ここから旭山動物園までどのぐらいかかりますか。
　　　　　　　　　　　　　あさひやまどうぶつえん

2 ホテルの人：そうですね。電車とバスで二時間半ぐらいです。
　　　　　　ひと　　　　　　でんしゃ　　　　　にじかんはん

3 メアリー：　　時間がかかりますね。
　　　　　　　じかん

4 ホテルの人：土曜日と日曜日はバスツアーがありますが……。
　　　　　　ひと　　どようび　　にちようび

5 メアリー：　　そうですか。いくらですか。

₆ ホテルの人：四千八百円です。
　　　　　　 ひと　 よんせんはっぴゃくえん

₇ メアリー：　いいですね。じゃあ、ツアーの予約をお願いします。
　　　　　　　　　　　　　　　　　　　 よ やく　　 ねが

₈ 　　　　　　土曜日のをお願いします。
　　　　　　　 ど よう び　　 ねが

Ⓘ

Mary: It is getting cold.

Takeshi: Yes. Mary, what will you do at winter break?

Mary: I am planning to go to Hokkaido or Kyushu, but I haven't decided yet.

Takeshi: That's nice.

Mary: Which do you think is better, Hokkaido or Kyushu?

Takeshi: I think Hokkaido is more interesting in winter. My friend said that the food was delicious there as well.

Mary: I see. By the way, are you going somewhere, Takeshi?

Takeshi: I don't have money, so I won't go anywhere.

Mary: Is that so? Then I'll buy a souvenir for you.

Takeshi: Wow, thank you.

Ⅱ

Mary: Excuse me, how long does it take from here to Asahiyama Zoo?

Hotel front desk: Let's see. It will take about two and half hours by train and bus.

Mary: It takes time, doesn't it?

Hotel front desk: There are bus tours on Saturday and Sunday.

Mary: Really? How much does it cost?

Hotel front desk: 4,800 yen.

Mary: Sounds good. Well, I would like to reserve the tour. The Saturday tour, please.

単語

たん　ご

Vocabulary

Nouns

きせつ	季節	season
はる	春	spring
あき	秋	fall
ぎゅうにゅう	牛乳	milk
ケーキ		cake
すし		sushi
てんぷら	天ぷら	tempura
りんご		apple
りょうり	料理	cuisine
サッカー		soccer
やきゅう	野球	baseball
いしゃ	医者	doctor
おかねもち	お金持ち	rich person
ゆうめいじん	有名人	celebrity
かお	顔	face
としうえ	年上	someone older
えき	駅	station
しんかんせん	新幹線	Shinkansen; "Bullet Train"
ちかてつ	地下鉄	subway
ふね	船	ship; boat
ひこうき	飛行機	airplane
* よやく	予約	reservation
* ツアー		tour
* どうぶつえん	動物園	zoo
* じかん	時間	time
せかい	世界	world
びよういん	美容院	beauty parlor
てぶくろ	手袋	gloves
せいかつ	生活	life; living
ことし	今年	this year

＊Words that appear in the dialogue

い - a d j e c t i v e s

あたたかい	暖かい	warm
すずしい	涼しい	cool (weather—not used for things)
つめたい	冷たい	cold (things/people)
おそい	遅い	slow; late
ねむい	眠い	sleepy

な - a d j e c t i v e

かんたん（な）	簡単	easy; simple

U - v e r b s

* かかる		to take (amount of time/money) (*no particle*)
とまる	泊まる	to stay (at a hotel, etc.) （〜に）
* なる		to become

R u - v e r b

* きめる	決める	to decide （〜を）

I r r e g u l a r   V e r b s

ごろごろする		to chill out at home; to stay home and do nothing
りょこうする	旅行する	to travel
れんしゅうする	練習する	to practice （〜を）

A d v e r b s   a n d   O t h e r   E x p r e s s i o n s

いちばん	一番	best
* どっち／どちら		which
はやく	早く／速く	(do something) early; fast
あるいて	歩いて	on foot
* 〜で		by (means of transportation); with (a tool)
どうやって		how; by what means
* どのぐらい		how much; how long
〜しゅうかん	〜週間	for . . . weeks
〜かげつ	〜か月	for . . . months
〜ねん	〜年	. . . years
このごろ		these days
〜ご	〜後	in . . . time; after . . .
* 〜か〜		or

会
L10

文法 Grammar
ぶん ぽう

1 Comparison between Two Items

In Japanese, adjectives do not change form in comparative sentences; there is no alteration as in "great/greater." You can express the idea of comparison by framing a sentence like:

> A のほうが　B より[1] (property)。　=　*A is more* (property) *than B.*

中国のほうが日本より大きいです。
ちゅうごく　　　　に ほん　　おお
China is larger than Japan.

If you want to ask a question comparing two items, you can say:

> A と B と　どちらのほう / どっちのほう[2] が　(property)。
> =　*Between A and B, which is more* (property)?

So a typical exchange looks like this:

A ：日本とカナダとどちらのほうが寒いですか。
　　に ほん　　　　　　　　　　　　　　さむ
　　Which is colder, Japan or Canada?

B ：カナダのほうが寒いです。
　　　　　　　　　　さむ
　　Canada is colder.

2 Comparison among Three or More Items

In comparison among three or more items, the degree qualifier いちばん is used.

> $\left\{ \begin{array}{l} A と B と C \\ \text{Category X} \end{array} \right\}$ の中で A がいちばん (property)。
> 　　　　　　　なか
> = *A is the most* (property) [*among* (the group of items)].

---

[1] In real life, the phrases A のほうが and B より often appear in the reverse order, making it very easy to be misled into believing the opposite of what is actually said. Don't rely on the word order, therefore, to decide which item is claimed to be superior. Listen carefully for the words のほうが and より.

[2] In place of どちらのほう and どっちのほう, you can also use どちら and どっち. Any one of these can be used in question sentences seeking comparisons between two items. どっち and どっちのほう are slightly more colloquial than どちら and どちらのほう.

A：カナダとフランスと日本の<u>中で</u>、どこが<u>いちばん</u>寒いですか。
　　Among Canada, France, and Japan, which country has the coldest climate?

B：カナダが<u>いちばん</u>寒いと思います。
　　Canada is the coldest, I think.

A：季節の<u>中</u>でいつが<u>いちばん</u>好きですか。
　　What season do you like best?

B：秋が<u>いちばん</u>好きです。
　　I like fall the most.

Note that the words のほう and どっち are not used in statements of comparison among three or more items. Normal question words like だれ, どれ, 何, いつ, and どこ are used instead.[3]

3 Adjective/Noun ＋ の

When a noun follows an adjective, and when it is clear what you are referring to, you can replace the noun with the indefinite noun の, "one," to avoid repetition. の mostly stands for things, not people.[4]

私は黒い<u>セーター</u>を持っています。赤い<u>の</u>も持っています。（の＝セーター）
I have a black sweater. I have a red one, too.

<u>ケーキ</u>がたくさんあります。好きな<u>の</u>を持っていってください。（の＝ケーキ）
We have a lot of cakes. Take the ones you like.

い-adjective な-adjective	＋ <u>noun</u>	→	い-adjective な-adjective	＋ <u>の</u>

---

[3] The tendency is to use どれ when a list of items is presented, and to use 何 when a group is referred to collectively. Compare:
りんごとみかんとさくらんぼの中で、どれがいちばん好きですか。
Which do you like best, apples, tangerines, or cherries?
くだものの中で、何がいちばん好きですか。
What fruit do you like best?

[4] When you want to refer indefinitely to people, use 人 instead of の, as in 頭がいい人 "smart people." The use of の to indicate people is largely limited to sentences like あそこで歌っているのは田中さんです (The one who is singing over there is Tanaka.), where you describe a person with ～のは first, and then name that person with ～です.

You can also use の in the sense of "mine," "yours," and so forth, referring to things owned by a person, or characterized by a place name, for example.

　　　A：これはソラさんの<u>かばん</u>ですか。　　　　　*Is this Sora's bag?*

　　　B：いいえ、それはメアリーさんの~~かばん~~です。　*No, that is Mary's.*

アメリカの<u>車</u>のほうが日本の<u>車</u>より大きいです。
American cars are larger than Japanese ones.

noun₁ の noun₂	→	noun₁ の ~~noun₂~~

4 ～つもりだ

つもり follows verbs in the present tense short forms to describe what a person is planning to do in the future. You can also use a verb in the negative plus つもり to describe what you are planning *not* to do, or what you do *not* intend to do.

verb (short, present) ＋ つもりだ	*(I) intend to do . . .*

（私は）週末にたけしさんとテニスをする<u>つもりです</u>。
I intend to play tennis with Takeshi this weekend.

山下先生はあした大学に来<u>ない</u>つもりです。
Professor Yamashita does not intend to come to school tomorrow.

You can also use the past tense to talk about your original intention, which did not materialize.

お寺を見に行く<u>つもりでしたが</u>、天気がよくなかったから、行きませんでした。
We were planning to visit a temple, but we didn't, because the weather was not good.

5 Adjective ＋ なる

The verb なる means "to become," indicating a change. なる follows nouns and both types of adjectives.

い-adjectives:	暖かい	→	暖か<u>く</u>なる	*to become warm/warmer*
な-adjectives:	静か（な）	→	静か<u>に</u>なる	*to become quiet/quieter*
nouns:	会社員	→	会社員<u>に</u>なる	*to become a company employee*

日本語の勉強が楽しくなりました。
にほんご べんきょう たの

Studying the Japanese language is fun now (though it was like torture before).

日本語の勉強が好きになりました。
にほんご べんきょう す

I have grown fond of studying the Japanese language.

With い-adjectives, the final い is dropped and く is added, just like in their negative conjugations. A common mistake is to use the な-adjectives pattern になる for い-adjectives and say, for example, × 暖かいになる.
あたた

When you use an adjective with なる, you may be describing an absolute change (e.g., "it has become warm, hence it is not cold any longer") or a relative change (e.g., "it has become warmer, but it is still cold"). If you want to make clear that you are talking in relative terms, you can use the pattern for comparison together with なる.

メアリーさんは前より日本語が上手になりました。
まえ にほんご じょうず

Mary has become better in Japanese than before.

6 どこかに / どこにも

In Lesson 8 we learned the Japanese expressions for "something" and "not . . . anything," 何か and 何も. As you must have noticed, these expressions are made up of the question word for things, 何, plus particles か and も. Other expressions for "some" and "any" in Japanese follow this pattern. Thus,
なに

something	何か___	someone	だれか___	somewhere	どこか___
	なに				
not anything	何___も	not anyone	だれ___も	not anywhere	どこ___も
	なに				

As we noted in Lesson 8, you do not need the particles は, が, or を with these words. You do need other particles, such as に, へ, and で. These particles appear in the places shown with underlines above.

A：どこか<u>へ</u>行きましたか。　　*Did you go anywhere?*
い

B：いいえ、どこ<u>へ</u>も行きませんでした。　　*No, I didn't go anywhere.*
い

A：だれか<u>に</u>会いましたか。　　*Did you see anybody?*
あ

B：いいえ、だれ<u>にも</u>会いませんでした。　　*No, I didn't see anybody.*
あ

A：何かしましたか。　　*Did you do anything?*
なに

B：いいえ、何<u>も</u>しませんでした。　　*No, I didn't do anything.*
なに

（を is not used.）

で

You can use the particle で with nouns that describe the means of transportation and the instruments you use.

はしでご飯を食べます。	*We eat our meals with chopsticks.*
日本語で話しましょう。	*Let's talk in Japanese.*
バスで駅まで行きました。	*I went to the station by bus.*
テレビで映画を見ました。	*I saw a movie on TV.*

Expression Notes

表現ノート
ひょう　げん

買ってきます ▶ In the dialogue, Mary tells Takeshi that she will get a souvenir for him during her trip to Hokkaido. You can use a verb *te*-form (買って in this example) + くる to describe an action performed somewhere else, followed by a movement to your current location.

バスツアーがありますが…… ▶ We sometimes use が and けど (but) at the end of a sentence when we want our partners to treat what we have just said as a given, common ground to build upon. These words often indicate the speaker's intention to give her partner a chance to react and speak up. By relegating the right to speak to one's partner, they also contribute to the politeness of one's utterance.

In the dialogue, the hotel employee lays out the relevant information on the table; there are two tours, one on Saturday and another on Sunday. が attached to her sentence indicates that she wants to build upon, and move forward with, these pieces of information. Instead of asking the obvious question, namely, どちらがいいですか, the hotel employee chooses not to finish her sentence, and lets her customer come forward with an answer immediately.

練習 Practice
れん しゅう

I バスのほうが電車より速いです ☞Grammar 1
でん しゃ　はや

A. Look at the pictures below and answer the following questions. 🔊 K10-07

Example Q：電車とバスとどちらのほうが速いですか。
でんしゃ　　　　　　　　　　　　　　はや

A：バスのほうが電車より速いです。
　　　　　　でんしゃ　はや

(a)
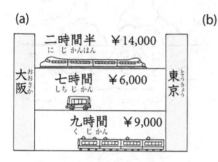

(b) (c)

Picture (a)

1. 新幹線とバスとどちらのほうが速いですか。
しんかんせん　　　　　　　　　　　　はや
2. 新幹線と電車とどちらのほうが遅いですか。
しんかんせん　でんしゃ　　　　　　　　おそ
3. 新幹線とバスとどちらのほうが安いですか。
しんかんせん　　　　　　　　　　　　やす
4. 電車とバスとどちらのほうが高いですか。
でんしゃ　　　　　　　　　　　　たか

Picture (b)

5. 田中さんと山田さんとどっちのほうが背が高いですか。
たなか　　やまだ　　　　　　　　　せ　たか
6. 山田さんと鈴木さんとどっちのほうが背が低いですか。
やまだ　　すずき　　　　　　　　　せ　ひく
7. 田中さんと鈴木さんとどっちのほうが若いですか。
たなか　　すずき　　　　　　　　　わか
8. 田中さんと山田さんとどっちのほうが年上ですか。
たなか　　やまだ　　　　　　　　　としうえ
9. 山田さんと鈴木さんとどっちのほうが髪が短いですか。
やまだ　　すずき　　　　　　　　　かみ　みじか

Picture (c)

10. 北海道と九州とどっちのほうが大きいですか。
ほっかいどう　きゅうしゅう　　　　　おお
11. 九州と四国とどっちのほうが小さいですか。
きゅうしゅう　しこく　　　　　　　　ちい

会
L10

B. Pair Work—Make questions using the following cues and ask your partner. When you answer the questions, add reasons for your answers if possible.

(Example) 夏／冬（好き）
なつ ふゆ す
→ A：夏と冬とどちら（のほう）が好きですか。
なつ ふゆ す
B：夏のほうが（冬より）好きです。／夏も冬も好きです。／
なつ ふゆ す なつ ふゆ す
夏も冬もきらいです。
なつ ふゆ
A：どうしてですか。
B：泳ぐのが好きですから。
およ す

1. すし／天ぷら（おいしい）
てん
2. 頭がいい人／かっこいい人（好き）
あたま ひと ひと す
3. 野球／サッカー（人気がある）
や きゅう にん き
4. 中国料理／日本料理（好き）
ちゅうごくりょう り に ほんりょう り す
5. 船／飛行機（好き）
ふね ひ こう き す
6. 日本の車／ドイツ（Germany）の車（いい）
に ほん くるま くるま
7. 漢字／カタカナ（かんたん）
かん じ
8. 春／秋（好き）
はる あき す
9. 冷たいお茶／熱いお茶（好き）
つめ ちゃ あつ ちゃ す
10. 日本の冬／あなたの国の冬（暖かい）
に ほん ふゆ くに ふゆ あたた
11. 日本の生活／あなたの国の生活（大変 or 楽しい）
に ほん せいかつ くに せいかつ たいへん たの

Ⅱ 新幹線がいちばん速いです ☞Grammar 2
しん かん せん はや

A. Look at the pictures on the previous page and answer the questions below. 🔊 K10-08

(Example) Q：新幹線とバスと電車の中で、どれがいちばん速いですか。
しんかんせん でんしゃ なか はや
A：新幹線がいちばん速いです。
しんかんせん はや

Picture (a)

1. 新幹線とバスと電車の中で、どれがいちばん遅いですか。
しんかんせん でんしゃ なか おそ
2. 新幹線とバスと電車の中で、どれがいちばん安いですか。
しんかんせん でんしゃ なか やす
3. 新幹線とバスと電車の中で、どれがいちばん高いですか。
しんかんせん でんしゃ なか たか

Picture (b)

4. この中で、だれがいちばん背が高いですか。
　　なか　　　　　　　　　　せ　たか

5. この中で、だれがいちばん若いですか。
　　なか　　　　　　　　　　わか

6. この中で、だれがいちばん年上ですか。
　　なか　　　　　　　　　　としうえ

7. この中で、だれがいちばん髪が長いですか。
　　なか　　　　　　　　　　かみ　なが

Picture (c)

8. この中で、どこがいちばん大きいですか。
　　なか　　　　　　　　　　おお

9. この中で、どこがいちばん小さいですか。
　　なか　　　　　　　　　　ちい

B. Pair Work—Make questions using the following cues and ask your partner.

(Example) 食べ物／好き
　　　　　た　もの　す
　→　Q：食べ物の中で、何がいちばん好きですか。
　　　　　　た　もの　なか　なに　　　　　　す
　　　　A：すしがいちばん好きです。
　　　　　　　　　　　　　　す

1. 果物／好き
　　くだもの　す

2. 世界の町／好き
　　せかい　まち　す

3. 有名人／好き
　　ゆうめいじん　す

4. 日本料理／きらい
　　にほんりょうり

5. 音楽／好き
　　おんがく　す

6. 季節／好き
　　きせつ　す

7. クラス／いい学生
　　　　　　　　がくせい

8. クラス／背が高い
　　　　　　せ　たか

9. クラス／よく話す
　　　　　　　　はな

会
L10

C. Group Work—Make a group of three or four people. Ask each other questions and make as many superlative sentences as possible about the group.

(Example) この中で、Aさんがいちばん若いです。
　　　　　　なか　　　　　　　　　　わか
　　　　この中で、Bさんがいちばん背が高いです。
　　　　　　なか　　　　　　　　　　せ　たか
　　　　この中で、Cさんがいちばんよくクラスに遅く来ます。
　　　　　　なか　　　　　　　　　　　　　　　　　おそ　き

D. Class Activity—First form pairs and make comparative and superlative question sentences with your partner. (You should know the answers.) Then ask questions to the class. The rest of the class answer the questions.

(Example) 富士山 (Mt. Fuji) とエベレスト (Mt. Everest) とどちらのほうが高いですか。
　　　　　ふじさん　　　　　　　　　　　　　　　　　　　　　　　　　　　たか
　　　　田中さんと山田さんとどちらのほうが若いですか。
　　　　たなか　　やまだ　　　　　　　　　　　わか
　　　　クラスの中で今日だれがいちばんお金を持っていますか。
　　　　　　　なか　きょう　　　　　　　　かね　も
　　　　世界の国の中でどこがいちばん小さいですか。
　　　　せかい　くに　なか　　　　　　　　ちい

Ⅲ これは私のです ☞Grammar 3

A. This is a refrigerator in a dormitory. Tell whose each thing is, using の. 🔊 K10-09

Example> このりんごはリーさん<u>の</u>です。

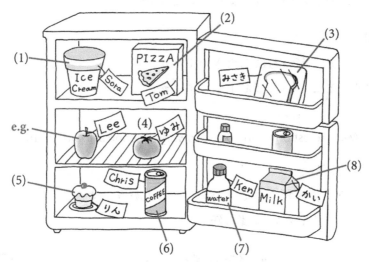

B. Mary and Yui did the following things before and during their trip. Describe what Yui did, using の. 🔊 K10-10

Example> メアリーさんは英語のガイドブック (guidebook) を持っていきました。

→ ゆいさんは日本語のを持っていきました。

	e.g.	1.	2.	3.	4.
メアリー	Guide Book Japan English	early	hot	cheap	red
ゆい	ガイドブック 日本 Japanese	late	cold	beautiful	black

1. メアリーさんは早い電車に乗りました。
2. メアリーさんはカフェで熱いコーヒーを飲みました。
3. メアリーさんは安い傘を買いました。
4. メアリーさんは赤い手袋を買いました。

C. You're at a flea market. You want to buy the items below. Ask the shopkeeper for help finding a better item using の.

(Example) 手袋 → A：すみません。手袋はありますか。
てぶくろ　　　　　てぶくろ

B：はい、あります。

A：ちょっと大きいですね。小さいのがありますか。
　　　　　　おお　　　　　　　ちい

B：これはどうですか。

A：いいですね。じゃあ、これをください。

B：ありがとうございます。

1. Tシャツ　　　4. ジーンズ
　 ティー

2. 靴　　　　　　5. 時計
　 くつ　　　　　　　とけい

3. 本
　 ほん

red　blue　black　white

Ⅳ 見に行くつもりです　☞Grammar 4
　　み　い

A. You are planning to do/not to do the following things next week. Tell what you will/will not do using ～つもりです。 🔊 K10-11

(Example) 月曜日に本を読むつもりです。
　　　　げつようび　ほん　よ

Monday	e.g. to read books	1. to practice the piano
Tuesday	2. to exercise	
Wednesday	3. to do laundry	
Thursday	4. to write a paper	5. not to go out
Friday	6. to eat dinner with friends	7. not to study Japanese
Saturday	8. to stay at a friend's house	9. not to go home
Sunday	10. not to get up early	11. to stay home do nothing (ごろごろする)

B. Answer the following questions.

Example Q：週末、映画を見に行きますか。
A：ええ、見に行きます。／
　　まだわかりませんが、見に行くつもりです。／
　　見に行かないつもりです。

1. 今日の午後、勉強しますか。
2. 週末、遊びに行きますか。
3. あさって、買い物をしますか。
4. 週末、料理を作りますか。
5. 三年後、日本にいますか。
6. 来年も日本語を勉強しますか。
7. 今度の休みに旅行しますか。

Ⅴ きれいになりました 👉Grammar 5

A. Describe the following pictures. 🔊 K10-12

Example きれい　→　きれいになりました。

e.g. きれい

(1) 眠い

(2) 元気

(3) 大きい

(4) 髪が短い

(5) ひま

(6) 暑い

(7) 涼しい

(8) 医者
いしゃ

(9) 春
はる

(10) お金持ち
かね も

B. Pair Work—Fill in the blanks and read the dialogue with your partner.

1. A：ちょっと寒いですね。
   さむ
   B：エアコンをつけたから、すぐ＿＿＿＿＿＿＿＿なりますよ。

2. A：髪が＿＿＿＿＿＿＿＿なりましたね。
   かみ
   B：ええ、きのう、美容院に行きました。
   びょういん い

3. A：子供の時、野菜がきらいでした。
   こども とき やさい
   B：私もきらいでした。でも今は＿＿＿＿＿＿＿なりました。
   わたし いま

4. A：たくさんお酒を飲みました。
   さけ の
   B：そうですね。顔が＿＿＿＿＿＿＿なりましたね。
   かお

5. A：このごろ＿＿＿＿＿＿＿なりましたね。
   B：ええ、もう冬ですね。
   ふゆ

6. A：日本語が＿＿＿＿＿＿＿なりましたね。
   にほんご
   B：ありがとうございます。でも、まだまだです。(I have a long way to go.)

Ⅵ どこかに行きましたか ☛Grammar 6

A. Takeshi was sick yesterday. Mary did a lot of things without him. Answer the questions based on the chart below. 🔊 K10-13

	Mary	Takeshi	
e.g. eat	sushi and tempura	nothing
drink	green tea and coffee	nothing
go	Osaka	nowhere
meet	Robert	nobody
do	watch a movie	nothing

(Example 1) Q：きのう、メアリーさんは何か食べましたか。

A：はい、すしと天ぷらを食べました。

(Example 2) Q：きのう、たけしさんは何か食べましたか。

A：いいえ、何も食べませんでした。

1. きのう、メアリーさんは何か飲みましたか。
2. きのう、たけしさんは何か飲みましたか。
3. きのう、メアリーさんはどこかに行きましたか。
4. きのう、たけしさんはどこかに行きましたか。
5. きのう、メアリーさんはだれかに会いましたか。
6. きのう、たけしさんはだれかに会いましたか。
7. きのう、メアリーさんは何かしましたか。
8. きのう、たけしさんは何かしましたか。

B. Pair Work—Ask your partner the following questions and continue the conversation.

(Example) A：週末、何かしましたか。

B：いいえ、何もしませんでした。Aさんは？

A：私は買い物をしました。

1. 先週の週末、どこかに行きましたか。
   <small>せんしゅう　しゅうまつ</small>
2. 先週の週末、だれかに会いましたか。
   <small>せんしゅう　しゅうまつ　　　あ</small>
3. 今日、何か食べましたか。
   <small>きょう　なに　た</small>
4. 今週の週末、何かするつもりですか。
   <small>こんしゅう　しゅうまつ　なに</small>
5. Make your own question, using どこか, だれか or 何か.
   <small>なに</small>

Ⅶ 自転車で行きます ☛Grammar 7
<small>じ てんしゃ　い</small>

A. Look at the pictures and answer each question as in the example below. 🔊 K10-14

> (Example) Q：うちから駅までどうやって行きますか。
> <small>えき　　　　　　　　　　い</small>
> A：うちから駅まで自転車で行きます。
> <small>えき　じ てんしゃ　い</small>

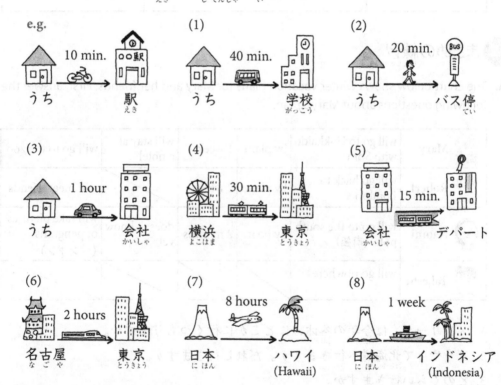

e.g.
10 min.
うち → 駅
<small>えき</small>

(1)
40 min.
うち → 学校
<small>がっこう</small>

(2)
20 min.
うち → バス停
<small>てい</small>

(3)
1 hour
うち → 会社
<small>かいしゃ</small>

(4)
30 min.
横浜 → 東京
<small>よこはま　とうきょう</small>

(5)
15 min.
会社 → デパート
<small>かいしゃ</small>

(6)
2 hours
名古屋 → 東京
<small>な ご や　とうきょう</small>

(7)
8 hours
日本 → ハワイ
<small>に ほん</small>　(Hawaii)

(8)
1 week
日本 → インドネシア
<small>に ほん</small>　(Indonesia)

会
L10

B. Use the same pictures and answer the questions as in the example below. 🔊 K10-15

> (Example) Q：うちから駅までどのぐらいかかりますか。
> <small>えき</small>
> A：うちから駅まで十分かかります。
> <small>えき　じゅっぷん</small>

C. Ask three classmates how they get from their house/hometown to school and fill in the chart.

[Example] Q：うちから大学までどうやって来ますか。

A：自転車で来ます。

Q：どのぐらいかかりますか。

A：十五分ぐらいかかります。

名前	どうやって	どのぐらい

Ⅷ まとめの練習

A. The chart below shows winter vacation plans for Mary and her friends. First, answer the following questions about Mary's plan.

Mary	will go to Hokkaido with Sora	by plane	1 week	will stay at a hotel	will go to the zoo
Robert	will go back to London	by plane	2 weeks		will meet friends
Naomi	will go to the south pole（南極）	by boat	2 months	doesn't know yet	will take pictures of penguins（ペンギン）
Takeshi	will go nowhere				

1. メアリーさんは今年の冬休みにどこかに行くつもりですか。
2. どうやって北海道へ行きますか。だれと行きますか。
3. どのぐらい行きますか。
4. どこに泊まりますか。
5. 北海道で何をするつもりですか。

How about the others' plans? Make pairs and ask questions.

B. Pair Work—Talk about your plans for the upcoming vacation.

C. Role Play—One of you is a hotel receptionist in Tokyo and the other is a customer. Using Dialogue Ⅱ as a model, make reservations for the following tours.

Destination	Time by regular transportation	Tour option 1 (price)	Tour option 2 (price)
Kamakura (鎌倉)	1 and half hours by train	Saturday (¥7,800)	Sunday (¥7,800)
Yokohama (横浜)	1 hour by subway and train	Day tour 昼のツアー (¥5,900)	Night tour 夜のツアー (¥6,500)
Asakusa (浅草)	30 minutes by bus	Walking tour ウォーキングツアー (¥4,300)	Bicycle tour 自転車のツアー (¥5,000)

D. You are talking to your friends who are currently in the following places. Ask him/her how the weather is like over there.

会
L10

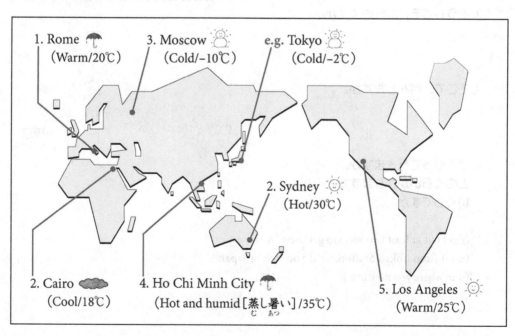

1. Rome (Warm/20℃)
3. Moscow (Cold/-10℃)
e.g. Tokyo (Cold/-2℃)
2. Sydney (Hot/30℃)
2. Cairo (Cool/18℃)
4. Ho Chi Minh City (Hot and humid [蒸し暑い]/35℃)
5. Los Angeles (Warm/25℃)

(Example) A：東京はどんな天気ですか。

B：雪です。

A：気温は何度ぐらいですか。

B：マイナス (minus) 二度ぐらいです。寒いですよ。

A：そうですか。

調べてみよう

Trip to Japan

You are going on a trip to Japan. Read travel guides and websites and decide on one destination. Answer the questions below.

1. どこに行きますか。地図 (map) のどこにありますか。
   (Show it on the map.)

2. どうしてそこに行きますか。

3. そこで、何をしますか。

4. どうやって行きますか。
   どのぐらいかかりますか。
   いくらですか。

   (Find out at least two ways to get there. Assume you
   travel from Tokyo Station, or if you live in Japan,
   from where you now live.)

東京
とうきょう

Culture Notes

日本の交通機関 Public Transportation in Japan
に ほん こう つう き かん

Japan's public transportation system is highly developed, especially within metropolitan areas and between major cities. The most common forms of public transportation are trains, buses, and, in major cities, subways. The Japan Railways Group (JR Group) has a train network covering almost all areas of the country. Travel by public transportation is enjoyable, safe, and efficient. Here are some tips for you.

Shinkansen

Japan Rail Pass

If you are in Japan on a "Temporary Visitor" entry permit and want to travel to different regions, consider getting a Japan Rail Pass, which offers unlimited travel on almost all JR lines (including bullet trains, except Nozomi and Mizuho) for a certain number of days.

If you are planning a budget trip during vacation time, the Seishun 18 Kippu (青春18きっぷ) may be the best option. This seasonal discount
せいしゅん
ticket gives you five days of unlimited rides on local and rapid-service JR trains for only 12,050 yen.

会
L10

Highway buses are another good way to travel between major cities. Compared with express rail services, highway bus travel usually takes longer hours but costs less. Also, if you travel on an overnight bus, you can save on accommodation costs.

Highway bus

写真提供：JR東海／JR四国／ジェイアールバス関東

Useful Expressions

駅で
えき

At the Station

Types of Trains

普通 —————— local
ふつう

急行 —————— express
きゅうこう

特急 —————— super express
とっきゅう

Destination

〜行き —————— bound for . . .
い

〜方面 —————— serving . . . areas
ほうめん

Types of Tickets and Seats

乗車券 —————— (boarding) ticket
じょうしゃけん

定期券 —————— commuter's pass
ていきけん

学割 —————— student discount
がくわり

指定席 —————— reserved seat
していせき

交通系ICカード —— rechargeable card such as Suica, Icoca, Pasmo, etc.
こうつうけいアイシー

自由席 —————— general admission seat
じゆうせき

一号車 —————— Car No. 1
いちごうしゃ

往復 —————— round trip
おうふく

片道 —————— one way
かたみち

Places in Stations

〜番線 —————— track number . . .
ばんせん

切符売り場 —— ticket vending area
きっぷうば

改札 —————— gate
かいさつ

ホーム —————— platform

売店 —————— shop; stand
ばいてん

出口 —————— exit
でぐち

入口 —————— entrance
いりぐち

階段 —————— stairs
かいだん

Miscellaneous Public Transportation Terms

乗り換え —————— transfer
のか

次は〜 —————— next (stop), . . .
つぎ

先発 —————— departing first
せんぱつ

次発 —————— departing second
じはつ

終電 —————— last train
しゅうでん

Announcements

まもなく発車します。	—— We will be leaving soon.
電車が参ります。	—— A train is arriving.
次は〜に止まります。	—— Next (we'll stop at) . . .
ドアが閉まります。ご注意ください。	—— The doors are closing. Please be careful.

Expressions

この電車は秋葉原に止まりますか。	—— Does this train stop at Akihabara?
終電は何時ですか。	—— What time is the last train?
東京までの指定席を一枚お願いします。	– One reserved ticket to Tokyo, please.
学割が使えますか。	—— Can I get a student discount?

*   *   *

A：鎌倉行きの電車はどれですか。
Which one is the train bound for Kamakura?

B：二番線です。
Track number two.

第11課　LESSON 11

休みのあと After the Vacation
やす

In this lesson, we will..

- Express what we want to do
- Talk about our experiences
- Introduce friends to each other
- Ask and talk about hometowns

会話 Dialogue
かい　わ

Yui and Mary meet after the vacation.

I 🔊 K11-01/02

1 ゆ　い：　メアリーさん、久しぶりですね。休みはどうでしたか。
　　　　　　　　　　　　 ひさ　　　　　　　　 やす

2 メアリー：　すごく楽しかったです。北海道で動物園に行ったり、
　　　　　　　　　 たの　　　　　　　 ほっかいどう　どうぶつえん　 い

3 　　　　　　買い物をしたりしました。
　　　　　　 か　 もの

4 ゆ　い：　いいですね。私も旅行したいです。
　　　　　　　　　　　　　　 わたし　りょこう

5 メアリー：　ゆいさんの休みは楽しかったですか。
　　　　　　　　　　　　 やす　　 たの

6 ゆ　い：　まあまあでした。一日だけドライブに行きましたが、
　　　　　　　　　　　　　　 いちにち　　　　　　　　　 い

7 　　　　　　毎日アルバイトをしていました。
　　　　　　 まいにち

II 🔊 K11-03/04

1 メアリー：　ゆいさん、友だちを紹介します。こちらはジョンさんです。
　　　　　　　　　　　　 とも　　　 しょうかい

2 　　　　　　ジョンさんは先月、日本に来ました。
　　　　　　　　　　　　 せんげつ　 にほん　 き

3 ジョン：　初めまして。
　　　　　　 はじ

4 ゆ　い：　初めまして、山川ゆいです。
　　　　　　 はじ　　　　　 やまかわ

Ⅲ 🔊 K11-05/06

1 ゆ い： ジョンさん、出身はどこですか。
2 ジョン： オーストラリアのケアンズです。
3 ゆ い： そうですか。
4 ジョン： ゆいさんはケアンズに行ったことがありますか。
5 ゆ い： いいえ、ありません。
6 ジョン： 山や海があって、きれいな所ですよ。グレートバリアリーフで有名です。
7 ゆいさんはどこの出身ですか。
8 ゆ い： 長野です。今度遊びに来てください。食べ物もおいしいですよ。
9 ジョン： ぜひ、行きたいです。

Ⅰ

Yui: Mary, I haven't seen you for a long time. How was your vacation?

Mary: It was really fun. I went to the zoo, did shopping and things like that in Hokkaido.

Yui: Sounds good. I want to travel, too.

Mary: Did you have a fun vacation, Yui?

Yui: It was okay. I went for a drive just for one day, but I was working part-time every day.

Ⅱ

Mary:Yui, I want to introduce you to a friend of mine. This is John. He came to Japan last month.

John: How do you do?

Yui: How do you do? I am Yui Yamakawa.

Ⅲ

Yui: John, where are you from?

John: I am from Cairns, Australia.

Yui: Is that so?

John: Have you been to Cairns?

Yui: No, I haven't.

John: It has mountains and the ocean and is a beautiful place. It's famous for the Great Barrier Reef. Where are you from, Yui?

Yui: I am from Nagano. Please come to visit me sometime. The food is good, too.

John: By all means, I would love to.

会
L11

単　語
たん　ご
K11-07 (J-E)
K11-08 (E-J)

Ｖ ｏ ｃ ａ ｂ ｕ ｌ ａ ｒ ｙ

Ｎ ｏ ｕ ｎ ｓ

がいこく	外国	foreign country
*オーストラリア		Australia
かわ	川	river
おんせん	温泉	spa; hot spring
つり		fishing
みずうみ	湖	lake
*やま	山	mountain
キャンプ		camp
*ドライブ		drive
じんじゃ	神社	shrine
びじゅつかん	美術館	art museum
しゃちょう	社長	president of a company
かしゅ	歌手	singer
ルームメイト		roommate
ホストファミリー		host family
しょうらい	将来	future
ゆめ	夢	dream
おまつり	お祭り	festival
おしょうがつ	お正月	New Year's
おかし	お菓子	snack; sweets
ビール		beer
おもちゃ		toy
こんがっき	今学期	this semester
らいがっき	来学期	next semester
じゅぎょう	授業	class
*こちら		this person (polite)

Ｕ - ｖ ｅ ｒ ｂ ｓ

うそをつく		to tell a lie
おなかがすく		to become hungry
かう	飼う	to own (a pet)　（～を）
サボる		to cut (classes)　（～を）
とる	取る	to take (a class); to get (a grade)　（～を）

＊Words that appear in the dialogue

ならう	習う	to learn（〜を）
のぼる	登る	to climb（place に）
はしる	走る	to run

Ru-verbs

| つかれる | 疲れる | to get tired |
| やめる | | to quit（〜を） |

Irregular Verbs

けんかする		to have a fight; to quarrel
* しょうかいする	紹介する	to introduce（person に person を）
ダイエットする		to go on a diet
ちこくする	遅刻する	to be late (for an appointment)（〜に）
りゅうがくする	留学する	to study abroad（place に）

Adverbs and Other Expressions

* しゅっしん	出身	coming from（place の）
* ひさしぶり	久しぶり	it has been a long time
* まあまあ		okay; so-so
もっと		more
あと	後	after (an event)（event の）
そして		and then
* 〜だけ		just . . . ; only . . .
〜てん	〜点	. . . points

L11

ADDITIONAL VOCABULARY

K11-09 (J-E)
K11-10 (E-J)

職業 (Occupations)
しょくぎょう

さっか（作家）writer
ジャーナリスト journalist
けいさつかん（警察官）police officer
しょうぼうし（消防士）firefighter
きょうし（教師）schoolteacher
けんきゅうしゃ（研究者）researcher
うちゅうひこうし（宇宙飛行士）astronaut
スポーツせんしゅ（スポーツ選手）athlete
だいとうりょう（大統領）president of a country

はいゆう（俳優）actor; actress
かんごし（看護師）nurse
シェフ chef
まんがか（漫画家）cartoonist

文 法 G r a m m a r

1 〜たい

You can use a verb stem (the verb form that goes before ます)＋たいです to describe your hope or aspiration.

今度の週末は、映画を見<u>たい</u>です。 or 映画が見<u>たい</u>です。
I want to see a film this weekend.

いつか中国に行き<u>たい</u>です。
I want to go to China someday.

> | verb stem ＋ たいです | *I want to do . . .* |

As you can see in the first example above, a verb that usually takes the particle を can have either the particle を or が when it is followed by たい. Particles other than を remain the same, as in the second example, which has に.

たい conjugates as an い-adjective. Here are examples of negative and past tense たい sentences.

あの人には会い<u>たくないです</u>。
I don't want to see that person.

お弁当が買い<u>たかった</u>から、コンビニに行きました。
I went to a convenience store, because I wanted to buy a boxed lunch.

If your wish is one you have entertained for some time, that is, if you "have wanted to," you can use たいと思っています instead of たいです.

留学し<u>たいと思っています</u>。
I've wanted to study abroad.

You usually do not use たいです to describe wishes held by others. Somebody else's wishes are usually reported in Japanese either as quotations, observations, or guesses. So if you want to say that somebody other than you wants to do something, you can use と言っていました with たい.

メアリーさんはチベットに行き<u>たい</u>と<u>言</u>っていました。
Mary said she wanted to go to Tibet.

To describe your observation to the effect that somebody wants to do something, you must use a special verb たがっている instead of たい. If a verb takes the particle を, the derived verb たがっている will retain を, unlike たい, with which we had a choice between the particles が and を.

メアリーさんは<u>着物</u>を<u>着</u>たがっています。
(It seems) Mary wants to wear a kimono.

The verb たがっている, which comes from the dictionary form たがる, indicates "I think that she wants to, because of the way she is behaving." We will have more to say about this type of sentence in Lesson 14.

I want to . . . /Do you want to . . . ?	*They want to . . .*
· verb stem + たいです	· verb stem + たがっています
· たい conjugates as an い-adjective	· たがる conjugates as an *u*-verb
· が or を for the direct object	· を only

2 ～たり～たりする

You already know that you can connect two clauses with the *te*-form of predicates, as in:

<u>大阪</u>で<u>買</u>い<u>物</u>をし<u>て</u>、<u>晩</u>ご<u>飯</u>を<u>食</u>べます。
In Osaka, I will do some shopping and eat dinner.

This sentence, however, tends to suggest that shopping and dining are *the only* activities you plan to perform in Osaka and that those two activities will be done in that order. If you want to avoid such implications and want to mention activities or events just *as examples*, and *in no set order*, you can use a special predicate form ～たり～たりする.

<u>大阪</u>で<u>買</u>い<u>物</u>をし<u>たり</u>、<u>晩</u>ご<u>飯</u>を<u>食</u>べ<u>たり</u>します。
In Osaka, I will do such things as shopping and eating dinner.

verb (short, past) + り、verb (short, past) + り
do such things as this and that

会 L11

To get the たり form of a predicate (したり and 食べたり in the example above), you just add り to the past tense short form of a predicate (した and 食べた). The helping verb する at the end of the sentence indicates the tense of the sentence. You can change a 〜たり〜たりする sentence into the past tense, or incorporate it in a bigger sentence, by working on the helping verb part.

週末は、勉強したり、友だちと話したりしました。
しゅうまつ　　べんきょう　　　とも　　　はな

I studied and talked with my friends, among other things, over the weekend.

踊ったり、音楽を聞いたりするのが好きです。
おど　　　おんがく　き　　　　　　　　す

I like dancing, listening to music, and so forth.

3　〜ことがある

The past tense short form of a verb ＋ ことがある describes that you did something, or something happened, in earlier times.

富士山に登ったことがあります。
ふ　じ　さん　のぼ

I have had the experience of climbing Mt. Fuji.

たけしさんは授業を休んだことがありません。
じゅぎょう　やす

Takeshi has never been absent from classes (in his life).

| verb (short, past, affirmative) ＋ ことがある　　　*have the experience of . . .* |

If somebody asks you a question using ことがありますか, you can just say あります/ありません or repeat the whole verbal complex (行ったことがあります/行ったことがありません),
い　　　　　　　　　　い
but not ことがあります without a verb.

A：ヨーロッパに行ったことがありますか。
い

Have you ever been to Europe?

B：はい、行ったことがあります。
い

はい、あります。

（× はい、ことがあります。）

Yes, I have.[1]

4 Noun A や Noun B

や connects two nouns, as does と. や suggests that the things referred to are proposed as examples, and that you are not citing an exhaustive list in much the same way that たり in Grammar 2 in p. 259 suggests that the two verbs are used as examples.

A や B	A and B, for example

京都や奈良に行きました。
I went to Kyoto and Nara (for example, and may have visited other places as well).

---

[1] We learned in Lesson 9 another way to describe past experiences or lack thereof: もう〜ました and まだ〜ていません. Use まだ〜ていません when you have not done something but expect to do it someday. In contrast, when you say 〜たことがありません, you do not think that you will eventually do it. So, unless you are an adventurer, it is funny to say まだ南極に行っていません (I haven't been to Antarctica yet) but it is perfectly normal to say 南極に行ったことがありません. On the affirmative side, もう食べました means that the result of the eating that took place is still felt now, probably that is why you are not hungry right now. 食べたことがあります means that you have had that experience, and the eating event may have taken place years ago.

表現ノート
ひょう　げん

は in negative sentences ▶ In negative sentences, you often find the particle は where you expect が or を. Observe the reply sentences in the dialogues below:

Q：山下先生はテレビを見ますか。 *Do you watch TV, Prof. Yamashita?*
やましたせんせい　　　　　　　み
A：いいえ、テレビ<u>は</u>見ません。 *No, I don't.*
　　　　　　　　　　　み

Q：コーヒーが好きですか。 *Do you like coffee?*
　　　　　　　す
A：いいえ、コーヒー<u>は</u>好きじゃないです。 *No, I don't.*
　　　　　　　　　　す

を and が, respectively, would not be ungrammatical in the above examples. Many Japanese speakers, however, find the は versions more natural.

The rule of thumb is that negative Japanese sentences tend to contain at least one は phrase. If you add 私は to the sentences above, therefore, the need for は
わたし
is already fulfilled, and Japanese speakers feel much less compelled to use は after テレビ and コーヒー.

は may also follow particles like で and に.

英語<u>では</u>話したくないです。 *I don't want to speak in English.*
えいご　　　はな
広島<u>には</u>行ったことがありません。 *I have never been to Hiroshima.*
ひろしま　　　い

だけ ▶ You can add だけ to numbers to talk about having just that many items. だけ implies that you have something up to the amount needed, but not more than that.

私はその人に一回<u>だけ</u>会ったことがあります。
わたし　　　ひと　いっかい　　あ

I have met that person just once.

一つ<u>だけ</u>質問があります。 *I have just one question.*
ひと　　　しつもん
三十分<u>だけ</u>寝ました。 *I slept for just thirty minutes.*
さんじゅっぷん　　ね

だけ suggests that you can live with that few, though the number admittedly could have been higher. We will learn another word in Lesson 14, namely, しか, which means "only" in the sense that you do not have enough of.

に ▶ You can use the particle に to indicate the occasion on which you do something.

晩ご飯<u>に</u>サラダを食べました。 *I ate salad <u>at</u> dinner.*
ばん　はん　　　　　　た

Expression Notes

に can also indicate the role you want something to play.

おみやげに絵葉書を買いました。　　　*I bought a postcard <u>as</u> a souvenir.*

ドライブ▶ ドライブ is used when you go somewhere by car for pleasure. To say "to have a drive" or "to go for a drive," use ドライブに行く or ドライブする.

湖までドライブに行きました／ドライブしました。
I went for a drive to the lake.

When you simply want to say "to drive a car" (not necessarily for pleasure), use 運転する instead.

日本で車を運転したことがありますか。
Have you ever driven a car in Japan?

夢▶ 夢, like the English word "dream," has two meanings. One is the dream you have while sleeping; the others the dream that you wish would come true. To say "I have a dream," in Japanese, you use the verb 見る for sleeping dreams, and 持っている or ある for your visions.

ゆうべこわい夢を見ました。　　　*I had a scary dream last night.*
夢を持っています／夢があります。　*I have a dream.*
あなたの将来の夢は何ですか。　　*What is your future dream?*

には▶ The particle は often follows the particle に in sentences describing a place in terms of the things that are found there.

(1) 東京<u>には</u>デパートがたくさんあります。
(2) 東京<u>に</u>デパートがたくさんあります。
There are many department stores in Tokyo.

There is a subtle difference between the two sentences. The first sentence is about the places: they answer questions (either explicitly asked, or implicitly) like "What is Tokyo like?" The second sentence, on the other hand, is an answer to a question like "Where do you find many department stores?"

See the grammar note discussing the difference between が and は in Lesson 8. In the case of the particle に, the contrast is between the simple に and the combination には. (See also the grammar note on counting people in Lesson 7.)

会
L11

練習 P r a c t i c e

I ハンバーガーを食べたいです ☛Grammar 1

A. Change the following phrases into 〜たい sentences. 🔊 K11-11

> (Example) ハンバーガーを食べる
>
> （はい）　→　ハンバーガーを食べたいです。
>
> （いいえ）　→　ハンバーガーを食べたくないです。

1. 湖に行く（はい）
2. 日本語を練習する（はい）
3. 温泉に行く（はい）
4. ゆっくり休む（いいえ）
5. 会社の社長になる（いいえ）

6. 日本で働く（はい）
7. 車を買う（はい）
8. 日本に住む（いいえ）
9. 留学する（はい）
10. 山に登る（いいえ）

B. Pair Work—Ask if your partner wants to do the things above. When you answer, give reasons as in the example.

> (Example) A：ハンバーガーを食べたいですか。
>
> B：はい、食べたいです。おなかがすいていますから。／
>
> いいえ、食べたくないです。さっき食べましたから。

C. Change the following phrases into 〜たい sentences in the past tense. 🔊 K11-12

> (Example) おもちゃの電車で遊ぶ
>
> （はい）　→　子供の時、おもちゃの電車で遊びたかったです。
>
> （いいえ）　→　子供の時、おもちゃの電車で遊びたくなかったです。

1. テレビを見る（はい）
2. 飛行機に乗る（はい）
3. ゲームをする（いいえ）
4. 犬を飼う（はい）
5. 学校をやめる（いいえ）

6. お祭りに行く（はい）
7. ピアノを習う（いいえ）
8. 車を運転する（はい）
9. 有名になる（はい）
10. ミッキー・マウスに会う（はい）

D. Pair Work—Ask if your partner wanted to do the things above during their childhood.

E. Pair Work—Ask your partner the following questions and report the answers as in the example. See p. 257 for occupation vocabulary.

Example　A：けんさんは何が食べたいですか。

　　　　B：ピザが食べたいです。

　　　→　A：けんさんはピザが食べたいと言っていました。

　　　　　　（けんさんはピザを食べたがっています。）

1. 昼ご飯に何が食べたいですか。
2. 何がいちばん買いたいですか。
3. どこにいちばん行きたいですか。
4. だれにいちばん会いたいですか。
5. 何を習いたいですか。
6. 今週の週末、何がしたいですか。
7. 今、何をしたくないですか。
8. 子供の時、何になりたかったですか。
9. 将来、何になりたいですか。
10. 来学期、何がしたいですか。

L11

F. Complete the following sentences.

1. 今日はいい天気だから、＿＿＿＿＿＿＿＿＿＿＿＿＿＿たいです。
2. あしたは休みだから、＿＿＿＿＿＿＿＿＿＿＿＿たいです。
3. 疲れたから、＿＿＿＿＿＿＿＿＿＿＿＿たくないです。
4. 田中さんはいじわるだから、一緒に＿＿＿＿＿＿＿＿＿たくないです。
5. 高校の時、もっと＿＿＿＿＿＿＿＿＿＿＿＿たかったです。

Ⅱ 掃除したり、洗濯したりします ☛Grammar 2
そう じ　　　　せん たく

A. Tell what the following people did on the weekend using 〜たり〜たりする. 🔊 K11-13

Example ジョン: went to a museum, ran, etc.

→ ジョンさんは、美術館に行ったり、走ったりしました。
　　　　　　　 び じゅつかん　 い　　　　　 はし

1. たけし: went camping, went for a drive, etc.
2. ウデイ: made sweets, played games at home, etc.
3. ソラ: went to Osaka to have fun, went to eat, etc.
4. けん: cleaned his room, did laundry, etc.
5. ロバート: met friends, watched movies, etc.
6. 山下先生: went to a hot spring, rested, etc.
　　やましたせんせい

B. Pair Work—Look at the picture and talk about what you want to do during the next vacation using 〜たり〜たり.

Example A：休みに何がしたいですか。
　　　　　　 やす　 なに
　　　　B：海でつりをしたり、ドライブをしたりしたいです。
　　　　　　 うみ
　　　　　それから……

C. Pair Work—Ask your partner the following questions. When you answer, use ～たり～たりする as in the example.

Example A：あした何をしますか。

B：宿題をしたり、カラオケに行ったりします。

1. 週末よく何をしますか。
2. デートの時、何をしますか。
3. あなたの国ではお正月に何をしますか。
4. 子供の時、よく何をしましたか。
5. 日本で何をしたいですか。
6. 冬休み／夏休みに何をしましたか。
7. クラスで何をしてはいけませんか。
8. 今学期の後、何をするつもりですか。
9. 何をするのが好きですか／きらいですか。

Ⅲ 有名人に会ったことがありますか ☛Grammar 3

A. The following are what John has or hasn't done. Make the sentences using ～ことがある。 🔊 K11-14

Example ○ eat tempura → 天ぷらを食べたことがあります。

× go to Tokyo → 東京に行ったことがありません。

1. ○ eat sushi
2. ○ study Korean
3. ○ work at a restaurant
4. × go to Hiroshima
5. × write a love letter （ラブレター）
6. ○ sleep in class
7. ○ climb Mt. Fuji
8. × drive a car in Japan
9. × see Japanese movies
10. × go to shrine

B. Pair Work—Make questions using 〜ことがある and ask your partner. Continue your conversation.

(Example) 日本のビールを飲む

→　A：日本のビールを飲んだことがありますか。

　　　　B：はい、あります。　　　｜　B：いいえ、ありません。

　　　　A：どうでしたか。　　　　｜　A：飲みたいですか。

　　　　B：おいしかったです。　　｜　B：ええ、飲みたいです。

1. ダイエットをする
2. テストで0点を取る
3. 英語を教える
4. 有名人に会う
5. カラオケに行く
6. ふぐ (blowfish) を食べる
7. 中国語を勉強する
8. 新幹線に乗る

9. うそをつく
10. 日本料理を作る
11. 遅刻する
12. 授業をサボる
13. 友だち／ルームメイト／
　　ホストファミリー とけんかする
14. 留学する
15. 川でつりをする

Ⅳ すしや天ぷらをよく食べます ☞Grammar 4

Pair Work—Ask your partner the following questions. When you answer, use 〜や〜 as in the example.

(Example) A：どんな日本料理をよく食べますか。

　　　　　B：すしや天ぷらをよく食べます。

1. どんなスポーツをよく見ますか。
2. どんな果物が好きですか。
3. どんな料理をよく作りますか。
4. あなたの大学の食堂には、どんな食べ物がありますか。
5. あなたの大学には、どこの国の人がいますか。
6. 外国に行ったことがありますか。どこですか。
7. 今、どんな授業を取っていますか。
8. 歌手の中で、だれが好きですか。

Ⅴ まとめの練習
れんしゅう

A. Talk about your dream for the future or what it was when you were a child.

1. あなたの夢は何ですか。
ゆめ なん

   〔Example〕 私は料理が好きだから、将来、シェフ (chef) になりたいです。
   わたし りょうり す しょうらい

   そして、日本でレストランを作って、そこで料理したいです。
   にほん つく りょうり

2. 子供の時の夢は何でしたか。
こども とき ゆめ なん

   〔Example〕 子供の時、歌手になりたかったです。歌が大好きでした。
   こども とき かしゅ うた だいす

   今も、よくカラオケで歌います。
   いま うた

B. Class Activity—Find someone who . . .

1. has seen celebrities _____

2. has never used chopsticks _____

3. wants to live in Japan in the future _____

4. wanted to be a hero (ヒーロー) as a child _____

5. wants to cut classes tomorrow _____

会
L11

C. Class Activity—Bring pictures of your hometown and describe it.

〔Example〕

私はロンドンの出身です。ロンドンはとても大きくてにぎやかです。
わたし しゅっしん おお

きれいな公園や有名な美術館やたくさんの劇場 (theater) があります。
こうえん ゆうめい びじゅつかん げきじょう

よくミュージカルを見たり、散歩したりしました。
み さんぽ

夏休みに帰って、友だちに会いたいです。
なつやす かえ とも あ

Culture Notes

お正月 New Year's
しょうがつ

お正月 (New Year's) is the biggest homecoming holiday in Japan. Japanese celebrate New Year's Day on January 1, unlike most other Asians, who go by the lunar calendar. Most businesses are closed on and around New Year's Day.

New Year's Eve is called 大晦日, and people try to finish their seasonal chores—cleaning the house thoroughly, writing greeting cards (年賀状), and so on—before this date. Dinner for New Year's Eve often includes 年越しそば (buckwheat noodles), as the long noodles symbolize the desire for longevity.

When saying good-bye to someone whom you do not expect to see again until the new year, the traditional parting phrase is よいお年を (Have a happy New Year!). When you meet somebody for the first time in the new year, you say あけましておめでとうございます (Happy New Year!).

Many people go to 神社 (Shinto shrines) and お寺 (Buddhist temples) for 初詣 or the "first worship of the year," which is likely to be their only visit to shrines and temples for the year, since Japan is a largely secular society.

Special dishes called お節料理 are eaten for New Year's. Each dish is said to signify a particular wish—black beans (黒豆) for diligence and health (a pun on the word まめ), herring roe (数の子) for having many offspring, and so forth. The staple food for New Year's is おもち (rice cake), which is toasted or served in 雑煮 (New Year's soup).

Children expect to receive お年玉, which are gifts of money from their parents, grandparents, aunts, uncles, and even family guests.

写真提供：（株）ジャパンタイムズ／フォトライブラリー

日本語のクラスで
In Japanese Class

Expressions

どちらでもいいです。—Both are fine.

同じです。————————Same thing.

だいたい同じです。——More or less the same.

ちょっと違います。——A little different.

使えません。————————Can't use it.

だめです。————————No good.

手をあげてください。—Raise your hand.

読んできてください。————————Read it before coming to class.

宿題を出してください。————————Hand in the homework.

10ページを開いてください。————Open the book to page 10.

教科書を閉じてください。————Close the textbook.

となりの人に聞いてください。——Ask the person sitting next to you.

やめてください。————————Please stop.

今日はこれで終わります。————That's it for today.

しつもんが
ありますか

会
L11

Vocabulary

しめきり–deadline

練習————exercise

意味————meaning

発音————pronunciation

文法————grammar

質問————question

答————answer

例————example

かっこ——( )(parentheses)

まる——○ (correct)

ばつ——× (wrong)

くだけた言い方——colloquial expression

かたい言い方————bookish expression

ていねいな言い方–polite expression

方言————————dialect

共通語————————common language

たとえば————for example

ほかに————————anything else

〜番————————number . . .

〜行目————line number . . .

二人ずつ————two people each

第12課 〳 L E S S O N 12

病 気 Feeling Ill
びょう き

In this lesson, we will...

● Give and ask for an explanation
● Complain about something being too much
● Express what we have to do

● Describe symptoms of illness
● Give advice

会 話 D i a l o g u e
かい わ

I Mary and Yui are talking at school. 🔊 K12-01/02

1 ゆ い： メアリーさん、元気がありませんね。
げん き

2 メアリー： うーん。ちょっとおなかが痛いんです。
いた

3 ゆ い： どうしたんですか。

4 メアリー： きのう友だちと晩ご飯を食べに行ったんです。
とも ばん はん た い

5 たぶん食べすぎたんです。
た

6 ゆ い： 大丈夫ですか。
だいじょう ぶ

7 メアリー： ええ。心配しないでください。……ああ、痛い。
しんぱい いた

8 ゆ い： 病院に行ったほうがいいですよ。
びょういん い

II Next day Mary is at a hospital. 🔊 K12-03/04

1 メアリー： 先生、おなかが痛くて熱もあるんです。インフルエンザでしょうか。
せんせい いた ねつ

*　　　　　　*　　　　　　*

2 医 者： インフルエンザじゃないですね。かぜです。
い しゃ

3 メアリー： よかった。あのう、もうすぐテニスの試合があるので、
し あい

4 練習しなきゃいけないんですが……。
れんしゅう

5 医 者： 二三日、運動しないほうがいいでしょう。
い しゃ に さんにち うんどう

6 メアリー： わかりました。

7 医 者： 今日は薬を飲んで、早く寝てください。
い しゃ きょう くすり の はや ね

8 メアリー： はい、ありがとうございました。

9 医者： お大事に。
　 い しゃ　　 だい じ

Ⓘ

Yui: You don't look well, Mary.

Mary: Um . . . I have a little stomachache.

Yui: What's the matter?

Mary: I went out to have dinner with my friend yesterday. I probably ate too much.

Yui: Are you all right?

Mary: Yes. Don't worry about it. Oh, it hurts.

Yui: You had better go to a hospital.

Ⓘ

Mary: Doctor, I have a stomachache and have a fever, too. Have I got the flu?

　　 *　　　 *　　　 *

Doctor: I don't think that you've got the flu. It is just a cold.

Mary: Good. Well, I will have a tennis tournament soon, so I have to practice, though . . .

Doctor: You had better not exercise for a couple of days.

Mary: I understand.

Doctor: Take medicine and go to bed early tonight.

Mary: Yes. Thank you so much.

Doctor: Take care.

会
L12

単語
たんご

V o c a b u l a r y

N o u n s

* おなか		stomach
あし	足	leg; foot
のど		throat
は	歯	tooth
* インフルエンザ		influenza
* かぜ	風邪	cold
せき		cough
ふつかよい	二日酔い	hangover
ホームシック		homesickness
アレルギー		allergy
ジュース		juice
たまご	卵	egg
ふく	服	clothes
もの	物	thing (concrete object)
プレゼント		present
きっぷ	切符	train ticket
〜だい	〜代	charge; fee
ようじ	用事	business to take care of
おてあらい	お手洗い	restroom
* しあい	試合	match; game
せいじ	政治	politics
せいせき	成績	grade (on a test, etc.)
かのじょ	彼女	she; girlfriend
かれ	彼	he; boyfriend
かれし	彼氏	boyfriend
いみ	意味	meaning

い - a d j e c t i v e s

せまい	狭い	narrow; not spacious
ひろい	広い	wide; spacious
わるい	悪い	bad
* いたい	痛い	hurt; painful

＊Words that appear in the dialogue

| あまい | 甘い | sweet |
| おおい | 多い | there are many . . . |

な-adjective

| すてき（な） | 素敵 | nice |

U-verbs

あるく	歩く	to walk
かぜをひく	風邪をひく	to catch a cold
*ねつがある	熱がある	to have a fever
のどがかわく	のどが渇く	to become thirsty
はらう	払う	to pay （～を）
なくす		to lose （～を）
きょうみがある	興味がある	to be interested (in . . .) (topic に)

Ru-verbs

| せきがでる | せきが出る | to cough |
| わかれる | 別れる | to break up; to separate (person と) |

Irregular Verbs

| きんちょうする | 緊張する | to get nervous |
| *しんぱいする | 心配する | to worry |

Adverbs and Other Expressions

*おだいじに	お大事に	Get well soon.
*げんきがない	元気がない	don't look well
できるだけ		as much as possible
*たぶん	多分	probably; maybe
*もうすぐ		very soon; in a few moments/days
はじめて	初めて	for the first time
*にさんにち	二三日	for two to three days
それに		moreover, . . .
おなじ	同じ	same

会

L12

文法 Grammar
ぶん ぽう

❶ 〜んです

There are two distinct ways to make a statement in Japanese. One way is to simply report the facts as they are observed. This is the mode of speech that we have learned so far. In this lesson, we will learn a new way: the mode of *explaining* things.

> short form (verbs/adjectives/nouns) + んです
> = explanation in terms of the verbs/adjectives/nouns

When you are late for an appointment, because the bus did not come on time, you could simply and bluntly report the fact by saying バスが来ませんでした, but you can sound more apologetic if you offer that as an *explanation* for your being late. You can say:

バスが来なかったんです。　*(As it happens,) the bus didn't come.*

An explanation therefore connects a fact (the bus not coming), to another element in the situation under discussion (you being late for the appointment). The sentence-final expression んです serves as the link between what the sentence says and what it accounts for. Compare:

あしたテストがあります。　*I have an exam tomorrow.* (a simple observation)
あしたテストがあるんです。　*I have an exam tomorrow. (So I can't go out tonight.)*

トイレに行きたいです。　*I want to go to the bathroom.* (declaration of one's wish)
トイレに行きたいんです。　*I want to go to the bathroom. (So tell me where it is.)*

んです itself is invariant and does not usually appear in the negative or the past tense forms,[1] but the predicate before it can be affirmative or negative, present tense or past tense.

成績がよくないんです。　(in response to the question "Why do you look so upset?")
せいせき
(As a matter of fact) My grade is not good.

試験が終わったんです。　(explaining to a person who has caught you smiling)
しけん お
The exam is over. (That's why I'm smiling.)

---

[1] In casual exchanges, んです appears in its short form, んだ. In casual questions, んですか is replaced by の. We will examine these further in Lesson 15.

When it follows a noun or a な-adjective in the present tense affirmative, な comes in between.

	report sentences	explanation sentences
な-adjectives:	静かです	静か<u>な</u>んです
nouns:	学生です	学生<u>な</u>んです

You can use んです in questions to invite clarifications from the person you are talking to. It is very often used together with question words, such as どうして (why) and どうした (what has happened).

> Ａ：どうして彼と別れた<u>ん</u>ですか。
> *Why did you break up with your boyfriend? (You've got to tell me.)*

> Ｂ：彼、ぜんぜんお風呂に入らないんです。
> *Oh, him. He never takes a bath. (That's a good enough reason, isn't it?)*

> Ａ：どうした<u>ん</u>ですか。
> *What happened? (You look shattered.)*

> Ｂ：うちの猫が死んだんです。[2]
> *My cat died. (That should explain how I look today.)*

You can also use んです to provide an additional comment on what has just been said.

> Ａ：かわいいノートですね。
> *That's a cute notebook.*

> Ｂ：ええ。日本で買った<u>ん</u>です。
> *You bet. I bought it in Japan (for your information).*

In the written language, you see のです instead of んです. It has the same functions but is stylistically more formal.

---

[2] A どうしたんですか question is best answered by a んです sentence with the subject marked with the particle が rather than は, as in this example. See Lesson 8 for a related discussion.

2 〜すぎる

Verb stems may be followed by the helping verb すぎる, which means "too much," or "to excess." すぎる conjugates as a regular *ru*-verb.

早く起きすぎました。   *I got up too early.*

食べすぎてはいけません。   *You must not eat too much.*

すぎる can also follow い- and な-adjective bases (the parts which do not change in conjugations); you drop the い and な at the end of the adjectives and then add すぎる.[3]

（高い）   この本は高すぎます。   *This book is too expensive.*

（静かな）   この町は静かすぎます。   *This town is too quiet.*

verb stem/adjective stem ＋ すぎる ... *too much*

You use すぎる when something is beyond normal or proper, suggesting that you do not welcome it. Thus 親切すぎます (too kind) for example is not a straightforward compliment. Use modifiers like とても and すごく if you simply want to say that something is in a high degree.

3 〜ほうがいいです

ほうがいいです "it is better (for you) to do . . ." is a sentence-final expression which you can use to give advice. ほうがいいです follows a verb in the short form. You usually use the past tense of a verb with ほうがいいです if the verb is in the affirmative. When the advice is in the negative, however, the verb is in the *present* tense.

verb (short, past, affirmative)	＋ ほうがいいです	*It is better.*
verb (short, present, negative)		*It is better not . . .*

もっと野菜を食べたほうがいいですよ。   *You'd better eat more vegetables.*

授業を休まないほうがいいですよ。   *It is better not to skip classes.*

---

[3] In addition to the verb conjugation, we also use the noun すぎ, as in 食べすぎです。

4 〜ので

You can use ので to give the reason for the situation described in the balance of the sentence. Semantically, ので is very similar to から. Stylistically, ので sounds slightly more formal than から and is used extensively in the written language.

> (reason) ので (situation)。　　(situation), *because* (reason).

いつも日本語で話すので、日本語が上手になりました。
My Japanese has improved, because I always speak Japanese.

宿題がたくさんあったので、きのうの夜、寝ませんでした。
I did not sleep last night, because I had a lot of homework.

The reason part of a ので sentence usually is in a short form. When ので follows a な-adjective or a noun in a present tense affirmative clause, な comes in between, as it did with the explanatory predicate んです.

その人はいじわるなので、きらいです。　　(Compare: いじわるだから)
I do not like that person, because he is mean.

今日は日曜日なので、銀行は休みです。　　(Compare: 日曜日だから)
Banks are closed, because today is a Sunday.

5 〜なければいけません / 〜なきゃいけません

We use なければいけません and なきゃいけません[4] to say that it is necessary to do something, or "must." The なければ variant is more formal and often seen in the written language, while the なきゃ variant is very colloquial and is mainly found in the spoken language.

試験があるから、勉強しなければいけません／なきゃいけません。
I have to study, because there will be an exam.

---

[4] There are more varieties for "must" sentences: なくちゃいけません, なくてはいけません, and ないといけません. You can also substitute なりません for いけません in the なければ and なきゃ combinations, like なければなりません, なきゃなりません.

なければ and なきゃ mean "if you do not do . . ." and いけません roughly means "you cannot go"; なければいけません and なきゃいけません therefore literally mean "you cannot go not doing . . ." with the double negatives giving rise to the affirmative sense of the mandate. な in なければ and なきゃ comes from the negative ない. Just drop the last い and replace it with ければ or きゃ.

verb	short negative	"must"
食べる	食べ<u>ない</u>	食べ<u>なければいけません</u> / 食べ<u>なきゃいけません</u>
言う	言わ<u>ない</u>	言わ<u>なければいけません</u> / 言わ<u>なきゃいけません</u>
する	し<u>ない</u>	し<u>なければいけません</u> / し<u>なきゃいけません</u>
くる	こ<u>ない</u>	こ<u>なければいけません</u> / こ<u>なきゃいけません</u>

You can change いけません to いけませんでした to say you *had to*. You can use the short form なきゃいけない in casual speech. You can further shorten it to just なきゃ.

けさは、六時に起きなきゃいけませんでした。　　　　(long form, past)
I had to get up at six this morning.

彼女が来るから、部屋を掃除しなきゃ（いけない）。　　(short form, present)
I must clean the room, because my girlfriend is coming.

6 ～でしょうか

If you ask somebody a question that they do not know the answer to, they may be embarrassed. You can avoid such awkward situations by phrasing the question using でしょうか, which adds a note of tentativeness and politeness.

A：あした、雨が降るでしょうか。
Would it rain tomorrow?

B：降ると思います。
I think it will.

でしょう means *probably*. By asking a でしょうか question, you are implying that you think the listener probably has a better-informed opinion, which you would appreciate.

でしょうか follows short form predicates (affirmative or negative, present or past). When it follows a noun or a な-adjective in a present tense affirmative sentence, it directly follows them, without だ in between.

来週は暖かいでしょうか。
らいしゅう　あたた
Would you say that it will be warm next week?

トマトは野菜でしょうか。　（×野菜だでしょうか）
　　　や さい　　　　　　　　　　や さい
Is a tomato a vegetable?

これ、もう話したでしょうか。
　　　　　　はな
Have I told you about this already?

You can use the non-interrogative でしょう to make a guess. You can add たぶん earlier in the sentence to signal that it is a guess.[5]

たぶんあしたは寒くないでしょう。
　　　　　　　　さむ
I bet it will not be cold tomorrow.

Expression Notes 12

表現ノート
ひょう　げん

うーん▶うーん, with the prolonged *u* syllable, indicates reflection and hesitation. It is often used when you cannot make up your mind or when you are about to give an answer which may be unfavorable to the person you are talking with.

A：結婚してください。
　　けっこん
B：うーん、まだ結婚したくないんです。もう少し待ってください。
　　　　　　　けっこん　　　　　　　　　　　　　すこ ま

会
L12

---

[5] In casual exchanges, you can use でしょう (with the question intonation, and most often pronounced as somewhat shorter でしょ) when you want to check if your partner agrees that you have the correct understanding about what you have just said.

ジョン、中国語がわかるでしょう？これ、読んで。
　　　ちゅうごく ご　　　　　　　　　　　　　　よ
John, you understand Chinese, right? Can you read this for me?

練 習 P r a c t i c e

I 頭が痛いんです ☛Grammar 1

A. You are in the following situations. Explain them using 〜んです. 🔊 K12-07

[Example]
頭が痛いです。
→　Q：どうしたんですか。
　　A：頭が痛いんです。

(1) 彼から電話が
　　ありました

(2) プレゼントを
　　もらいました

(3) あしたは休みです

(4) きのうは
　　誕生日でした

(5) 試験が難しく
　　なかったです

(6) のどが痛いです

いたい…

(7) かぜをひきました

(8) 切符をなくしました

train ticket

(9) あした試験があります

(10) せきが出ます

(11) 彼女と別れました

(12) お手洗いに行きたいです

B. Respond to the comments using 〜んです. 🔊 K12-08

(Example)

すてきな車ですね。

My father's → 父のなんです。

(1) きれいな花ですね。

I received them from my friend.

(2) 新しい靴ですね。

Italian ones （イタリア）

(3) かわいい服ですね。

I made it.

会 L12

(4) いいかばんですね。

It was cheap.

(5) かっこいい彼氏ですね。

kind

C. Pair Work—Your partner has said something nice about what you have. Respond using ～んです.

> (Example) Ｂ：すてきな時計ですね。
>
> Ａ：友だちにもらったんです。

D. Pair Work—Make up dialogues asking for reasons.

> (Example) I went to Tokyo last week.
>
> → Ａ：先週東京に行きました。
>
> Ｂ：どうして東京に行ったんですか。
>
> Ａ：母がアメリカから来たんです。

1. I am very tired.
2. I have no money.
3. I want to marry my boyfriend/girlfriend.
4. I am going to Japan to study.
5. He is good at Chinese.
6. I don't want to watch that movie.

Ⅱ 食べすぎました ☞Grammar 2

A. Describe the following pictures using ～すぎる. Use "verb＋すぎる" for (1) through (4) and "adjective＋すぎる" for (5) through (10). 🔊 K12-09

> (Example 1) 作りすぎました。
>
> (Example 2) この部屋はせますぎます。

e.g.1　　　　e.g.2　　　　(1)　　　　(2)

(3)　(4)　(5)　(6)

(7)　(8)　(9)　(10)

B. Look at the verbs below. Think about the results of over doing these things and make sentences as in the example.

(Example) 食べる　→　食べすぎたから、おなかが痛いんです。
　　　た　　　　　　　た　　　　　　　　　　　　　　いた

1. お酒を飲む　　　　　4. 本を読む　　　　　7. 歌を歌う
　　さけ　の　　　　　　　　ほん　よ　　　　　　　うた　うた
2. 勉強する　　　　　　5. 走る　　　　　　　8. 緊張する
　　べんきょう　　　　　　はし　　　　　　　　きんちょう
3. パソコンを使う　　　6. 甘い物を食べる　　9. 服を買う
　　　　　　つか　　　　　　あま　もの　た　　　　ふく　か

C. Group Work—Complain about your classes, town, school, dormitory (寮), cafeteria, etc.
　　　　　　　　　　　　　　　　　　　　　　　　　　　　　　　　りょう

(Example) Ａ：このクラスは宿題が多すぎます。
　　　　　　　　　　　　しゅくだい　おお
　　　　Ｂ：私もそう思います。それに、試験は難しすぎます。
　　　　　　わたし　　おも　　　　　　　しけん　むずか
　　　　Ｃ：それから、授業は八時半に始まります。早すぎます。
　　　　　　　　　　じゅぎょう　はちじはん　はじ　　　　　　はや

Ⅲ 薬を飲んだほうがいいです　☞Grammar 3
　　くすり　の

A. Using the cues below, give advice to a friend who has a headache. Decide if you should use the affirmative or the negative. K12-10

(Example) 薬を飲む　→　Ｂ：頭が痛いんです。
　　　　　くすり　の　　　　　　あたま　いた
　　　　　　　　　　　　　Ａ：薬を飲んだほうがいいですよ。
　　　　　　　　　　　　　　　くすり　の

1. 早く寝る　　　　　3. 病院に行く　　　　5. うちに帰る
　　はや　ね　　　　　　びょういん　い　　　　　　　かえ
2. 遊びに行く　　　　4. 仕事を休む　　　　6. 運動する
　　あそ　い　　　　　　しごと　やす　　　　　うんどう

B. Pair Work—Give advice to your partner in the following situations, using 〜ほうがいい.

(Example) 日本語が上手になりたい

→ 　B：日本語が上手になりたいんです。

　　　A：日本人の友だちを作ったほうがいいですよ。／

　　　できるだけ英語を話さないほうがいいですよ。

1. ホームシックだ　　　4. お金がない　　　7. 歯が痛い

2. やせたい　　　　　　5. 成績が悪い　　　8. 教科書をなくした

3. 友だちとけんかした　6. 二日酔いだ　　　9. いつも授業に遅刻する

C. Pair Work—You are a health counselor. Someone who hasn't been feeling well is at your office. Ask the following questions. Complete this form first, then give your advice using 〜ほうがいい.

a. よく運動しますか。　　　　　　　はい　　いいえ

b. よく甘い物を食べますか。　　　　はい　　いいえ

c. よく野菜を食べますか。　　　　　はい　　いいえ

d. 朝ご飯を食べますか。　　　　　　はい　　いいえ

e. よくお酒を飲みますか。　　　　　はい　　いいえ

f. たばこを吸いますか。　　　　　　はい　　いいえ

g. よく歩きますか。　　　　　　　　はい　　いいえ

h. 何時間ぐらい寝ますか。　　　　＿＿＿＿＿時間

i. どんな料理をよく食べますか。　＿＿＿＿＿

Ⅳ いい天気なので、散歩します ☞Grammar 4
てん き さん ぼ

A. Connect the two sentences using 〜ので. 🔊K12-11

Example いい天気です／散歩します → いい天気なので、散歩します。
てん き さん ぼ てん き さん ぼ

1. 安いです／買います
やす か

2. あの授業はおもしろくないです／サボりたいです
じゅぎょう

3. 今週は忙しかったです／疲れています
こんしゅう いそが つか

4. かぜでした／バイトを休みました
やす

5. 彼女はいつも親切です／人気があります
かのじょ しんせつ にん き

6. 政治に興味がありません／新聞を読みません
せい じ きょう み しんぶん よ

7. 友だちと同じ授業を取っています／一緒に勉強します
とも おな じゅぎょう と いっしょ べんきょう

8. のどがかわきました／ジュースが飲みたいです
の

9. 歩きすぎました／足が痛いです
ある あし いた

10. ホテルの部屋は広かったです／よかったです
へ や ひろ

B. Make sentences using the cues below as reasons, according to the example.

Example かぜをひきました → かぜをひいたので、授業を休みました。
じゅぎょう やす

1. お金がありません
かね

2. おなかがすいています

3. 卵アレルギーです
たまご

4. 用事があります
よう じ

5. 単語の意味がわかりません
たん ご い み

6. 疲れました
つか

C. Fill in the blanks with appropriate words.

1. _____ ので、人気があります。
にん き

2. _____ ので、かぜをひきました

3. _____ ので、別れました。
わか

4. _____ ので、日本に住みたくないです。
に ほん す

5. _____ ので、遅刻しました
ち こく

6. _____ ので、緊張しています。
きんちょう

7. _____ ので、_____。

Ⓥ 七時に起きなければいけません/起きなきゃいけません ☞Grammar 5
しち じ お お

A. You have a busy day tomorrow. You have to do the following things. Make sentences according to the example. 🔊 K12-12

Example 七時に起きる → 七時に起きなければいけません。
しち じ お しち じ お

1. 八時にうちを出る
  はち じ で
2. 九時に授業に出る
  く じ じゅぎょう で
3. 一時に先生に会う
  いち じ せんせい あ
4. 二時から英語を教える
  に じ えい ご おし
5. 午後、図書館に行って、本を借りる
  ご ご としょかん い ほん か
6. 電気代を払いに行く
  でん き だい はら い
7. 夜、宿題をする
  よる しゅくだい
8. 晩ご飯の後、薬を飲む
  ばん はん あと くすり の

B. Answer the following questions.

1. 日本語の授業で何をしなければいけませんか。
  に ほん ご じゅぎょう なに
2. かっこよくなりたいんです。何をしなければいけませんか。
  なに
3. 友だちが遊びに来ます。何をしなければいけませんか。
  とも あそ き なに
4. あしたは初めてのデートです。何をしなければいけませんか。
  はじ なに
5. 子供の時、何をしなければいけませんでしたか。
  こ ども とき なに

C. Using the cues in A, tell your friend what you must do tomorrow. 🔊 K12-13

Example 七時に起きる → 七時に起きなきゃいけない。
しち じ お しち じ お

D. Pair Work—Your partner invites you to do the following things together on a certain time. Turn down the invitation and explain your reason using 〜なきゃいけない.

Example play tennis

→ A：あしたの朝、一緒にテニスをしませんか。
  あさ いっしょ
  B：すみません。あしたはうちにいなきゃいけないんです。

1. do homework
2. eat lunch
3. drink coffee

4. study in the library
5. go to karaoke
6. travel

Ⅵ 日本は寒いでしょうか　☞Grammar 6
に　ほん　　さむ

A. You are at the study abroad counselor's office. You are worried about your upcoming trip to Japan. Ask the counselor the following questions, using でしょうか. K12-14

(Example) 日本は寒いですか。
に　ほん　　さむ
→　日本は寒いでしょうか。
　　に　ほん　　さむ

1. 冬は雪が降りますか。
ふゆ　ゆき　ふ
2. 授業はいつ始まりますか。
じゅぎょう　　　　はじ
3. 先生は厳しいですか。
せんせい　きび
4. 日本語のクラスは大変ですか。
に　ほん　ご　　　　　　　たいへん
5. アニメ (animation) のサークルがありますか。
6. 部屋代はいくらですか。
へ　や　だい
7. ホストファミリーは英語を話しますか。
えい　ご　　はな
8. アルバイトをしてもいいですか。
9. 薬を持っていったほうがいいですか。
くすり　も

B. Pair Work—You are talking with a matchmaker, who is going to introduce a partner to you. Ask as many questions as possible using でしょうか about that person, such as their appearances, age, etc. Decide if you want to date them.

(Example) A：その人の仕事は何でしょうか。
　　　　　ひと　しごと　なん
B：歌手です。でも、あまり有名じゃないと思います。
　か しゅ　　　　　　　　　　　ゆうめい　　　　　おも
(more questions and answers)
⋮
A：そうですか！会いたいです。／うーん、ちょっと。
　　　　　　　　あ

Ⅶ まとめの練習
れんしゅう

A. Using Dialogue I as a model, make skits in the following situations.

—Your friend looks sad.

—Your friend looks happy.

B. Pair Work—A and B are deciding when they can play tennis together. Play the role of A and B. Discuss your schedules and find the day on which both of you are available. Refer to the next page for B's schedule.

(Example) A：来週の月曜日に一緒にテニスをしませんか。
らいしゅう　げつようび　いっしょ

B：来週の月曜日はちょっと……。英語を教えなきゃいけないんです。
らいしゅう　げつようび　　　　　　　えいご　おし

日曜日はどうですか。
にちようび

A's schedule

21 Sun.	write a paper
22 Mon.	
23 Tue.	read books
24 Wed.	
25 Thu.	
26 Fri.	meet the teacher
27 Sat.	

C. Role Play—Visiting a Doctor's Office

Using Dialogue Ⅱ as a model, act the role of a doctor or a patient.

Doctor—Fill out the medical report below and give advice to the patient.

Patient—Describe the symptoms you have and answer the doctor's questions.

Name: _____		**Age:** _____	
Symptoms:	☐ Sore throat	☐ Cough	
	☐ Headache	☐ Fever	
	☐ Stomachache	☐ Allergy	
	☐ Any other pain	☐ Others	

Pair Work Ⅶ B. (p. 290)

Example A：来週の月曜日に一緒にテニスをしませんか。
らいしゅう　げつようび　　　　いっしょ

B：来週の月曜日はちょっと……。英語を教えなきゃいけないんです。
らいしゅう　げつようび　　　　　　　　えいご　　おし
日曜日はどうですか。
にちようび

B's schedule

21 Sun.	
22 Mon.	teach English
23 Tue.	
24 Wed.	go to the hospital
25 Thu.	
26 Fri.	
27 Sat.	clean rooms, do laundry, etc.

会
L12

Culture Notes

日本の気候 The Japanese Climate
(に　ほん　　き　こう)

Japan has four seasons: spring (March−May), summer (June−August), autumn (September−November), and winter (December−February). The seasons in Japan can be very different depending on where you go.

	Naha	Tokyo	Sapporo
Cherry trees blossom	Mid-January	Late March	Early May
Rainy season starts	Early May	Mid-June	No rainy season
First snowfall	No snow	January	October
January temperatures	High: 19.6 Low: 15.0	High: 9.4 Low: 0.6	High: 0 Low: −5.5
August temperatures	High: 31.2 Low: 26.4	High: 32.5 Low: 24.6	High: 25.0 Low: 18.3
Annual precipitation	2469.5 mm	1445.5 mm	1282.0 mm

(2018)

Winter is sunny and dry on the Pacific coast, but cloudy and snowy on the Sea of Japan coast. Spring is rather short because daily temperatures rise quickly and the season is cut short by the arrival of the rainy season (梅雨), which lasts for about a month and a half. Summer in most parts of Japan is hot and very humid, and almost tropical in some places. Typhoons (台風) make occasional landfalls in summer and early fall.
(つゆ)　　(たいふう)

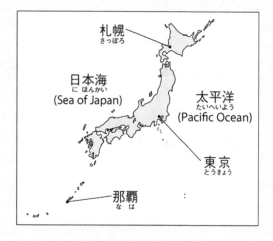

Temperature, including body temperature, is measured in Celsius. Here is a conversion scale for those of you who are more used to the Fahrenheit system.

Useful Expressions

健 康 と 病 気
けんこう と びょうき
H e a l t h   a n d   I l l n e s s

At the Clinic's Reception

Patient:	すみません。初めてなんですが。 *Excuse me. This is my first visit.*
Receptionist:	はい、保険証を見せてください。 *Okay. Please show me your health insurance certificate.*

*　　　*　　　*

Patient:	これは何の薬ですか。 *What kind of medicine are these?*
Receptionist:	痛み止めです。食後に飲んでください。 *These are painkillers. Please take one after meals.*
Patient:	わかりました。 *I see.*
Receptionist:	お大事に。 *Please take care.*

Expressions for Illness（病気）and Injuries（けが）

下痢です。	I have diarrhea.
便秘です。	I am constipated.
生理です。	I have my period.
花粉症です。	I have hay fever.
（〜に）アレルギーがあります。	I have an allergy to . . .
虫歯があります。	I have a bad tooth.
くしゃみが出ます。	I sneeze.
鼻水が出ます。	I have a runny nose.
背中がかゆいです。	My back itches.
発疹があります。	I have rashes.

めまいがします。———————————— I feel dizzy.

吐<ruby>吐<rt>は</rt></ruby>きました。———————————— I threw up.

<ruby>気分<rt>きぶん</rt></ruby>が<ruby>悪<rt>わる</rt></ruby>いです。———————————— I am not feeling well.

やけどをしました。———————————— I burned myself.

<ruby>足<rt>あし</rt></ruby>を<ruby>骨折<rt>こっせつ</rt></ruby>しました。———————————— I broke my leg.

けがをしました。———————————— I hurt myself.

Vocabulary

● Doctor's office

<ruby>内科<rt>ないか</rt></ruby>———————— physician

<ruby>皮膚科<rt>ひふか</rt></ruby>———————— dermatologist

<ruby>外科<rt>げか</rt></ruby>———————— surgeon

<ruby>産婦人科<rt>さんふじんか</rt></ruby>———————— obstetrician and gynecologist

<ruby>整形外科<rt>せいけいげか</rt></ruby>———————— orthopedic surgeon

<ruby>眼科<rt>がんか</rt></ruby>（<ruby>目医者<rt>めいしゃ</rt></ruby>）—— ophthalmologist

<ruby>歯科<rt>しか</rt></ruby>（<ruby>歯医者<rt>はいしゃ</rt></ruby>）—— dentist

<ruby>耳鼻科<rt>じびか</rt></ruby>———————— otorhinolaryngologist; ENT doctor

● Miscellaneous

<ruby>抗生物質<rt>こうせいぶっしつ</rt></ruby>———————— antibiotic

レントゲン———————— X-ray

<ruby>手術<rt>しゅじゅつ</rt></ruby>———————— operation

<ruby>注射<rt>ちゅうしゃ</rt></ruby>———————— injection

<ruby>体温計<rt>たいおんけい</rt></ruby>———————— thermometer

<ruby>点滴<rt>てんてき</rt></ruby>———————— intravenous feeding

読み書き編
よ　　か　　へん

R e a d i n g   a n d   W r i t i n g

第1課
だい いっか

ひらがな *Hiragana*

あ *a*	い *i*	う *u*	え *e*	お *o*
か *ka*	き *ki*	く *ku*	け *ke*	こ *ko*
さ *sa*	し *shi*	す *su*	せ *se*	そ *so*
た *ta*	ち *chi*	つ *tsu*	て *te*	と *to*
な *na*	に *ni*	ぬ *nu*	ね *ne*	の *no*
は *ha*	ひ *hi*	ふ *fu*	へ *he*	ほ *ho*
ま *ma*	み *mi*	む *mu*	め *me*	も *mo*
や *ya*		ゆ *yu*		よ *yo*
ら *ra*	り *ri*	る *ru*	れ *re*	ろ *ro*
わ *wa*				を *o*
ん *n*				

I *Hiragana* Practice

A. Choose the correct *hiragana*. 🔊 Y01-1

1. *yo* ま　よ
2. *ho* は　ほ
3. *me* ぬ　め
4. *su* む　す
5. *ki* さ　き
6. *chi* さ　ち
7. *ta* た　に
8. *ro* ろ　る
9. *e* え　ん

B. Match the words. 🔊 Y01-2

Person's name		Place name	
1. たなか ・	・ Sakuma	6. くまもと・	・ Morioka
2. やまもと・	・ Tanaka	7. おかやま・	・ Yokohama
3. さくま ・	・ Morikawa	8. もりおか・	・ Mito
4. たかはし・	・ Takahashi	9. よこはま・	・ Okayama
5. もりかわ・	・ Yamamoto	10. みと ・	・ Kumamoto

C. Listen to the recording and add diacritical marks ゛ and ゜ to the *hiragana* where needed.

🔊 Y01-3

1. いちこ　　　　*ichigo* (strawberry)

2. たんこ　　　　*dango* (dumpling)

3. さふとん　　　*zabuton* (cushon)

4. かいこくしん　*gaikokujin* (foreigner)

5. たんほほ　　　*tanpopo* (dandelion)

6. かんへき　　　*ganpeki* (cliff)

D. Listen to the recording and circle the matching *hiragana* word. 🔊 Y01-4

1. *shashin* (photograph) （ しやしん ・ しゃしん ）

2. *dokusho* (reading) （ どくしょ ・ どくしよ ）

3. *kyori* (distance) （ きょり ・ きより ）

4. *hiyasu* (to chill) （ ひゃす ・ ひやす ）

5. *chairo* (brown) （ ちゃいろ ・ ちやいろ ）

6. *onna no hito* (woman) （ おんなのひと ・ おっなのひと ）

7. *kitte* (stamp) （ きて ・ きって ）

8. *motto* (more) （ もつと ・ もっと ）

E. Read the following pairs, paying attention to the long vowels. 🔊 Y01-5

1. おばさん — おばあさん
   (aunt)   (grandmother)

2. おじいさん — おじさん
   (grandfather)   (uncle)

3. しゅじん — しゅうじん
   (husband)   (prisoner)

4. おや — おおや
   (parent)   (landlord)

5. せいき — せき
   (century)   (seat)

F. Put the *hiragana* in the right order to make sense.

Example だともち → と も だ ち

1. わんで ＿＿ ＿＿ ＿＿

2. ごいえ ＿＿ ＿＿ ＿＿

3. んほに ＿＿ ＿＿ ＿＿

4. えなま ＿＿ ＿＿ ＿＿

5. んせせい ＿＿ ＿＿ ＿＿ ＿＿

6. がだいく ＿＿ ＿＿ ＿＿ ＿＿

Ⅱ Reading Practice

Read the following people's self-introductions and answer the questions. Refer to the vocabulary list on pp. 38-40. 🔊 Y01-6

(1)
たなか まいです。
かいしゃいんです。

(2)
はらだ りょうです。
だいがくせいです。
せんこうは れきしです。

(3)
かとう ゆうとです。
だいがくいんせいです。
せんこうは けいざいです。

(4)
わたしの なまえは
きたの ひろみです。
こうこうの
さんねんせいです。

(5)
やまだ まことです。
だいがくせいです。
せんこうは にほんごです。

Questions:

1. Who is an office worker?

2. Whose major is Japanese?

3. Who is a high school student?

4. What is Harada's major?

Ⅲ Writing Practice

Read Aoi's self-introduction and write your own.

はじめまして、まえかわ あおいです。
にほんじんです。
だいがくの いちねんせいです。
せんこうは えいごです。
よろしくおねがいします。

第2課
だい に か

カタカナ *Katakana*

ア *a*	イ *i*	ウ *u*	エ *e*	オ *o*
カ *ka*	キ *ki*	ク *ku*	ケ *ke*	コ *ko*
サ *sa*	シ *shi*	ス *su*	セ *se*	ソ *so*
タ *ta*	チ *chi*	ツ *tsu*	テ *te*	ト *to*
ナ *na*	ニ *ni*	ヌ *nu*	ネ *ne*	ノ *no*
ハ *ha*	ヒ *hi*	フ *fu*	ヘ *he*	ホ *ho*
マ *ma*	ミ *mi*	ム *mu*	メ *me*	モ *mo*
ヤ *ya*		ユ *yu*		ヨ *yo*
ラ *ra*	リ *ri*	ル *ru*	レ *re*	ロ *ro*
ワ *wa*				ヲ *o*
ン *n*				

I *Katakana* Practice

A. Choose the correct *katakana*. 🔊 Y02-1

1. *o* オ ア   4. *shi* シ ツ   7. *ru* レ ル

2. *nu* ヌ メ   5. *ku* ワ ク   8. *ho* モ ホ

3. *sa* テ サ   6. *ma* マ ム   9. *yu* エ ユ

B. Match the following words and pictures. 🔊 Y02-2

1. (　) オレンジジュース   7. (　) サンドイッチ

2. (　) フライドポテト   8. (　) ステーキ

3. (　) ケーキ   9. (　) カレー

4. (　) サラダ   10. (　) ピザ

5. (　) チョコレートパフェ   11. (　) トースト

6. (　) コーヒー   12. (　) アイスティー

C. Match each country with its capital city.

Countries	Capital cities

1. マレーシア ・ ・ オタワ
2. オランダ ・ ・ ワシントンＤＣ
3. アメリカ ・ ・ ニューデリー
4. エジプト ・ ・ アムステルダム
5. オーストラリア・ ・ クアラルンプール
6. スウェーデン ・ ・ ブエノスアイレス
7. インド ・ ・ キャンベラ
8. アルゼンチン ・ ・ カイロ
9. カナダ ・ ・ ストックホルム

D. Put the *katakana* in the right order to make sense.

(Example) マホス → <u>ス マ ホ</u>

1. トノー ＿＿ ＿＿ ＿＿
2. ンペ ＿＿ ＿＿
3. ニュメー ＿＿ ＿＿ ＿＿ ＿＿
4. ンジーズ ＿＿ ＿＿ ＿＿ ＿＿

Ⅱ Reading Practice

Mary wrote about four of the things below. Identify the items she wrote about. 🔊 Y02-3

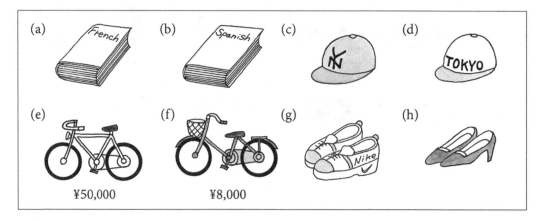

1. （　　） これは わたしの ぼうしじゃないです。
キャシーさんの ぼうしです。
ニューヨークヤンキースの ぼうしです。

2. （　　） これは わたしの じてんしゃです。
オーストラリアの じてんしゃです。
たかいです。

3. （　　） これは ミシェルさんの ほんです。
スペインごの ほんじゃないです。
フランスごの ほんです。

4. （　　） これは ジャクソンさんの くつです。
イタリアの くつじゃないです。
アメリカの くつです。

Ⅲ Writing Practice

Make your own name tag.[1]

(Example)

メアリー・ハート

メアリー・ハート

---

[1] **Your name in Japanese**
Japanese have only one given name and one surname, which is placed first, as in:
　　たなか たけし　　[last—first]
Foreign names are normally written in *katakana* and in their native order. A dot " ・ " or a space is often used between the first name and last name.
　　Mary Hart　→　メアリー・ハート　or　メアリー ハート　[first—last]
East Asian names such as Korean or Chinese can be written in kanji.
　　Yao Ming　→　ヨウ メイ　or　姚 明　[last—first]
For double surnames, "=" is often used between the two names.
　　John Smith-Jones　→　ジョン・スミス=ジョーンズ

第3課

まいにちのせいかつ Daily Life

001	一 (one)	▶いち　いっ ▷ひと	一(いち) one　一時(いちじ) one o'clock 一年生(いちねんせい) first-year student 一分(いっぷん) one minute　一つ(ひとつ) one
			(1) 一
002	二 (two)	▶に ▷ふた	二(に) two　二時(にじ) two o'clock 二年生(にねんせい) second-year student　二つ(ふたつ) two 二日間(ふつかかん) two days
			(2) 一　二
003	三 (three)	▶さん ▷みっ	三(さん) three　三時(さんじ) three o'clock 三年生(さんねんせい) third-year student 三月(さんがつ) March　三つ(みっつ) three
			(3) 一　二　三
004	四 (four)	▶し ▷よん　よ よっ	四(よん) four　四時(よじ) four o'clock 四年生(よねんせい) fourth-year student 四月(しがつ) April　四つ(よっつ) four
			(5) 1　冂　冈　四　四
005	五 (five)	▶ご ▷いつ	五(ご) five　五時(ごじ) five o'clock 五月(ごがつ) May　五歳(ごさい) five years old 五つ(いつつ) five
			(4) 一　丆　五　五
006	六 (six)	▶ろく　ろっ ▷むっ	六(ろく) six　六時(ろくじ) six o'clock 六百(ろっぴゃく) six hundred 六分(ろっぷん) six minutes　六つ(むっつ) six
			(4) 丶　亠　广　六
007	七 (seven)	▶しち ▷なな	七(しち／なな) seven　七時(しちじ) seven o'clock 七月(しちがつ) July　七つ(ななつ) seven 七人(ななにん／しちにん) seven people
			(2) 一　七
008	八 (eight)	▶はち　はっ ▷やっ	八(はち) eight　八時(はちじ) eight o'clock 八百(はっぴゃく) eight hundred 八歳(はっさい) eight years old　八つ(やっつ) eight
			(2) ノ　八

009	九 (nine)	▶きゅう　く ▷ここの	九(きゅう) nine　　九時(くじ) nine o'clock 九月(くがつ) September　　九歳(きゅうさい) nine years old 九つ(ここのつ) nine
			(2) ノ　九
010	十 (ten)	▶じゅう 　じゅっ　じっ ▷とお	十(じゅう) ten　　十時(じゅうじ) ten o'clock 十月(じゅうがつ) October 十歳(じゅっさい／じっさい) ten years old　　十(とお) ten
			(2) 一　十
011	百 (hundred)	▶ひゃく 　びゃく 　ぴゃく	百(ひゃく) hundred　　三百(さんびゃく) three hundred 六百(ろっぴゃく) six hundred　　八百(はっぴゃく) eight hundred
			(6) 一　ア　ア　万　百　百
012	千 (thousand)	▶せん　ぜん	千(せん) thousand　　三千(さんぜん) three thousand 八千(はっせん) eight thousand 千円(せんえん) one thousand yen
			(3) ′　二　千
013	万 (ten thousand)	▶まん	一万(いちまん) ten thousand 十万(じゅうまん) one hundred thousand 百万(ひゃくまん) one million
			(3) 一　フ　万
014	円 (yen; circle)	▶えん ▷まる	百円(ひゃくえん) one hundred yen 円(えん) circle　　円高(えんだか) strong yen 円い(まるい) round
			(4) ｜　冂　冂　円
015	時 (time)	▶じ ▷とき	一時(いちじ) one o'clock　　時間(じかん) time; ... hours 子どもの時(こどものとき) in one's childhood 時々(ときどき) sometimes　　時計(とけい) watch; clock
			(10) ｜　冂　日　日　日′　日十　昨　昨　時　時

(▶ indicates the *on-yomi* [pronunciation originally borrowed from Chinese] and ▷ indicates the *kun-yomi* [native Japanese reading].)

I 漢字の練習 (Kanji Practice)
かん じ　　れん しゅう

A. Read the price of the following items in kanji and write it in numerals.

Example チョコレート　　(1) ハンカチ　　(2) せんす

百五十円　　　　　　六百五十円　　　　　千八百円

（¥ 150 ）　　　　　（¥　　　　）　　　　（¥　　　　　）

(3) きもの　　　　　(4) テレビ　　　　　(5) いえ

七十一万四千円　　　十二万三千円　　　　三千九百万円

（¥　　　　　）　　　（¥　　　　　　）　　（¥　　　　　　　）

B. Write the following prices in kanji.

Example ¥5,420　→　　五千四百二十円

1. ¥30　＿＿＿＿＿＿＿＿　　6. ¥12,500　＿＿＿＿＿＿＿＿＿＿＿＿

2. ¥140　＿＿＿＿＿＿＿＿　　7. ¥168,000　＿＿＿＿＿＿＿＿＿＿＿＿

3. ¥251　＿＿＿＿＿＿＿＿　　8. ¥3,200,000　＿＿＿＿＿＿＿＿＿＿＿

4. ¥6,070　＿＿＿＿＿＿＿　　9. ¥57,000,000　＿＿＿＿＿＿＿＿＿＿

5. ¥8,190　＿＿＿＿＿＿＿

Ⅱ まいにちのせいかつ

A student writes about his daily routine. Read the passage and find out about his schedule and fill in the blanks below. 🔊 Y03

1 　　わたしはまいにち七時におきます。うちであさごはんをた
2 べます。八時にだいがくへいきます。九時ににほんごをべん
3 きょうします。十二時半にだいがくでひるごはんをたべます。
4 ときどきコーヒーをのみます。四時にとしょかんでほんをよ
5 みます。六時ごろうちへかえります。十時にテレビをみます。
6 十二時ごろねます。

7:00 　　_____

(　　) go to the university

9:00 　　_____

(　　) eat lunch

4:00 　　_____

6:00 　　_____

(　　) watch TV

(　　) 　_____

Ⅲ 書く練習 (Writing Practice)

Write about your daily routine. Use the above passage as a model.

第4課 LESSON 4
メアリーさんのしゅうまつ Mary's Weekend

016	日	▶に　にち 　にっ ▷び　ひ　か (day; sun)	日本(にほん) Japan　日曜日(にちようび) Sunday 毎日(まいにち) every day　母の日(ははのひ) Mother's Day 日記(にっき) diary　三日(みっか) three days
			(4) ｜ 冂 月 日
017	本	▶ほん ▷もと (book; basis)	本(ほん) book　日本(にほん) Japan 日本語(にほんご) Japanese language 山本さん(やまもとさん) Mr./Ms. Yamamoto
			(5) 一 十 オ 木 本
018	人	▶じん　にん ▷ひと (person)	日本人(にほんじん) Japanese people 一人で(ひとりで) alone　この人(このひと) this person 三人(さんにん) three people
			(2) ノ 人
019	月	▶げつ　がつ ▷つき (moon; month)	月曜日(げつようび) Monday　一月(いちがつ) January 月(つき) moon　今月(こんげつ) this month 一か月(いっかげつ) one month
			(4) ｊ 刀 月 月
020	火	▶か ▷ひ　び (fire)	火曜日(かようび) Tuesday 火(ひ) fire　火山(かざん) volcano　花火(はなび) fireworks 火星(かせい) Mars
			(4) ・ ⺌ ⺌ 火
021	水	▶すい ▷みず (water)	水曜日(すいようび) Wednesday　水(みず) water 水泳(すいえい) swimming　水道(すいどう) water supply 水着(みずぎ) bathing suit
			(4) 亅 オ 水 水
022	木	▶もく ▷き (tree)	木曜日(もくようび) Thursday 木(き) tree　木村さん(きむらさん) Mr./Ms. Kimura
			(4) 一 十 オ 木
023	金	▶きん ▷かね (gold; money)	金曜日(きんようび) Friday お金(おかね) money　料金(りょうきん) charge お金持ち(おかねもち) rich person
			(8) ノ 入 人 合 全 全 金 金

024	土 (soil)	▶ど　と ▷つち	土曜日（どようび）Saturday 土（つち）soil　土地（とち）land　粘土（ねんど）clay
			(3) 一　十　土
025	曜 (weekday)	▶よう	日曜日（にちようび）Sunday 曜日（ようび）day of the week
			(18) ｜ 冂 冊 日 日 日 日 日 日 日 日 日 日 日 日 日 曜 曜
026	上 (up)	▶じょう ▷うえ　のぼ	上（うえ）top; above 上手な（じょうずな）good at　屋上（おくじょう）rooftop 上る（のぼる）to go up
			(3) ｜ 卜 上
027	下 (down)	▶か ▷した　くだ	下（した）under 地下鉄（ちかてつ）subway　下手な（へたな）poor at 下さい（ください）Please give/do . . .
			(3) 一　丁　下
028	中 (middle)	▶ちゅう 　じゅう ▷なか	中（なか）inside 中国（ちゅうごく）China　中学（ちゅうがく）junior high school 一年中（いちねんじゅう）all year around
			(4) ｜ 冂 口 中
029	半 (half)	▶はん	三時半（さんじはん）half past three 半分（はんぶん）half　半年（はんとし）half a year 半額（はんがく）half price
			(5) 丶　丷　丷　半　半

（▶ indicates the *on-yomi* and ▷ indicates the *kun-yomi*.）

Ⅰ 漢字の練習 (Kanji Practice)
かん　じ　　れんしゅう

A. Match the kanji with the English equivalents.

1. 水曜日 ・   ・ Sunday

2. 金曜日 ・   ・ Monday

3. 日曜日 ・   ・ Tuesday

4. 月曜日 ・   ・ Wednesday

5. 土曜日 ・   ・ Thursday

6. 木曜日 ・   ・ Friday

7. 火曜日 ・   ・ Saturday

B. Look at the picture and choose the appropriate kanji for the blanks.

上　　下　　中

1. レストランはビルの＿＿＿＿＿です。
   (building)

2. 日本語学校はレストランの＿＿＿＿＿です。
   ご　がっこう

3. スーパーはレストランの＿＿＿＿＿です。

Ⅱ おかあさんへのメモ

メアリーさんはおかあさんにメモをかきました。
Read the memo and answer the questions.

1. メアリーさんはきょうなにをしますか。

2. うちでばんごはんをたべますか。

3. 何時ごろかえりますか。
   なん

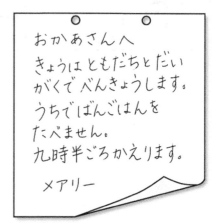

おかあさんへ
きょうは ともだちと だい
がくで べんきょうします。
うちで ばんごはんを
たべません。
九時半ごろ かえります。

　　　　メアリー

Ⅲ メアリーさんのしゅうまつ

Read the following passage about Mary's weekend. 🔊 Y04

1　　金曜日に日本人のともだちとこうえんにいきました。こうえんでともだちとはなしました。それから、レストランへいきました。たくさんたべました。

　　土曜日は一人でおてらへいきました。たくさんみせがありま
5　した。みせでおまんじゅうをかいました。

　　日曜日はおそくおきました。おかあさんもおそくおきました。わたしはあさ、ざっしをよみました。それから、おかあさんとひるごはんをたべました。ごごは日本語をべんきょうしました。
9　レポートもかきました。

みせ	shop; store
おまんじゅう	sweet bun
おそく	(do something) late

Answer the following activities in the order Mary did them.

(　) → (　) → (　) → (　) → (　)

(a) studied Japanese	(b) went to a restaurant	(c) went to a park
(d) bought sweet buns	(e) read a magazine	

Ⅳ 書く練習 (Writing Practice)

A. You are going out. Write a memo to someone in your house, telling when you will be back and whether you will have dinner at home.

B. Write about your weekend. Use the above passage as a model.

第5課　りょこう Travel

030	山	▶さん ▷やま (mountain)	山(やま) mountain 山川さん(やまかわさん) Mr./Ms. Yamakawa 富士山(ふじさん) Mt. Fuji (3) 丨 凵 山
031	川	▷かわ　がわ (river)	川(かわ) river　山川さん(やまかわさん) Mr./Ms. Yamakawa 小川さん(おがわさん) Mr./Ms. Ogawa (3) 丿 丿丨 川
032	元	▶げん　がん ▷もと (origin)	元気な(げんきな) fine 元日(がんじつ) the first day of the year　地元(じもと) local (4) 一 二 テ 元
033	気	▶き (spirit)	元気な(げんきな) fine　天気(てんき) weather 電気(でんき) electricity　気持ち(きもち) feeling 人気(にんき) popularity (6) ′ ～ ⌐ 气 気 気
034	天	▶てん (heaven)	天気(てんき) weather 天国(てんごく) heaven　天皇(てんのう) Japanese emperor 天才(てんさい) genius (4) 一 二 チ 天
035	私	▶し ▷わたし (I; private)	私(わたし) I 私立大学(しりつだいがく) private university (7) ′ ⌐ 千 チ 禾 私 私
036	今	▶こん ▷いま (now)	今(いま) now　今日(きょう) today 今晩(こんばん) tonight　今月(こんげつ) this month 今年(ことし) this year (4) 丿 人 今 今
037	田	▷た　だ (rice field)	田中さん(たなかさん) Mr./Ms. Tanaka 山田さん(やまださん) Mr./Ms. Yamada 田んぼ(たんぼ) rice field (5) 丨 冂 冖 用 田

038	女 (woman)	▶じょ ▷おんな	女の人(おんなのひと) woman 女性(じょせい) woman　女の子(おんなのこ) girl 長女(ちょうじょ) the eldest daughter
			(3) く　夕　女
039	男 (man)	▶だん ▷おとこ	男の人(おとこのひと) man 男性(だんせい) man　男の子(おとこのこ) boy 男子学生(だんしがくせい) male student
			(7) 丨　冂　冂　甲　田　男　男
040	見 (to see)	▶けん ▷み	見る(みる) to see 見物(けんぶつ) sightseeing　花見(はなみ) flower viewing 意見(いけん) opinion
			(7) 丨　冂　冃　月　目　貝　見
041	行 (to go)	▶こう　ぎょう ▷い	行く(いく) to go 銀行(ぎんこう) bank　一行目(いちぎょうめ) first line 旅行(りょこう) travel
			(6) ′　夕　イ　彳　彳　行
042	食 (to eat)	▶しょく ▷た	食べる(たべる) to eat 食べ物(たべもの) food　食堂(しょくどう) cafeteria 食事(しょくじ) meal　朝食(ちょうしょく) breakfast
			(9) ノ　ヘ　ム　今　今　含　食　食　食
043	飲 (to drink)	▶いん ▷の	飲む(のむ) to drink 飲み物(のみもの) drink 飲酒運転(いんしゅうんてん) drunken driving
			(12) ノ　ヘ　ム　今　今　含　食　食　食　飲　飲　飲

(▶ indicates the *on-yomi* and ▷ indicates the *kun-yomi*.)

Ⅰ 漢字の練習 (Kanji Practice)

A. Use each part below to write a kanji incorporating it.

Example 目 → 見

1. 艮
2. 欠
3. ム
4. 二
5. 力
6. 气
7. 八
8. 良
9. メ
10. 田

B. Match the following sentences with the pictures.

1. (　) えいがを見ます。
2. (　) コーヒーを飲みます。
3. (　) ハンバーガーを食べます。
4. (　) 男の人と女の人がいます。
5. (　) 山と川があります。
6. (　) 今日はいい天気です。
7. (　) 銀行に行きます。
　　　　ぎんこう

(a) (b) (c) (d)
(e) (f) (g)

C. Match the kanji with the reading.

1. (　) 一日
2. (　) 二日
3. (　) 三日
4. (　) 四日
5. (　) 五日
6. (　) 六日
7. (　) 七日
8. (　) 八日
9. (　) 九日
10. (　) 十日
11. (　) 二十日

(a) いつか　(b) ここのか　(c) ついたち　(d) とおか　(e) なのか　(f) はつか
(g) ふつか　(h) みっか　(i) むいか　(j) ようか　(k) よっか

Ⅱ たのしいりょこう

A. Match the following *katakana* words with the English equivalents.

1. コーヒー　・　　　　　　　　・ cake
2. コンサート・　　　　　　　　・ coffee
3. ウィーン　・　　　　　　　　・ cafe
4. カフェ　　・　　　　　　　　・ classical music
5. クラシック・　　　　　　　　・ concert
6. ケーキ　　・　　　　　　　　・ Vienna

B. Read Moe's post below. Write ○ for the things she did or does and write × for the things she didn't or doesn't do in Vienna. Y05-1

山田もえ
1月6日 17:35 ·

1　今、ウィーンにいます。
　ここはちょっとさむいです。
　ウィーンはとてもきれいなまちです。

　きのうはおしろを見ました。
5　ふるかったですが、とてもきれいでした。
　たくさんしゃしんをとりました。

　よるはクラシックのコンサートに行きました。よかったです。

　ウィーンにはカフェがたくさんあります。
10　まいにちカフェでコーヒーを飲みます。
　ケーキも食べます。すごくおいしいです。

👍❤️ 田中 ようこさん、他15人　　　　コメント2件

👍 いいね！　　💬 コメントする　　↪ シェア

1. (　　) see an old castle
2. (　　) go to see a ballet
3. (　　) take pictures
4. (　　) drink beer at the cafe
5. (　　) enjoy sweets
6. (　　) eat at McDonald's

おしろ　castle
〜が　　..., but
よる　　night

C. Robert wrote a postcard to his former host mother. Read the postcard below and answer the following questions in Japanese. 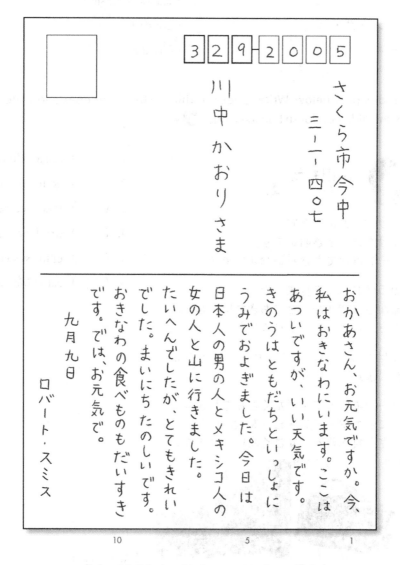 Y05-2

1. ロバートさんは今どこにいますか。

2. どんな天気ですか。

3. きのうは なにをしましたか。

4. 今日は なにをしましたか。だれとしましたか。

〒329-2005

さくら市今中
三－一－四〇七

川中 かおり さま

おかあさん、お元気ですか。今、私はおきなわにいます。ここはあついですが、いい天気です。きのうは ともだちといっしょにうみでおよぎました。今日は日本人の男の人とメキシコ人の女の人と山に行きました。たいへんでしたが、とてもきれいでした。まいにちたのしいです。おきなわの食べものもだいすきです。では、お元気で。

九月九日

ロバート・スミス

～さま	Mr./Ms. (used in letter writing)	男の人 man
メキシコ Mexico	女の人 woman	山 mountain
たいへん（な）tough	では、お元気で Take care.

Ⅲ 書く練習 (Writing Practice)
か れんしゅう

The following are your Japanese friends' addresses in your pocket notebook. Copy their addresses on the postcards and write about your vacation.

名 前 な まえ	住　　所 じゅう　しょ	
今中なみ いまなか	〒753-0041	山口県山口市東山 36-8 やまぐちけんやまぐち し ひがしやま
上田元気 うえ だ げん き	〒112-0002	東京都文京区小石川 7-7 とうきょう と ぶんきょう く こ いしかわ

読
L5

Japanese addresses

Japanese addresses start with the postal code, followed by the prefecture, city, and district as follows:

(1) 〒 (2) 753−0041

(3) 山口県 (4) 山口市 (5) 東山 (6) 36−8
　　やまぐちけん　　やまぐち し　　ひがしやま

(7) 今中なみ (8) 様
　　いまなか　　　さま

(1) postal symbol	(4) city, village, etc.	(7) name
(2) postal code	(5) district	(8) "Mr./Ms."
(3) prefecture	(6) block number and house number	

Note that, like all Japanese texts, addresses can be written vertically as well as horizontally.

第6課

LESSON 6

私のすきなレストラン My Favorite Restaurant

044	東 (east)	▶とう ▷ひがし	東(ひがし) east　東口(ひがしぐち) east exit 東京(とうきょう) Tokyo　関東(かんとう) Kanto area 東洋(とうよう) the East
			(8) 一 厂 厅 盲 盲 审 東 東
045	西 (west)	▶せい　さい ▷にし	西(にし) west　西口(にしぐち) west exit 北西(ほくせい) northwest　関西(かんさい) Kansai area 西洋(せいよう) the West
			(6) 一 厂 丌 丙 西 西
046	南 (south)	▶なん ▷みなみ	南(みなみ) south　南口(みなみぐち) south exit 南東(なんとう) southeast　南極(なんきょく) Antarctica 東南アジア(とうなんアジア) Southeast Asia
			(9) 一 十 广 内 内 南 南 南 南
047	北 (north)	▶ほく　ほっ ▷きた	北(きた) north　北口(きたぐち) north exit 東北(とうほく) Tohoku area　北極(ほっきょく) North Pole 北海道(ほっかいどう) Hokkaido
			(5) 一 ＋ ｊ 北 北
048	口 (mouth)	▶こう ▷ぐち　くち	北口(きたぐち) north exit 口(くち) mouth　人口(じんこう) population 入り口／入口(いりぐち) entrance
			(3) 丨 冂 口
049	出 (to exit)	▶しゅっ 　しゅつ ▷で　だ	出る(でる) to exit　出口(でぐち) exit　出かける(でかける) to go out　出す(だす) to take something out 出席(しゅっせき) attendance　輸出(ゆしゅつ) export
			(5) 丨 屮 中 出 出
050	右 (right)	▶う　ゆう ▷みぎ	右(みぎ) right 右折(うせつ) right turn　左右(さゆう) right and left 右手(みぎて) right hand　右側(みぎがわ) right side
			(5) ノ ナ オ 右 右
051	左 (left)	▶さ ▷ひだり	左(ひだり) left 左折(させつ) left turn　左手(ひだりて) left hand 左利き(ひだりきき) left-handed
			(5) 一 ナ ナ 左 左

052	分	▶ふん　ぷん ぶん ▷わ (minute; to divide)	五分（ごふん）five minutes 十分（じゅっぷん／じっぷん）ten minutes 自分（じぶん）oneself　分ける（わける）to divide
			(4) ノ 八 分 分
053	先	▶せん ▷さき (ahead)	先生（せんせい）teacher 先週（せんしゅう）last week　先に（さきに）ahead 先月（せんげつ）last month　先輩（せんぱい）senior member
			(6) ノ ⺊ ⺍ 生 牛 先
054	生	▶せい　しょう ▷う (birth)	学生（がくせい）student　先生（せんせい）teacher 生まれる（うまれる）to be born 一生に一度（いっしょうにいちど）once in a life time
			(5) ノ ⺊ 牛 牛 生
055	大	▶だい　たい ▷おお (big)	大学生（だいがくせい）college student　大きい（おおきい）big 大変な（たいへんな）tough　大人（おとな）adult 大使館（たいしかん）embassy
			(3) 一 ナ 大
056	学	▶がく　がっ ▷まな (learning)	大学（だいがく）university　学生（がくせい）student 学校（がっこう）school　学ぶ（まなぶ）to study 学部（がくぶ）department; faculty
			(8) ` ゛ ゛ ⺍ 学 学 学
057	外	▶がい ▷そと (outside)	外国（がいこく）foreign country 外国人（がいこくじん）foreigner 外（そと）outside　海外（かいがい）overseas
			(5) ノ ク タ 列 外
058	国	▶こく　ごく こっ ▷くに (country)	外国（がいこく）foreign country　中国（ちゅうごく）China 国（くに）country　韓国（かんこく）South Korea 国会（こっかい）the Diet
			(8) ｜ 冂 冂 冂 冐 国 国 国

(▶ indicates the *on-yomi* and ▷ indicates the *kun-yomi*.)

Ⅰ 漢字の練習 (Kanji Practice)

A. Combine the following kanji to make compound words. You can use the same kanji more than once.

[Example] 外 + 国 → 外国

気　生　外　先　学　天　日　国　今　大

B. Indicate where each place is located on the map.

1. (　　) レストラン・アルデンテ：えきの中にあります。南口の近くです。
2. (　　) ロイヤルホテル：えきの東口を出て、まっすぐ五分ぐらいです。
3. (　　) 山下先生のうち：北口を出て、右へ十分ぐらいです。
4. (　　) こうえん：西口をまっすぐ十五分ぐらい行ってください。
5. (　　) 大学：北口を出て、左へ十分ぐらい行ってください。

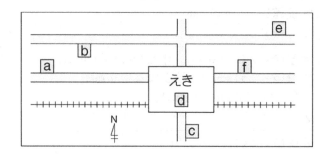

えき　　　　station
出る　　　　to exit
まっすぐ　　straight

Ⅱ でんごんばん (Bulletin Board)

Look at the bulletin board on the next page and answer the questions.

1. If you want to buy a bicycle, who are you going to contact?
2. Where will the party be held? Are you going to bring anything?
3. How do you get to the concert hall?
4. What can you do for winter break (from December to January)?

ホームステイ
プログラム

東北_{とうほく}のまちでホームステイをしませんか。

十二月二十八日(日) 〜 一月三日(土)

きれいな山と川の近_{ちか}くです。

えいごをおしえてください。

日本人の大学生です。

misakit@genkinihongo.com

みさき

<u>セール!!</u>

じてんしゃ

¥8,000

あたらしいです。
でんわしてください。
(よる7時〜11時)

山田　597-1651

ハロウィーン パーティー

ところ：山下先生のうち
じかん：6時〜
ともだちをつれてきてもいいですよ！
飲みものをもってきてください。

イタリアンレストラン
マンジャーレ

ランチ 1,200 円

Aセット （サラダ・コーヒー）
Bセット （パン・コーヒー）

ギターコンサート

11月12日(金)
6：30〜

西コンサートホール
(西駅_{えき}3出口を出て左へ3分)

読
L6

Ⅲ 私のすきなレストラン

Naomi writes about her favorite restaurant. Read the passage and answer the questions.

🔊 Y06

15　　　　　10　　　　　5　　　　　1

私のすきなレストラン

　私のすきなレストランは、イタリア
りょうりのマンジャーレです。えきの
南口を出て、右へ五分ぐらいです。ち
いさいレストランです。シェフはイタ
リア人のアントニオさんです。アント
ニオさんはとてもおもしろい人です。
アントニオさんのりょうりはとてもお
いしいです。私はよくマンジャーレに
行きます。マンジャーレでワインを飲
んで、ピザを食べます。アイスクリー
ムもおいしいです。ここでいつもたく
さん食べます。りょうりはやすいです
から。外国人もたくさんきます。みな
さんもきてください。

イタリア	Italy	ピザ	pizza
りょうり	cooking; dish	いつも	always
シェフ	chef	みなさん	everyone
ワイン	wine		

A. Where is the restaurant?

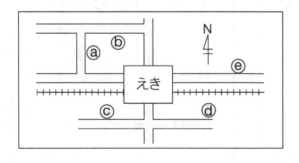

B. Circle the food or drink the writer has at the restaurant.

ピザ	パスタ	アイスクリーム
ワイン	ビール	ステーキ

C. Choose the correct answer.

1. マンジャーレは $\left\{\begin{array}{l}\text{大きい}\\\text{ちいさい}\end{array}\right\}$ レストランです。

2. マンジャーレは $\left\{\begin{array}{l}\text{たかい}\\\text{やすい}\end{array}\right\}$ です。

3. アントニオさんは $\left\{\begin{array}{l}\text{おもしろい}\\\text{つまらない}\end{array}\right\}$ 人です。

4. マンジャーレに外国人が $\left\{\begin{array}{l}\text{きます。}\\\text{きません。}\end{array}\right\}$

読 L6

IV 書く練習 (Writing Practice)
か れんしゅう

A. You are organizing a party. Write a flyer about the party. Be sure to include: what kind of party it is, what time it starts, where it is held, what to bring, how to get there, and so on.

B. Write about your favorite restaurant. You may include the following.

(1) name of the restaurant

(2) how to get there

(3) description of the restaurant, such as people who work there and what the place is like

(4) what you recommend (what is good)

第7課　LESSON 7

メアリーさんのてがみ Mary's Letter

059	京 (capital)	▶きょう	東京 (とうきょう) Tokyo　京子 (きょうこ) Kyoko 京都 (きょうと) Kyoto 上京する (じょうきょうする) to go to the capital
			(8) 丶 一 一 一 一 一 一 一 一 京 京 京
060	子 (child)	▶し ▷こ	子ども (こども) child　京子 (きょうこ) Kyoko 女の子 (おんなのこ) girl　男の子 (おとこのこ) boy 女子学生 (じょしがくせい) female student
			(3) 了 了 子
061	小 (small)	▶しょう ▷ちい	小さい (ちいさい) small 小学校 (しょうがっこう) elementary school 小学生 (しょうがくせい) elementary school student
			(3) 亅 小 小
062	会 (to meet)	▶かい ▷あ	会う (あう) to meet　会社 (かいしゃ) company 会社員 (かいしゃいん) office worker 会議 (かいぎ) meeting　教会 (きょうかい) church
			(6) ノ 人 今 今 会 会
063	社 (company)	▶しゃ じゃ	会社 (かいしゃ) company 神社 (じんじゃ) shrine　社会 (しゃかい) society 入社 (にゅうしゃ) entry to a company
			(7) 丶 ㇹ ネ ネ ネ 补 社
064	父 (father)	▶ふ ▷ちち とう	父 (ちち) father　お父さん (おとうさん) father 父母 (ふぼ) father and mother　祖父 (そふ) grandfather
			(4) 丿 八 グ 父
065	母 (mother)	▶ぼ ▷はは かあ	母 (はは) mother　お母さん (おかあさん) mother 母語 (ほご) mother tongue　祖母 (そぼ) grandmother
			(5) ㇄ 口 口 母 母
066	高 (high)	▶こう ▷たか	高い (たかい) expensive; high　高校 (こうこう) high school 高校生 (こうこうせい) high school student 最高 (さいこう) the best
			(10) 丶 一 一 一 一 一 高 高 高 高

067	校 (school)	▶こう	学校（がっこう）school　高校（こうこう）high school 高校生（こうこうせい）high school student 中学校（ちゅうがっこう）junior high school
			(10) 一 十 オ オ オ' オ' オ゛ オ゛ 朴 枚 校
068	毎 (every)	▶まい	毎日（まいにち）every day 毎週（まいしゅう）every week　毎晩（まいばん）every night 毎年（まいねん／まいとし）every year
			(6) ノ 一 ヒ 勾 匃 毎
069	語 (word)	▶ご	日本語（にほんご）Japanese language 英語（えいご）English language 敬語（けいご）honorific expressions
			(14) ` 一 二 三 言 言 言 訂 訂 訝 語 語 語 語
070	文 (sentence)	▶ぶん	文学（ぶんがく）literature 作文（さくぶん）composition　文字（もじ）letter; character 文化（ぶんか）culture　文法（ぶんぽう）grammar
			(4) ` 一 ナ 文
071	帰 (to return)	▶き ▷かえ	帰る（かえる）to return 帰国（きこく）going home　帰宅（きたく）returning home 帰り（かえり）return
			(10) ' リ リ' リ゛ リ゛ リ゛ リ゛ 归 帰 帰
072	入 (to enter)	▶にゅう ▷はい い いり	入る（はいる）to enter 入リ口／入口（いりぐち）entrance 入れる（いれる）to put something in　輸入（ゆにゅう）import
			(2) ノ 入

（▶ indicates the *on-yomi* and ▷ indicates the *kun-yomi*.）

読
L7

I 漢字の練習
かん　じ　　れんしゅう

A. Fill in the blanks with the appropriate kanji.

1. 日本＿＿＿＿学　　高＿＿＿＿三年生　　＿＿＿＿と母
ねん

| 父 | 文 | 校 |

2. ＿＿＿＿日、＿＿＿＿は六時におきます。

| 母 | 毎 |

3. 日本＿＿＿＿はよくおふろに＿＿＿＿ります。

| 人 | 入 |

4. 東＿＿＿＿に行きました。食べものは＿＿＿＿かったです。

| 京 | 高 |

B. Which new kanji from this lesson include the *katakana* below?

Example) エ → 左

1. ヨ →

2. ネ →

3. ム →

4. ロ →

C. Word Search—Find seven kanji compounds from this lesson and six review compounds.

Example) 先生

帰	父	文	学	山	西
行	食	高	校	女	田
東	会	出	口	毎	日
京	社	母	天	時	本
右	中	元	気	先	語
外	国	人	左	生	男

II メアリーさんのてがみ

Mary wrote a letter to Professor Nishikawa, her Japanese teacher back home. 🔊 Y07

西川京子先生へ

西川先生、お元気ですか。アリゾナはあついですか。日本はすこしさむいです。今、私は日本のかぞくと大学のちかくにすんでいます。ここは小さくて、しずかなまちです。

私のかぞくは四人です。みんなとてもしんせつで、たのしいです。お父さんはコンピューターの会社ではたらいています。いそがしくて、毎日おそく帰ります。お母さんはとてもおもしろい人です。いっしょによくはなします。いもうとは高校生です。らいねん大学ですから、よくべんきょうします。毎日学校から帰って、すぐじゅくへ行きます。日本の高校生はたいへんですね。

おにいさんは東京の大学に行っていますから、あまり会いません。

私は今、日本語と日本文学のクラスをとっています。テニスサークルにも入っています。とてもおもしろいです。

西川先生はいつ日本に帰りますか。日本で会いましょう。たのしみにしています。からだに気をつけてください。

十一月三日

メアリー・ハート

すこし	a little
みんな	all
～から	from ...
じゅく	cram school
文学	literature
とる	to take (a class)
（～を）たのしみにする	to look forward (to)
からだに気をつける	to take care of oneself

Summarize what Mary wrote about the following topics in Japanese.

1. Japan: _____

2. Her town: _____

3. Father: _____

4. Mother: _____

5. Sister: _____

6. Brother: _____

7. School: _____

Ⅲ 書く練習
（か）（れんしゅう）

A. Write about the following topics.

1. 日本は／私の国は_____

_____

2. 私のまちは_____

_____

3. かぞくは_____

_____

4. ともだちは_____

_____

B. Write a letter to a Japanese friend or teacher. Describe your town, school, family, friends, and so on.

第8課 LESSON 8

日本の会社員 Japanese Office Workers

073	員 (member)	▶いん	会社員（かいしゃいん）office worker 店員（てんいん）store clerk　会員（かいいん）member 駅員（えきいん）station attendant
		(10)	` 冖 冖 冃 冃 冒 冒 員 員 員
074	新 (new)	▶しん ▷あたら	新しい（あたらしい）new　新聞（しんぶん）newspaper 新幹線（しんかんせん）Bullet Train 新鮮な（しんせんな）fresh
		(13)	` 亠 亠 立 立 辛 辛 亲 亲 新 新 新
075	聞 (to listen)	▶ぶん ▷き	聞く（きく）to listen　新聞（しんぶん）newspaper 聞こえる（きこえる）can be heard
		(14)	l 「 「 『 『 『 門 門 門 門 門 聞 聞 聞
076	作 (to make)	▶さく ▷つく	作る（つくる）to make 作文（さくぶん）composition　作品（さくひん）artistic piece 作者（さくしゃ）author
		(7)	ノ イ 亻 仁 乍 作 作
077	仕 (to serve)	▶し ▷つか	仕事（しごと）job 仕返し（しかえし）revenge 仕える（つかえる）to serve; to work under
		(5)	ノ イ 亻 什 仕
078	事 (thing)	▶じ ▷ごと　こと	仕事（しごと）job 事（こと）thing　火事（かじ）fire　食事（しょくじ）meal 返事（へんじ）reply
		(8)	一 一 ㅜ 写 写 写 事 事
079	電 (electricity)	▶でん	電車（でんしゃ）train　電気（でんき）electricity; light 電話（でんわ）telephone　電池（でんち）battery 電子レンジ（でんしレンジ）microwave oven
		(13)	一 一 厂 币 币 币 雨 雨 雪 雪 雷 雷 電
080	車 (car)	▶しゃ ▷くるま	車（くるま）car　電車（でんしゃ）train 自転車（じてんしゃ）bicycle　車いす（くるまいす）wheelchair 駐車場（ちゅうしゃじょう）parking lot
		(7)	一 一 厂 币 币 百 車

081	休	▶きゅう ▷やす (to rest)	休む (やすむ) to be absent; to rest 休み (やすみ) holiday; absence 休日 (きゅうじつ) holiday
			(6) ノ イ 仁 什 付 休
082	言	▶げん ▷い　こと (to say)	言う (いう) to say 言語学 (げんごがく) linguistics　方言 (ほうげん) dialect 言葉 (ことば) word; language
			(7) 丶 ニ ニ 言 言 言 言
083	読	▶どく ▷よ (to read)	読む (よむ) to read 読書 (どくしょ) reading books 読み物 (よみもの) reading matter
			(14) 丶 ニ ニ ニ 言 言 言 計 計 計 計 詰 詩 読
084	思	▶し ▷おも (to think)	思う (おもう) to think 不思議な (ふしぎな) mysterious 思い出す (おもいだす) to recall; to remember
			(9) 丨 冂 冋 冊 用 田 甲 思 思 思
085	次	▶じ ▷つぎ (next)	次 (つぎ) next 次女 (じじょ) second daughter 目次 (もくじ) table of contents　次回 (じかい) next time
			(6) 丶 冫 冫 汐 次 次
086	何	▷なに　なん (what)	何 (なに) what　何時 (なんじ) what time 何人 (なんにん) how many people 何か (なにか) something
			(7) ノ イ 仁 仁 佢 佢 何

(▶ indicates the *on-yomi* and ▷ indicates the *kun-yomi*.)

I 漢字の練習
かん　じ　れんしゅう

A. Using the parts below to write as many kanji as possible.

Example メ → 文　父

1. 言　　2. 木　　3. 日　　4. 田　　5. イ　　6. 口

B. Match the following phrases with an appropriate verb.

1. 新聞を　・　　　　　　　　　・作る
2. 音楽を　・　　　　　　　　　・休む
   おんがく
3. 仕事を　・　　　　　　　　　・読む
4. 日本語はおもしろいと・　　　　・する
5. ハンバーガーを・　　　　　　・思う
6. 電車に　・　　　　　　　　　・聞く
7. クラスを・　　　　　　　　　・のる

II 日本の会社員

A. 留学生のウデイさんはアンケートを作って、日本人の会社員に聞きました。
りゅう
Read the following questionnaire.

アンケート

1. 仕事のストレスがありますか。

　□はい　　　　□いいえ

2. よく残業をしますか。
　　ざんぎょう

　□よくする　　□ときどきする

　□ぜんぜんしない

3. 仕事の後、何をしますか。
　　　あと

4. 休みはたいてい何をしますか。

アンケート	questionnaire
ストレス	stress
残業（ざんぎょう）	overtime work
〜の後（〜のあと）	after ...

B. How would you answer the above questions?

C. ウデイさんはアンケートについてレポートを書きました。
Read the report below and answer the questions. 🔊 Y08

日本の会社員

ウデイ・クマール

　私は電車で毎日会社員を見ます。みんなとても疲れていると思います。この間、新聞で「日本の会社員とストレス」の話を読みました。私はアンケートを作って、会社員十人に聞きました。

　まず、「仕事のストレスがありますか」と聞きました。七人は「はい」と答えました。「仕事が大変で、休みがあまりない」と言っていました。次に、「よく残業をしますか」と聞きました。三人は「よく残業をする」と言っていました。四人は「ときどき残業をする」と言っていました。次に「仕事の後、何をしますか」と聞きました。五人は「何もしない。すぐ家に帰る」と言っていました。二人は「お酒を飲みに行く」と言っていました。最後に「休みはたいてい何をしますか」と聞きました。六人は「疲れているから、家にいる」と言っていました。

　日本の会社員はたくさん仕事をして、ストレスもあります。だから、休みもあまり出かけません。アンケートをして、日本の会社員はとても大変だと思いました。

疲れている（つかれている）	to be tired	答える（こたえる）	to answer
この間（このあいだ）	the other day	次に	secondly
話（はなし）	story; talk	最後に（さいごに）	lastly
まず	first of all		

1. ウデイさんは新聞で何の話を読みましたか。

2. ウデイさんはだれにアンケートをしましたか。

3. 何人いましたか。

    (a) 仕事のストレスがある。 …… ＿＿＿＿人

    (b) よく残業をする。 …… ＿＿＿＿人

    (c) ときどき残業をする。 …… ＿＿＿＿人

    (d) 仕事の後、お酒を飲む。…… ＿＿＿＿人

    (e) 休みの日は出かけない。…… ＿＿＿＿人

4. アンケートの後、ウデイさんはどう思いましたか。

5. ウデイさんのレポートを読んで、あなたはどう思いましたか。

読
L8

Ⅲ 書く練習

Make a questionnaire and ask several people the questions. Then, write a report based on the results.

第9課

LESSON 9

ソラさんの日記 Sora's Diary
にっき

087	午 (noon)	▶ご (noon)	午前(ごぜん) A.M.　午後(ごご) P.M.; in the afternoon 午前中(ごぜんちゅう) in the morning 正午(しょうご) noon
			(4) ノ 一 二 午
088	後 (after)	▶ご ▷あと　うし (after)	午後(ごご) P.M.; in the afternoon　〜の後(のあと) after ... 後で(あとで) later　後ろ(うしろ) back; behind 最後に(さいごに) lastly
			(9) ノ ク イ 彳 谷 往 後 後 後
089	前 (before)	▶ぜん ▷まえ (before)	前(まえ) before; front　午前(ごぜん) A.M. 名前(なまえ) name 前売り(まえうり) advance sale
			(9) ` ` 一 亠 广 广 广 前 前 前
090	名 (name)	▶めい　みょう ▷な (name)	名前(なまえ) name 有名な(ゆうめいな) famous　名刺(めいし) name card 氏名(しめい) full name　名字(みょうじ) family name
			(6) ノ ク タ タ 名 名
091	白 (white)	▶はく ▷しろ (white)	白い(しろい) white 白紙(はくし) blank sheet　白(しろ) white color 白鳥(はくちょう) swan
			(5) ノ イ 白 白 白
092	雨 (rain)	▶う ▷あめ (rain)	雨(あめ) rain 雨期(うき) rainy season　梅雨(つゆ) rainy season 大雨(おおあめ) heavy rain
			(8) 一 厂 厅 币 雨 雨 雨 雨
093	書 (to write)	▶しょ ▷か (to write)	書く(かく) to write 辞書(じしょ) dictionary　教科書(きょうかしょ) textbook 図書館(としょかん) library
			(10) 一 一 ヨ ヨ ヨ 聿 聿 書 書 書
094	友 (friend)	▶ゆう ▷とも (friend)	友だち(ともだち) friend 親友(しんゆう) best friend　友人(ゆうじん) friend 友情(ゆうじょう) friendship
			(4) 一 ナ 方 友

095	間	▶かん　げん ▷あいだ (between)	時間 (じかん) time　　二時間 (にじかん) two hours 間 (あいだ) between　　人間 (にんげん) human being 一週間 (いっしゅうかん) one week
			(12) 丨 冂 冂 冃 冃 門 門 門 門 間 間 間
096	家	▶か ▷いえ (house)	家 (いえ) house 家族 (かぞく) family　　家 (うち) house; home 家内 (かない) my wife　　作家 (さっか) author
			(10) 丶 宀 宀 宀 宇 宇 宇 家 家 家
097	話	▶わ ▷はな　はなし (to speak)	話す (はなす) to speak　　話 (はなし) talk; story 電話 (でんわ) telephone 会話 (かいわ) conversation
			(13) 丶 二 二 章 言 言 言 訂 訂 訂 話 話
098	少	▶しょう ▷すこ　すく (little)	少し (すこし) little 少ない (すくない) few　　少々 (しょうしょう) a little 少女 (しょうじょ) girl　　少年 (しょうねん) boy
			(4) 丿 小 小 少
099	古	▶こ ▷ふる (old)	古い (ふるい) old (for things) 中古 (ちゅうこ) secondhand　　古代 (こだい) ancient times
			(5) 一 十 十 古 古
100	知	▶ち ▷し (to know)	知る (しる) to know 知人 (ちじん) acquaintance 知り合い (しりあい) acquaintance
			(8) 丿 ㇒ ㇜ 矢 矢 知 知 知
101	来	▶らい ▷く　き　こ (to come)	来る (くる) to come　　来ます (きます) to come 来ない (こない) not to come 来週 (らいしゅう) next week　　来日 (らいにち) visit to Japan
			(7) 一 ㇐ ㇜ 平 来 来 来

読
L9

(▶ indicates the *on-yomi* and ▷ indicates the *kun-yomi*.)

I 漢字の練習
かんじ れんしゅう

A. Fill in the blanks with the appropriate kanji.

1. この＿＿＿いＴシャツは五＿＿＿円でした。 〔 百　白 〕

2. ＿＿＿さいケーキを＿＿＿し食べました。 〔 小　少 〕

3. 一時＿＿＿音楽を＿＿＿きました。 〔 聞　間 〕
   おんがく

4. 日本＿＿＿を＿＿＿します。 〔 話　語 〕

B. Choose the most appropriate word for each blank.

1. はじめまして。私の＿＿＿＿はキムです。 〔 名前　午前 〕

2. 毎日たいてい＿＿＿＿＿七時ごろおきます。 〔 午後　午前 〕

3. このかさは古いから、＿＿＿＿＿かさをかいます。

   〔 大きい　新しい 〕

4. 今日はいい＿＿＿＿だった。でも、あしたは＿＿＿＿がふると思う。

   〔 元気　天気　白　雨 〕

5. メアリーのお父さんを＿＿＿＿＿いますか。 〔 帰って　知って 〕

II ソラさんの日記
にっき

ソラさんは日記を書きました。 🔊 Y09-1
にっき

11月25日(土)　雨

　今日は朝から雨がふっていた。午前中は友だちにメールを書い
あさ
て、一時間ぐらい音楽を聞いた。
おんがく
　昼ごろメアリーの家へ行った。白くて、大きい家だった。メア
ひる

リーのホストファミリーの山本さんに会った。お父さんはせが高
くて、やせている人だった。

　家で晩ご飯を食べた。お母さんは「何もありませんが」と言っ
ていたが、たくさんごちそうがあった。晩ご飯はとてもおいしかっ
た。お母さんは料理がすごく上手だと思う。

　晩ご飯の後、いろいろな話をした。そして、きれいな着物をもらっ
た。お母さんは少し古いと言っていたが、すごくきれいだ。メア
リーのホストファミリーはとてもしんせつで楽しかった。

日記（にっき）	diary	いろいろ（な）	various
午前中（ごぜんちゅう）	in the morning	話をする	to have a talk
昼（ひる）	noon	そして	and then
ホストファミリー	host family	着物（きもの）	kimono; Japanese
ごちそう	excellent food		traditional dress

読
L9

A. Put the following pictures in the right order according to Sora's diary.

（　　）→（　　）→（　　）→（　　）→（　　）

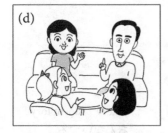

B. Make each of the following statements with ◯ if true, or with ✕ if false.

1. (　　) ソラさんは新しい着物をもらった。
2. (　　) お父さんはせがひくくて、やせている。
3. (　　) 晩ご飯は何もなかった。
4. (　　) ソラさんはお母さんの料理が好きだ。
5. (　　) 天気がよくなかった。
6. (　　) メアリーさんのホストファミリーの名前は山田だ。

C. ソラさんはメアリーさんのホストファミリーにメールを書きました。
Read the following mail. Y09-2

< 　　　　　　⤓　🗑　✉　⋯

ありがとうございました　　☆

 Sora Kim　11:30　　　　↩　⋯
To yamamoto22@genkinihongo.com

1　山本さま

きのうはどうもありがとうございました。
とてもたのしかったです。

りょうではあまり日本のりょうりを食べませんが、
5　お母さんのりょうりはとてもおいしかったです。
それから、きものをありがとうございました。
とてもきれいなきものですね。

かんこくにもあそびに来てください。
私はソウルのおもしろいところを知っていますから、
10　あんないします。

ソラ・キム
sora@genkinihongo.com

りょう　dormitory
あんないする
　　to show someone around

Ⅲ 書く練習
<small>か れんしゅう</small>

A. What did you do yesterday? Write a journal.

B. Write a thank-you mail to someone.

Useful Expressions:

いろいろおせわになりました。(Thank you for everything.)

体に気をつけてください。(Please take care of yourself.)
<small>からだ</small>

お会いできるのを楽しみにしています。(I am looking forward to seeing you.)
<small>たの</small>

～おめでとう（ございます）。(Congratulations on . . .)

（お）たんじょうびおめでとう。(Happy Birthday)

読
L9

第10課

昔話「かさじぞう」 The Folktale *Kasajizo*
むかしばなし

102 住	▶じゅう ▷す (to live)	住む（すむ）to live 住所（じゅうしょ）address 移住する（いじゅうする）to immigrate	
		(7) ノ イ イ 仁 住 住 住	
103 正	▶しょう せい ▷ただ (right)	お正月（おしょうがつ）New Year 正しい（ただしい）right　正午（しょうご）noon 正解（せいかい）correct answer	
		(5) 一 丁 下 正 正	
104 年	▶ねん ▷とし (year)	三年生（さんねんせい）third-year student 来年（らいねん）next year　今年（ことし）this year 年（とし）year	
		(6) ノ ト 仁 仁 年 年	
105 売	▶ばい ▷う (to sell)	売る（うる）to sell 売店（ばいてん）stand; stall 自動販売機（じどうはんばいき）vending machine	
		(7) 一 十 士 产 声 声 売	
106 買	▶ばい ▷か (to buy)	買う（かう）to buy 買い物（かいもの）shopping　売買（ばいばい）selling and buying	
		(12) 丶 一 冂 冂 罒 罒 買 買 買 買 買 買	
107 町	▶ちょう ▷まち (town)	町（まち）town　北山町（きたやまちょう）Kitayama Town 町長（ちょうちょう）mayor of a town	
		(7) ｜ 冂 冂 田 田 町 町	
108 長	▶ちょう ▷なが (long)	長い（ながい）long 長男（ちょうなん）the eldest son 社長（しゃちょう）company president	
		(8) ｜ 厂 厂 厓 長 長 長 長	
109 道	▶どう ▷みち (way)	道（みち）way; road 書道（しょどう）calligraphy　柔道（じゅうどう）judo 北海道（ほっかいどう）Hokkaido	
		(12) 丶 丷 丷 兰 产 首 首 首 首 ㆑ 道 道	

110	雪 (snow)	▶せつ ▷ゆき	雪（ゆき）snow 新雪（しんせつ）new snow　雪だるま（ゆきだるま）snowman (11) 一 一 一 戸 戸 雪 雪 雪 雪 雪 雪
111	立 (to stand)	▶りつ ▷た	立つ（たつ）to stand 国立大学（こくりつだいがく）national university 私立高校（しりつこうこう）private high school (5) 丶 一 十 立 立
112	自 (self)	▶じ	自分（じぶん）oneself 自動車（じどうしゃ）automobile　自転車（じてんしゃ）bicycle 自由（じゆう）freedom (6) 丶 亻 冂 白 自 自
113	夜 (night)	▶や ▷よる　よ	夜（よる）night 夜中（よなか）middle of night　今夜（こんや）tonight 夜明け（よあけ）dawn (8) 丶 一 广 疒 疒 夜 夜 夜
114	朝 (morning)	▶ちょう ▷あさ	朝（あさ）morning　今朝（けさ）this morning 朝食（ちょうしょく）breakfast　毎朝（まいあさ）every morning (12) 一 十 十 古 吉 directly 卓 直 卓 朝 朝 朝
115	持 (to hold)	▶じ ▷も	持つ（もつ）to carry; to hold　持ってくる（もってくる）to bring 所持品（しょじひん）belongings 気持ち（きもち）feeling (9) 一 十 扌 扌 扩 护 拦 持 持

（▶ indicates the *on-yomi* and ▷ indicates the *kun-yomi*.）

読
L10

Ⅰ 漢字の練習
かんじ　れんしゅう

A. Add strokes to the kanji below and turn them into new kanji from this lesson.

Example 二 → 立

1. 上 →   3. 雨 →   5. 白 →   7. 貝 →

2. 田 →   4. 月 →   6. 土 →   8. 自 →

B. Write each antonym in kanji.

1. 買う　　　⇔ _____   3. みじかい ⇔ _____

2. すわる　　⇔ _____   4. 夜　　　⇔ _____

C. Fill in the blanks with the appropriate kanji from the list, and add *hiragana* where necessary.

売　雪　住　買　長　立　持

1. 町で_____をしました。
   　　　　　shopping

2. かさを_____ていますか。
   　　　　have

3. 本屋では本を_____ています。
   　や　　　(are) sell(ing)

4. よく_____がふります。
   　　　snow

5. おじいさんの話は_____。
   　　　　　　　　was long

6. 駅の近くに_____でいます。
   　えき　ちか　　live

7. 私の後ろに女の人が_____。
   　　　　　　　　was standing

Ⅱ かさじぞう

A. Answer the following questions.

1. 日本ではお正月に何をすると思いますか。

2. (Picture 1) これはおじぞうさんです。何だと思いますか。

3. (Picture 2) このおじいさんとおばあさんがこの話の主人公 (main characters) です。どんな人だと思いますか。どんな生活をしていると思いますか。
   しゅじんこう
   かつ

1

2

B. Read the Japanese folktale "かさじぞう" on pp. 344-345. 🔊 Y10

C. Put the following pictures in the right order.

(　) → (　) → (　) → (　) → (　) → (　)

(a)

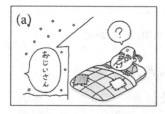

(b)

(c)

(d)

(e)

(f)

むかしむかし	once upon a time
かさ	bamboo hat
お正月	New Year's
年	year
おもち	rice cake
売る	to sell
かなしい	sad
山道（やまみち）	mountain road
じぞう／おじぞうさん	guardian deity of children
雪	snow
かぶせる	to put (a hat) on a person's head (*person* に *a hat* を)
自分	oneself
とる	to take off
いいこと	good deed
声（こえ）	voice
戸（と）	door
びっくりする	to be surprised
しあわせ（な）	happy

「このかさは古いですが、どうぞ。」と言って、おじぞうさんにかぶせました。

うちに帰って、おじいさんはおばあさんにおじぞうさんの話をしました。

おばあさんは「おじいさん、いいことをしましたね。」と言いました。

その夜おそく、おじいさんはだれかの声を聞きました。

「おじいさん、おじいさん。」

おじいさんは戸を開けて、びっくりしました。六人のおじぞうさんが立っていました。おじぞうさんはお正月のおもちをたくさん持っていました。

お正月の朝になりました。おじいさんとおばあさんはおもちをたくさん食べました。二人はとてもしあわせでした。

D. Mark each of the following statements with ○ if true, or with × if false.

1. （　　） おじいさんとおばあさんはお金持ちだった。
2. （　　） だれもおじいさんのかさを買わなかった。
3. （　　） おじいさんはおじぞうさんにかさを売った。
4. （　　） 雪の中でおじいさんはおじぞうさんを六つ見た。
5. （　　） おじいさんは新しいかさを六つ持っていた。
6. （　　） おばあさんはおじいさんの話を聞いて、かなしくなった。
7. （　　） おじぞうさんはお金をたくさん持ってきた。
8. （　　） おじいさんとおばあさんのお正月はとてもよかった。

かさじぞう

むかしむかし、山の中におじいさんとおばあさんが住んでいました。あしたはお正月です。新しい年がはじまります。でも、おじいさんとおばあさんはお金がなかったから、お正月のおもちもありませんでした。二人はかさを売って、おもちを買うつもりでした。

おじいさんはかさを持って、町に売りに行きました。でも、だれもかさを買いませんでした。おじいさんはかなしくなりました。雪がたくさんふっていました。

おじいさんは長い山道を歩いて帰りました。雪の中におじぞうさんが六つ立っていました。

「あっ！ おじぞうさんだ！」

おじいさんは「おじぞうさん、さむくないですか。」と聞きました。おじぞうさんは何も言いませんでした。

「どうぞかさを使ってください。」

おじいさんはおじぞうさんのあたまの上にかさをかぶせました。「一つ、二つ、三つ、四つ、五つ。」かさは五つでした。一人のおじぞうさんはかさがありませんでした。おじいさんは自分のかさをとりました。

Ⅲ 書く練習（れんしゅう）

Choose one topic from the list below and write what you do/did on these days.

お正月	クリスマス (Christmas)	ハロウィーン (Halloween)
誕生日（たんじょうび） (Birthday)	バレンタインデー (Valentine's Day)	
ラマダン (Ramadan)	ハヌカー (Chanukkah)	
ディーワーリー (Diwali)	Others	

第11課

友だち・メンバー募集 Looking for Friends/Members
ぼ しゅう

	手 (hand)	▶しゅ ▷て	手紙 (てがみ) letter　歌手 (かしゅ) singer 手 (て) hand　手話 (しゅわ) sign language 上手な (じょうずな) good at
116			(4) 一 二 三 手
117	紙 (paper)	▶し ▷がみ　かみ	手紙 (てがみ) letter 紙 (かみ) paper　和紙 (わし) Japanese paper 表紙 (ひょうし) cover page　折り紙 (おりがみ) origami
			(10) く 幺 幺 糸 糸 糸 紅 紙 紙
118	好 (favorite; to like)	▶こう ▷す　この	好きな (すきな) to like　大好きな (だいすきな) to love 好意 (こうい) goodwill　好み (このみ) liking; taste 好物 (こうぶつ) favorite food
			(6) く 夕 女 女 好 好
119	近 (near)	▶きん ▷ちか	近く (ちかく) near; nearby　近所 (きんじょ) neighborhood 最近 (さいきん) recently 中近東 (ちゅうきんとう) the Middle and Near East
			(7) 一 丘 斤 斤 沂 近 近
120	明 (bright)	▶めい ▷あか	明るい (あかるい) cheerful; bright 明日 (あした) tomorrow　説明 (せつめい) explanation 発明 (はつめい) invention　文明 (ぶんめい) civilization
			(8) 丨 冂 日 日 日 明 明 明
121	病 (ill; sick)	▶びょう	病院 (びょういん) hospital　病気 (びょうき) illness 重病 (じゅうびょう) serious illness 急病 (きゅうびょう) sudden illness
			(10) ' 亠 广 广 疒 疒 疒 病 病 病
122	院 (institution)	▶いん	病院 (びょういん) hospital 大学院 (だいがくいん) graduate school 美容院 (びよういん) beauty parlor
			(10) ' ろ 阝 阝 阝 阼 阼 阼 院
123	映 (to reflect)	▶えい ▷うつ	映画 (えいが) movie 映画館 (えいがかん) movie theater 映る (うつる) to be reflected
			(9) 丨 冂 日 日 日 町 叻 映 映

124	画	▸が　かく	映画(えいが) movie
			画家(がか) painter　計画(けいかく) plan
			漫画(まんが) comic
		(picture)	(8) 一　厂　厅　而　而　面　面　画　画
125	歌	▸か ▷うた	歌う(うたう) to sing　歌(うた) song　歌手(かしゅ) singer
			国歌(こっか) national anthem　歌舞伎(かぶき) Kabuki
			歌詞(かし) lyrics
		(to sing)	(14) 一　「　「　「　「　可　可　哥　哥　哥　哥　歌　歌　歌
126	市	▸し ▷いち	川口市(かわぐちし) Kawaguchi City
			市役所(しやくしょ) city hall　市長(しちょう) mayor
			市場(いちば) market
		(city)	(5) 丶　亠　广　方　市
127	所	▸じょ　しょ ▷ところ 　どころ	いろいろな所(ところ) various places
			近所(きんじょ) neighborhood
			台所(だいどころ) kitchen　住所(じゅうしょ) address
		(place)	(8) 一　ㄋ　�　戸　戸　所　所　所
128	勉	▸べん ▷つと	勉強する(べんきょうする) to study
			勉める(つとめる) to try hard　勤勉な(きんべんな) diligent
		(to make efforts)	(10) ノ　ク　ケ　名　免　免　多　免　免　勉
129	強	▸きょう　ごう ▷つよ	勉強する(べんきょうする) to study
			強い(つよい) strong　強情な(ごうじょうな) obstinate
			強盗(ごうとう) robbery　強力な(きょうりょくな) powerful
		(strong)	(11) フ　コ　弓　弘　犸　弦　弦　弦　強　強　強
130	有	▸ゆう ▷あ	有名な(ゆうめいな) famous
			有料(ゆうりょう) toll; fee　有る(ある) to exist
			有能な(ゆうのうな) talented
		(to exist)	(6) ノ　ナ　オ　有　有　有
131	旅	▸りょ ▷たび	旅行(りょこう) travel　旅館(りょかん) Japanese inn
			一人旅(ひとりたび) traveling alone　旅券(りょけん) passport
		(travel)	(10) 丶　亠　ㄗ　方　ガ　方　方　旅　旅　旅

(▸ indicates the *on-yomi* and ▷ indicates the *kun-yomi*.)

Ⅰ 漢字の練習
かん じ　れんしゅう

A. Combine the parts below to form the new kanji from this lesson.

B. Put one kanji in each box to make compounds.

(1) 歌 ☐
　　　 紙

(2) ☐ く
　　 所

(3) 有 ☐
　　　 前

(4) ☐ 院
　　 気

Ⅱ 友だち・メンバー募集
ぼ しゅう

A. 質問に答えてください。(Answer the following questions.)
しつもん　こた

1. あなたは友だちやメンバーを募集したことがありますか。
ぼ しゅう

2. 友だちやメンバーを募集している人に、メールや手紙を書いたことがあり
ぼ しゅう
ますか。

B. 右ページの「友だち・メンバー募集」を読みましょう。🔊 Y11-1
ぼ しゅう

C. 次の人はだれですか。その人の名前を書いてください。

1. The person who likes movies 　　　　　　　(　　　　　　) さん

2. The person who likes children 　　　　　　(　　　　　　) さん

3. The person who works for a company 　　(　　　　　　) さん

4. The person who wants to go to the concert 　(　　　　　　) さん

5. The person who likes outdoor activities 　　(　　　　　　) さん

友だち・メンバー募集
<ruby>募集<rt>ぼしゅう</rt></ruby>

いっしょにボランティアをしませんか

つくば市のボランティアサークルです。週末に近所の病院でボランティアをしています。子どもに勉強を<ruby>教<rt>おし</rt></ruby>えたり、いっしょに歌を歌ったりしています。子どもが大好きな人、ボランティアを<ruby>始<rt>はじ</rt></ruby>めませんか。

ひろクン

アウトドアが好きな人

会社員です。川口市に住んでいます。アウトドアが好きで、休みの日には車で近くの山や川に行きます。<ruby>将<rt>しょう</rt></ruby><ruby>来<rt>らい</rt></ruby>は外国の山に<ruby>登<rt>のぼ</rt></ruby>りたいと思っています。山に<ruby>登<rt>のぼ</rt></ruby>るのが好きな人、メールください。

ゆう

映画について話しませんか？

22<ruby>歳<rt>さい</rt></ruby>の大学生です。ホラー映画が大好きです。<ruby>週末<rt>しゅうまつ</rt></ruby>はバイトがあるから、いつも<ruby>平日<rt>へいじつ</rt></ruby>に一人で映画を見に行きます。いっしょに映画を見て、話しませんか？<ruby>将来<rt>しょうらい</rt></ruby>はホラー映画を作りたいです。

<ruby>貞子<rt>さだこ</rt></ruby>

いっしょにバンドをやりませんか

ロックが好きな明るい女の子です。ギターをひくのが好きで、<ruby>将来<rt>しょうらい</rt></ruby>は歌手になりたいと思っています。私といっしょにバンドをやりませんか。それからコンサートもいっしょに行きましょう！

カオリン

～募集（ぼしゅう）	looking for...	ホラー	horror
ボランティア	volunteer	平日（へいじつ）	weekday
近所	neighborhood	バンド	band
アウトドア	outdoor activities	明るい	cheerful

読
L11

D. 質問に答えてください。

1. ひろクンは、病院で何をしていますか。

2. ゆうは車を運転しますか。

3. 貞子はどんな映画が好きですか。

4. カオリンは何になりたいと思っていますか。

5. あなたはどの人と友だちになりたいですか。どうしてですか。

E. 「友だち・メンバー募集」を見て、エバさんはゆうさんにメッセージを書きました。
メッセージを読んで、質問に答えてください。 🔊 Y11-2

はじめまして。 1

私はメキシコ人の留学生です。一月に日本に来ました。今、
日本語や日本文化を勉強しています。

私もアウトドアが大好きで、山に登ったり、つりをしたりす
るのが好きです。旅行も好きです。日本では、まだあまり旅 5
行していませんが、これからいろいろな所に行くつもりです。
古いお寺や神社を見たいと思っています。日本の有名なお祭
りも見たいです。

日本人の友だちをたくさん作って、日本語でいろいろなこと
を話したいと思っています。よかったら、お返事ください。 10

エバ

文化（ぶんか）	culture
これから	from now on
こと	things; matters
お返事（おへんじ）	reply

1. エバさんはいつ日本に来ましたか。

2. エバさんは何をするのが好きですか。

3. エバさんは日本でどこに行きたいと思っていますか。

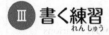

Ⅲ 書く練習

A. Describe who you are in detail and what kind of members/friends you are looking for. Make a catchy title.

B. Respond to one of the ads in Ⅱ-B or the ads posted by your classmates.

第12課 LESSON 12

七夕 *Tanabata* Festival
たなばた

132	昔 (ancient times)	▷むかし	昔(むかし) old times 昔話(むかしばなし) old tale　大昔(おおむかし) ancient times
			(8) 一 十 艹 爿 昔 昔 昔 昔
133	々 (symbol of repetition of a kanji)		昔々(むかしむかし) once upon a time 人々(ひとびと) people 時々(ときどき) sometimes　色々な(いろいろな) various
			(3) ノ 夕 々
134	神 (God)	▶じん しん こう ▷かみ	神さま(かみさま) God　神社(じんじゃ) shrine 神道(しんとう) Shinto 神戸市(こうべし) Kobe City
			(9) ` ㇇ 礻 礻 礻 衤 初 神 神 神
135	早 (early)	▶そう ▷はや	早い(はやい) early 早起きする(はやおきする) to get up early 早朝(そうちょう) early morning
			(6) 丿 口 日 日 旦 早
136	起 (to get up)	▶き ▷お	起きる(おきる) to get up 起こす(おこす) to wake someone up 再起動(さいきどう) reboot
			(10) 一 十 土 丰 丰 丰 走 起 起 起
137	牛 (cow)	▶ぎゅう ▷うし	牛(うし) cow 牛乳(ぎゅうにゅう) milk　牛肉(ぎゅうにく) beef 子牛(こうし) calf; veal
			(4) ノ 匕 仁 牛
138	使 (to use)	▶し ▷つか	使う(つかう) to use 大使(たいし) ambassador　使用中(しようちゅう) "Occupied" お使い(おつかい) errand
			(8) ノ イ 仁 佂 佂 佂 使 使
139	働 (to work)	▶どう ▷はたら ばたら	働く(はたらく) to work 共働き(ともばたらき) both husband and wife working 労働(ろうどう) labor
			(13) ノ イ 仁 佂 佂 伂 佲 佲 伸 俥 働 働 働

140	連 (to link)	▶れん ▷つ	連れて帰る (つれてかえる) to bring (a person) back 国連 (こくれん) United Nations 連休 (れんきゅう) consecutive holidays
			(10) 一 厂 戸 戸 亘 亘 車 車 連 連
141	別 (to separate)	▶べつ ▷わか	別れる (わかれる) to separate　別に (べつに) not in particular 特別な (とくべつな) special　差別 (さべつ) discrimination 別々に (べつべつに) separately
			(7) 丶 ロ ロ � 号 別 別
142	度 (time; degrees)	▶ど	一度 (いちど) once　今度 (こんど) near future 温度 (おんど) temperature　三十度 (さんじゅうど) 30 degrees 態度 (たいど) attitude
			(9) 丶 亠 广 广 庐 庐 庐 度 度
143	赤 (red)	▶せき ▷あか	赤 (あか) red color　赤い (あかい) red 赤ちゃん (あかちゃん) baby　赤道 (せきどう) the equator 赤十字 (せきじゅうじ) the Red Cross
			(7) 一 十 土 于 耂 赤 赤
144	青 (blue)	▶せい ▷あお	青 (あお) blue color　青い (あおい) blue 青年 (せいねん) youth　青空 (あおぞら) blue sky 青信号 (あおしんごう) green light
			(8) 一 十 キ 主 丰 青 青 青
145	色 (color)	▶しき しょく ▷いろ	色 (いろ) color 色々な (いろいろな) various　景色 (けしき) scenery 特色 (とくしょく) characteristic
			(6) 丿 ㄅ ㄅ 各 名 色

読 L12

(▶ indicates the *on-yomi* and ▷ indicates the *kun-yomi*.)

I 漢字の練習
かんじ れんしゅう

A. Match each reading with its kanji and translation.

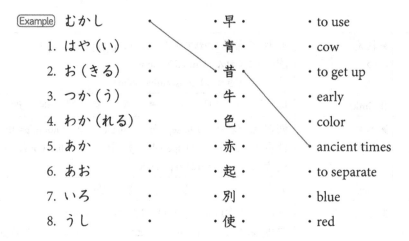

(Example) むかし	・早・	・to use
1. はや（い） ・	・青・	・cow
2. お（きる） ・	昔・	・to get up
3. つか（う） ・	・牛・	・early
4. わか（れる） ・	・色・	・color
5. あか ・	・赤・	・ancient times
6. あお ・	・起・	・to separate
7. いろ ・	・別・	・blue
8. うし ・	・使・	・red

B. Which new kanji from this lesson include the *katakana* below?

1. マ →   2. ネ →   3. カ →   4. ヌ →

C. Which new kanji from this lesson shares the same component as each pair of kanji below?

(Example) 朝　前 → 青

1. 住　仕   2. 道　近   3. 万　旅

II 七夕
たなばた

A. 絵 (picture) を見てください。これは何だと思いますか。七夕の日に作ります。
え　　　　　　　　　　　　　　　　　　　　　　　　　　　たなばた

B. 七夕の話を読みましょう。 🔊 Y12

七月七日は七夕です。これは七夕の話です。

昔々、天に神さまが住んでいました。娘が一人いて、名前はおりひめでした。おりひめはとてもまじめで、毎日、朝早く起きてははたを織っていました。

ある日、神さまは思いました。「おりひめはもう大人だ。結婚したほうがいい。」

神さまはまじめな男の人を見つけました。天の川の向こうに住んでいる人で、名前はひこぼしでした。ひこぼしは牛を使って、畑で働いていました。

おりひめとひこぼしは結婚しました。二人はとても好きになりました。いつもいっしょにいて、ぜんぜん働きませんでした。神さまは怒りました。でも二人は仕事をしませんでした。

神さまはとても怒って、おりひめを家に連れて帰りました。二人は別れなければいけませんでした。おりひめはひこぼしに会いたくて、毎日泣いていました。神さまは二人がかわいそうだと思って、言いました。

「おりひめ、ひこぼし、あなたたちは一年に一度だけ会ってもいい。それは七月七日の夜だ。おりひめ、あなたはその日、天の川の向こうに行ってもいい。でも、朝までに帰らなければいけない。」

一年に一度、七夕の夜におりひめとひこぼしは会います。二人の願いはかなうのです。

この日、私たちは赤や青などいろいろな色のたんざくに願いを書きます。七夕の日の願いはかなうと人々は言います。ある子供は「いい成績を取りたい」と書きます。ある人は「すてきな人に会いたい」と書きます。あなたは七夕の日にどんな願いを書きますか。

天（てん）	the heavens; the sky	怒る（おこる）	to get angry
神さま	God	連れて帰る	to bring (a person) back
娘（むすめ）	daughter	泣く（なく）	to cry
まじめ（な）	serious; sober; diligent	かわいそう（な）	pitiful
はたを織る（おる）	to weave	一年に一度	once a year
ある〜	one ... （ある日 one day）	〜までに	by ...
大人（おとな）	adult	願い（ねがい）	wish
見つける（みつける）	to find	かなう	to be realized
天の川（あまのがわ）	the Milky Way	私たち（わたしたち）	we
向こう（むこう）	the other side; over there	〜など	and so forth
牛	cow	たんざく	strip of fancy paper
畑（はたけ）	farm	人々	people

C. 質問に答えてください。
しつもん　こた

1. おりひめはどんな人ですか。

2. ひこぼしはどんな人ですか。

3. どうして神さまは怒りましたか。
おこ

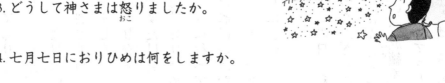

4. 七月七日におりひめは何をしますか。

5. どうして私たちは七夕の日にたんざくに願いを書きますか。
たなばた　　　　　　　　　　ねが

6. 神さまはやさしい人だと思いますか。どうしてですか。

Ⅲ 書く練習

れんしゅう

あなたの願いを五つ書いてください。
ねが

巻末
かん まつ
Appendix

文法さくいん Grammar Index
ぶんぽう

単語さくいん1　Vocabulary Index (J-E)
たんご

会……会話・文法編
　　　(Conversation and Grammar section)
読……読み書き編
　　　(Reading and Writing section)
G……あいさつ (Greetings)
(e)……Useful Expressions
I・II・III……問題番号 (読み書き編)
　　　(number of exercise in the
　　　Reading and Writing section)
[u] u-verb　[ru] ru-verb　[irr.] irregular verb

アイスクリーム　ice cream　会L3
あいだ　間　between　会L4
あう　会う　to meet; to see (a person) [u]
　　　会L4
アウトドア　outdoor activities　読L11-II
あおい　青い　blue　会L9, 会L9(e)
あかい　赤い　red　会L9, 会L9(e)
あおしんごう　青信号　green light
　　　会L9(e)
あかるい　明るい　cheerful　読L11-II
あき　秋　fall　会L10
あける　開ける　to open (something) [ru]
　　　会L6
あさ　朝　morning　会L3
あさごはん　朝ご飯　breakfast　会L3
あさって　the day after tomorrow
　　　会L4(e), 会L8
あし　足　leg; foot　会L7(e), 会L12
アジアけんきゅう　アジア研究　Asian
　studies　会L1
あした　明日　tomorrow　会L3, 会L4(e)
あそこ　over there　会L2
あそぶ　遊ぶ　to play; to spend time
　pleasantly [u]　会L6
あたたかい　暖かい　warm　会L10
あたま　頭　head　会L7(e)
あたまがいい　頭がいい　bright; smart;
　clever　会L7
あたらしい　新しい　new　会L5
あつい　熱い　hot (thing)　会L5
あつい　暑い　hot (weather)　会L5
(〜の) あと　後　after (an event)
　　　読L8-II, 会L11
あとで　後で　later on　会L6
あなた　you　会L4
あに　兄　(my) older brother　会L7
あね　姉　(my) older sister　会L7
あの　that ... (over there)　会L2
あのう　um ...　会L1

アボカド　avocado　会L8(e)
あまい　甘い　sweet　会L12
あまのがわ　天の川　the Milky Way
　　　読L12-II
あまり + negative　not much　会L3
あめ　雨　rain　会L8
アメリカ　U.S.A.　会L1
あらう　洗う　to wash [u]　会L8
ありがとう　Thank you.　会G
ありがとうございます　Thank you.
　(polite)　会G
ある　there is ... [u]　会L4
ある〜　one ...　読L12-II
あるいて　歩いて　on foot　会L10
あるく　歩く　to walk [u]　会L12
アルバイト　part-time job　会L4
あれ　that one (over there)　会L2
アレルギー　allergy　会L8(e), 会L12
アンケート　questionnaire　読L8-II
あんないする　案内する　to show
　(someone) around [irr.]　読L9-II

いい　good　会L3
いいえ　No.; Not at all.　会G
いいこ　いい子　good child　会L9
いいこと　good deed　読L10-II
いう　言う　to say [u]　会L8
いえ　家　home; house　会L3
〜いき　〜行き　bound for ...　会L10(e)
イギリス　Britain　会L1, 会L2
いく　行く　to go [u]　会L3
いくら　how much　会L2
いしゃ　医者　doctor　会L1, 会L10
いじわる (な)　意地悪　mean-spirited
　　　会L9
いす　chair　会L2(e), 会L4
いそがしい　忙しい　busy (people/days)
　　　会L5
いそぐ　急ぐ　to hurry [u]　会L6
いたい　痛い　hurt; painful　会L12
いただきます　Thank you for the meal.
　(before eating)　会G
いたみどめ　痛み止め　painkiller
　　　会L12(e)
イタリア　Italy　読L6-III
いちがつ　一月　January　会L4(e)
いちご　strawberry　会L8(e)
いちごうしゃ　一号車　Car No. 1
　　　会L10(e)
いちじ　一時　one o'clock　会L1, 会L1(e)
いちじかん　一時間　one hour　会L4

いちねんせい　一年生　first-year student
　　　会L1
いちねんにいちど　一年に一度　once a
　year　読L12-II
いちばん　一番　best　会L10
いつ　when　会L3
いつか　五日　the fifth day of a month
　　　会L4(e)
いっしょに　一緒に　together　会L5
いつつ　五つ　five　会L9
いってきます　I'll go and come back.　会G
いってらっしゃい　Please go and come
　back.　会G
いっぷん　一分　one minute　会L1(e)
いつも　always　読L6-III, 会L8
いぬ　犬　dog　会L4
いま　今　now　会L1
いみ　意味　meaning　会L11(e), 会L12
いもうと (さん)　妹 (さん)　younger
　sister　会L1, 会L7
いらっしゃいませ　Welcome (to our
　store).　会L2
いりぐち　入口　entrance　会L10(e)
いる　(a person) is in ...; stays at ... [ru]
　　　会L4
いる　to need [u]　会L8
いろ　色　color　会L9
いろいろ (な)　various　読L9-II
インド　India　会L1
インフルエンザ　influenza　会L12

ううん　uh-uh; no　会L8
うえ　上　on　会L4
うし　牛　cow　読L12-II
うしろ　後ろ　back　会L4
うそをつく　to tell a lie [u]　会L11
うた　歌　song　会L7
うたう　歌う　to sing [u]　会L7
うち　home; house; my place　会L3
うちゅうひこうし　宇宙飛行士
　astronaut　会L11
うみ　海　sea　会L5
うる　売る　to sell [u]　読L10-II
うん　uh-huh; yes　会L8
うんてんする　運転する　to drive [irr.]
　　　会L8
うんどうする　運動する　to exercise
　[irr.]　会L9

エアコン　air conditioner　会L6

えいが 映画 movie 会L3
えいご 英語 English language 会L2
ええ yes 会L3
えき 駅 station 読L6-I, 会L10
エジプト Egypt 会L1
L サイズ（エルサイズ） size L 会L5
〜えん 〜円 ...yen 会L2

おいしい delicious 会L2
おうふく 往復 round trip 会L10(e)
おおい 多い there are many... 会L12
おおきい 大きい large 会L5
オーストラリア Australia 会L1, 会L11
おかあさん お母さん mother
　　　　　　　　　　会L1, 会L2
おかえり（なさい） Welcome home. 会G
おかし お菓子 snack; sweets 会L11
おかね お金 money 会L6
おかねもち お金持ち rich person
　　　　　　　　　　　　会L10
おきる 起きる to get up [ru] 会L3
おこる 怒る to get angry [u] 読L12-II
おさけ お酒 sake; alcoholic drink 会L3
おじいさん grandfather; old man 会L7
おしえる 教える to teach; to instruct
　[ru] 会L6
おじぞうさん guardian deity of children
　　　　　　　　　　　読L10-II
おしょうがつ お正月 New Year's
　　　　　　　　読L10-II, 会L11
おしり buttocks 会L7(e)
おしろ お城 castle 読L5-II
おそい 遅い slow; late 会L10
おそく 遅く (do something) late
　　　　　　　読L4-III, 会L8
おそくなる 遅くなる to be late [u]
　　　　　　　　　　　会L8
おだいじに お大事に Get well soon.
　　　　　　　　　　　会L12
おちゃ お茶 green tea 会L3
おてあらい お手洗い restroom 会L12
おてら お寺 temple 会L4
おとうさん お父さん father 会L1, 会L2
おとうと（さん） 弟（さん） younger
　brother 会L1, 会L7
おとこのひと 男の人 man
　　　　　　　読L5-II, 会L7
おととい the day before yesterday 会L4(e)
おととし the year before last 会L4(e)
おとな 大人 adult 読L12-II
おどる 踊る to dance [u] 会L9
おなか stomach 会L7(e), 会L12
おなかがすく to become hungry [u]
　　　　　　　　　　　会L11

おなじ 同じ same 会L12
おにいさん お兄さん older brother
　　　　　　　　会L1, 会L7
おねえさん お姉さん older sister
　　　　　　　　会L1, 会L7
おねがいします（〜を） ..., please. 会L2
おばあさん grandmother; old woman
　　　　　　　　　　　会L7
おはよう Good morning. 会G
おはようございます Good morning.
　(polite) 会G
おふろ お風呂 bath 会L8
おふろにはいる お風呂に入る to take
　a bath [u] 会L8
おへんじ お返事 reply 読L11-II
おべんとう お弁当 boxed lunch 会L9
おぼえる 覚える to memorize [ru]
　　　　　　　　　　　会L9
おまつり お祭り festival 会L11
おまんじゅう sweet bun 読L4-III
おみやげ お土産 souvenir 会L5
おもう 思う to think [u] 会L8
おもしろい 面白い interesting; funny
　　　　　　　　　　　会L5
おもち rice cake 読L10-II
おもちゃ toy 会L11
おやすみ（なさい） Good night. 会G
およぐ 泳ぐ to swim [u] 会L5
おりる 降りる to get off [ru] 会L6
オレンジ orange 会L9(e)
おわる 終わる (something) ends [u]
　　　　　　　　　　　会L9
おんがく 音楽 music 会L3
おんせん 温泉 spa; hot spring 会L11
おんなのひと 女の人 woman
　　　　　　　読L5-II, 会L7

〜か〜 or 会L10
〜が ..., but 読L5-II, 会L7
カーテン curtain 会L2(e)
がいこく 外国 foreign country 会L11
かいさつ 改札 gate 会L10(e)
かいしゃ 会社 company 会L7
かいしゃいん 会社員 office worker
　　　　　　　　会L1, 会L8
かいだん 階段 stairs 会L10(e)
かいもの 買い物 shopping 会L4
かう 買う to buy [u] 会L4
かう 飼う to own (a pet) [u] 会L11
かえす 返す to return (a thing) [u]
　　　　　　　　　　　会L6
かえる 帰る to go back; to return [u]
　　　　　　　　　　　会L3
かお 顔 face 会L7(e), 会L10

かおがあおい 顔が青い to look pale
　　　　　　　　　　会L9(e)
かかる to take (amount of time/money)
　[u] 会L10
かく 書く to write [u] 会L4
がくせい 学生 student 会L1
がくわり 学割 student discount
　　　　　　　　　　会L10(e)
〜かげつ 〜か月 for...months 会L10
かける（めがねを） to put on (glasses) [ru]
　　　　　　　　　　　会L7
かさ bamboo hat 読L10-II
かさ 傘 umbrella 会L2
かし 菓子 snack; sweets 会L11
かしゅ 歌手 singer 会L11
かぜ 風邪 cold 会L12
かぜをひく 風邪をひく to catch a cold
　[u] 会L12
かぞく 家族 family 会L7
かた 肩 shoulder 会L7(e)
かたいいいかた かたい言い方
　bookish expression 会L11(e)
かたみち 片道 one way 会L10(e)
かっこ parenthesis 会L11(e)
かっこいい good-looking 会L5
がっこう 学校 school 会L3
かど 角 corner 会L6(e)
かなう to be realized [u] 読L12-II
カナダ Canada 会L1
かなしい 悲しい sad 読L10-II
かね 金 money 会L6
かねもち 金持ち rich person 会L10
かのじょ 彼女 she; girlfriend 会L12
かばん bag 会L2
カフェ cafe 会L3
かぶき 歌舞伎 Kabuki; traditional
　Japanese theatrical art 会L9
かぶせる to put (a hat) on a person's head
　[ru] 読L10-II
かぶる to put on (a hat) [u] 会L7
かふんしょう 花粉症 hay fever
　　　　　　　　　　会L12(e)
かみ 髪 hair 会L7, 会L7(e)
かみさま 神様 God 読L12-II
カメラ camera 会L8
かようび 火曜日 Tuesday 会L4, 会L4(e)
〜から from... 読L7-II, 会L9
カラオケ karaoke 会L8
からだにきをつける 体に気をつける
　to take care of oneself [ru] 読L7-II
かりる 借りる to borrow [ru] 会L6
かれ 彼 he; boyfriend 会L12
かれし 彼氏 boyfriend 会L12
かわ 川 river 会L11
かわいい cute 会L7

かわいそう（な）　pitiful　読L12-II
がんか　眼科　ophthalmologist　会L12(e)
かんこく　韓国　Korea　会L1, 会L2
かんごし　看護師　nurse　会L1, 会L11
かんじ　漢字　kanji; Chinese character
　　　会L6
かんたん（な）　簡単　easy; simple　会L10
かんぱい　乾杯　Cheers! (a toast)　会L8

きいろい　黄色い　yellow　会L9(e)
きおん　気温　temperature (weather)
　　　会L8
きく　聞く　to ask [u]　会L5
きく　聞く　to listen; to hear [u]　会L3
きせつ　季節　season　会L10
きた　北　north　会L6(e)
ギター　guitar　会L9
きっぷ　切符　train ticket　会L12
きっぷうりば　切符売り場　ticket
　　vending area　会L10(e)
きのう　昨日　yesterday　会L4, 会L4(e)
きぶんがわるい　気分が悪い　not to feel
　　well　会L12(e)
きめる　決める　to decide [ru]　会L10
きもの　着物　kimono; Japanese
　　traditional dress　読L9-II
キャベツ　cabbage　会L8(e)
キャンプ　camp　会L11
きゅうこう　急行　express　会L10(e)
ぎゅうにく　牛肉　beef　会L8(e)
ぎゅうにゅう　牛乳　milk　会L10
きゅうふん　九分　nine minutes　会L1(e)
きゅうり　cucumber　会L8(e)
きょう　今日　today　会L3, 会L4(e)
きょうかしょ　教科書　textbook　会L6
きょうし　教師　schoolteacher　会L11
きょうだい　兄弟　brothers and sisters
　　　会L7
きょうつうご　共通語　common
　　language　会L11(e)
きょうみがある　興味がある　to be
　　interested (in) [u]　会L12
〜ぎょうめ　〜行目　line number ...
　　　会L11(e)
きょねん　去年　last year　会L4(e), 会L9
きらい（な）　嫌い　disgusted with; to
　　dislike　会L5
きる　切る　to cut [u]　会L8
きる　着る　to put on (clothes above your
　　waist) [ru]　会L5
きれい（な）　beautiful; clean　会L5
きんいろ　金色　gold　会L9(e)
ぎんいろ　銀色　silver　会L9(e)
ぎんこう　銀行　bank　会L2

きんじょ　近所　neighborhood　読L11-II
きんちょうする　緊張する　to get
　　nervous [irr.]　会L12
きんようび　金曜日　Friday
　　　会L4, 会L4(e)

くがつ　九月　September　会L4(e)
くじ　九時　nine o'clock　会L1(e)
くしゃみ　sneeze　会L12(e)
くすり　薬　medicine　会L9
くすりをのむ　薬を飲む　to take
　　medicine [u]　会L9
くだけたいいかた　くだけた言い方
　　colloquial expression　会L11(e)
ください（〜を）　Please give me ...　会L2
くだもの　果物　fruit　会L5
くち　口　mouth　会L7, 会L7(e)
くつ　靴　shoes　会L2
くに　国　country; place of origin　会L6
くび　首　neck　会L7(e)
くもり　曇り　cloudy weather　会L8
〜ぐらい　about (approximate
　　measurement)　会L4
クラス　class　会L4
グリーン　green　会L9(e)
くる　来る　to come [irr.]　会L3
くるま　車　car　会L7
グレー　gray　会L9(e)
くろい　黒い　black　会L9, 会L9(e)

けいざい　経済　economics　会L1, 会L2
けいさつかん　警察官　police officer
　　　会L11
ケーキ　cake　会L10
ゲーム　game　会L4
けが　injury　会L12(e)
げか　外科　surgeon　会L12(e)
けさ　今朝　this morning　会L8
けしゴム　消しゴム　eraser　会L2(e)
けす　消す　to turn off; to erase [u]　会L6
けっこうです　結構です　That would be
　　fine.; That wouldn't be necessary.　会L6
けっこんする　結婚する　to get married
　　[irr.]　会L7
げつようび　月曜日　Monday
　　　会L4, 会L4(e)
げり　下痢　diarrhea　会L12(e)
けんかする　to have a fight; to quarrel [irr.]
　　　会L11
げんき（な）　元気　healthy; energetic
　　　会L5
げんきがない　元気がない　don't look
　　well　会L12

けんきゅうしゃ　研究者　researcher
　　　会L11

〜ご　〜後　in ... time; after ...　会L10
〜ご　〜語　... language　会L1
こうえん　公園　park　会L4
こうこう　高校　high school　会L1
こうこうせい　高校生　high school
　　student　会L1
こうせいぶっしつ　抗生物質　antibiotic
　　　会L12(e)
こうつうけいICカード　交通系ICカー
　　ド　rechargeable card such as Suica,
　　Icoca, Pasmo, etc.　会L10(e)
こえ　声　voice　読L10-II
コーヒー　coffee　会L3
ゴールド　gold　会L9(e)
ごがつ　五月　May　会L4(e)
こくさいかんけい　国際関係
　　international relations　会L1
こくばん　黒板　blackboard　会L2(e)
ここ　here　会L2
ごご　午後　P.M.　会L1
ここのか　九日　the ninth day of a month
　　　会L4(e)
ここのつ　九つ　nine　会L9
ごじ　五時　five o'clock　会L1(e)
ごぜん　午前　A.M.　会L1
ごぜんちゅう　午前中　in the morning
　　　読L9-II
こたえ　答　answer　会L11(e)
こたえる　答える　to answer [ru]　読L8-II
ごちそう　excellent food　読L9-II
ごちそうさま（でした）　Thank you for
　　the meal. (after eating)　会G
こちら　this person (polite)　会L11
こっせつする　骨折する　to break (a
　　bone)　会L12(e)
こと　things; matters　読L11-II
ことし　今年　this year　会L4(e), 会L10
こども　子供　child　会L4
この　this ...　会L2
このあいだ　この間　the other day
　　　読L8-II
このごろ　these days　会L10
ごはん　ご飯　rice; meal　会L4
ごふん　五分　five minutes　会L1(e)
ごめんなさい　I'm sorry.　会L4
これ　this one　会L2
これから　from now on　読L11-II
〜ごろ　at about ...　会L3
ごろごろする　to chill out at home; to stay
　　home do nothing [irr.]　会L10
こわい　怖い　frightening　会L5

こんいろ　紺色　navy　会L9(e)	
こんがっき　今学期　this semester　会L11	
こんげつ　今月　this month	
	会L4(e), 会L8
コンサート　concert　会L9	
こんしゅう　今週　this week	
	会L4(e), 会L6
こんど　今度　near future　会L9	
こんにちは　Good afternoon.　会G	
こんばん　今晩　tonight　会L3	
こんばんは　Good evening.　会G	
コンビニ　convenience store　会L2	
コンピューター　computer　会L1, 会L2	

さ

サークル　club activity　会L7	
サーフィン　surfing　会L5	
～さい　～歳　...years old　会L1	
さいごに　最後に　lastly　読L8-II	
さいふ　財布　wallet　会L2	
さかな　魚　fish　会L2	
さくぶん　作文　essay; composition　会L9	
さけ　酒　sake; alcohol　会L3	
さっか　作家　writer　会L11	
サッカー　soccer　会L10	
ざっし　雑誌　magazine　会L3	
さびしい　寂しい　lonely　会L9	
サボる　to cut (classes) [u]　会L11	
～さま　～様　Mr./Ms. ...　読L5-II	
さむい　寒い　cold (weather)　会L5	
さようなら　Good-bye.　会G	
さらいげつ　再来月　the month after	
next　会L4(e)	
さらいしゅう　再来週　the week after	
next　会L4(e)	
さらいねん　再来年　the year after next	
	会L4(e)
～さん　Mr./Ms. ...　会L1	
さんがつ　三月　March　会L4(e)	
ざんぎょう　残業　overtime work　読L8-II	
さんじ　三時　three o'clock　会L1(e)	
さんじっぷん/さんじゅっぷん　三十分	
thirty minutes　会L1(e)	
ざんねん（ですね）　残念（ですね）	
That's too bad.　会L8	
さんふじんか　産婦人科　obstetrician	
and gynecologist　会L12(e)	
さんぷん　三分　three minutes　会L1(e)	
さんぽする　散歩する　to take a walk	
[irr.]　会L9	

し

～じ　～時　o'clock　会L1	
しあい　試合　match; game　会L12	
しあわせ（な）　幸せ　happy　読L10-II	

ジーンズ　jeans　会L2	
シェフ　chef　読L6-III, 会L11	
しか　歯科　dentist　会L12(e)	
しがつ　四月　April　会L4(e)	
じかん　時間　time　会L10	
～じかん　～時間　...hours　会L4	
しけん　試験　exam　会L9	
じしょ　辞書　dictionary　会L2(e)	
しずか（な）　静か　quiet　会L5	
じぞう　guardian deity of children	
	読L10-II
した　下　under　会L4	
しちがつ　七月　July　会L4(e)	
しちじ　七時　seven o'clock　会L1(e)	
しっています　知っています　I know	
	会L7
じっぷん　十分　ten minutes　会L1(e)	
しつもん　質問　question　会L11(e)	
していせき　指定席　reserved seat	
	会L10(e)
じてんしゃ　自転車　bicycle　会L2	
しぬ　死ぬ　to die [u]　会L6	
じはつ　次発　departing second　会L10(e)	
じびか　耳鼻科　otorhinolaryngologist;	
ENT doctor　会L12(e)	
じぶん　自分　oneself　読L10-II	
しめきり　締め切り　deadline　会L11(e)	
しめる　閉める　to close (something) [ru]	
	会L6
じゃあ　then ...; if that is the case, ...　会L2	
ジャーナリスト　journalist　会L11	
じゃがいも　potato　会L8(e)	
しゃしん　写真　picture; photograph　会L4	
しゃちょう　社長　president of a	
company　会L11	
シャワー　shower　会L6	
シャワーをあびる　シャワーを浴びる	
to take a shower [ru]　会L6	
じゅういちがつ　十一月　November	
	会L4(e)
じゅういちじ　十一時　eleven o'clock	
	会L1(e)
じゅういちにち　十一日　the eleventh	
day of a month　会L4(e)	
じゅういっぷん　十一分　eleven minutes	
	会L1(e)
じゅうがつ　十月　October　会L4(e)	
～しゅうかん　～週間　for ... weeks	
	会L10
じゅうきゅうふん　十九分　nineteen	
minutes　会L1(e)	
じゅうごふん　十五分　fifteen minutes	
	会L1(e)
じゅうさんぷん　十三分　thirteen	
minutes　会L1(e)	

じゅうじ　十時　ten o'clock　会L1(e)	
じゆうせき　自由席　general admission	
seat　会L10(e)	
しゅうでん　終電　last train　会L10(e)	
じゅうななふん　十七分　seventeen	
minutes　会L1(e)	
じゅうにがつ　十二月　December	
	会L4(e)
じゅうにじ　十二時　twelve o'clock	
	会L1(e)
じゅうにふん　十二分　twelve minutes	
	会L1(e)
じゅうはちふん/じゅうはっぷん　十八	
分　eighteen minutes　会L1(e)	
しゅうまつ　週末　weekend　会L3	
じゅうよっか　十四日　the fourteenth	
day of a month　会L4(e)	
じゅうよんぷん　十四分　fourteen	
minutes　会L1(e)	
じゅうろっぷん　十六分　sixteen	
minutes　会L1(e)	
じゅぎょう　授業　class　会L11	
じゅく　塾　cram school　読L7-II	
しゅくだい　宿題　homework　会L5	
しゅじゅつ　手術　operation　会L12(e)	
しゅっしん　出身　coming from　会L11	
じゅっぷん　十分　ten minutes　会L1(e)	
しゅふ　主婦　housewife　会L1	
ジュース　juice　会L12	
しょうかいする　紹介する　to introduce	
[irr.]　会L11	
しょうがつ　正月　New Year's	
	読L10-II, 会L11
じょうしゃけん　乗車券　(boarding)	
ticket　会L10(e)	
じょうず（な）　上手　skillful; good at ...	
	会L8
しょうぼうし　消防士　firefighter　会L11	
しょうらい　将来　future　会L11	
しょくご　食後　after meals　会L12(e)	
しょくどう　食堂　cafeteria; dining	
commons　会L7	
しり　buttocks　会L7(e)	
しりません　知りません　I do not know	
	会L7
しる　知る　to get to know [u]　会L7	
シルバー　silver　会L9(e)	
しろ　城　castle　読L5-II	
しろい　白い　white　会L9, 会L9(e)	
しろくろ　白黒　black and white　会L9(e)	
～じん　～人　...people　会L1	
しんかんせん　新幹線　Shinkansen;	
"Bullet Train"　会L10	
しんごう　信号　traffic light　会L6(e)	
じんじゃ　神社　shrine　会L11	

しんせつ (な)　親切　kind　会L7
しんぱいする　心配する　to worry [irr.]
　　　　会L12
しんぶん　新聞　newspaper　会L2

すいか　watermelon　会L8(e)
すいようび　水曜日　Wednesday
　　　　会L4, 会L4(e)
スーパー　supermarket　会L4
すき (な)　好き　fond of; to like　会L5
スキー　ski　会L9
すぐ　right away　会L6
すごく　extremely　会L5
すこし　少し　a little　読L7-II
すし　sushi　会L10
すずしい　涼しい　cool (weather)　会L10
すてき (な)　素敵　nice　会L12
すてる　捨てる　to throw away [ru]　会L8
ストレス　stress　読L8-II
スペイン　Spain　会L8
スポーツ　sports　会L3
スポーツせんしゅ　スポーツ選手
　　athlete　会L11
スマホ　smartphone; mobile　会L2
すみません　Excuse me.; I'm sorry.　会G
すむ　住む　to live [u]　会L7
する　to do [irr.]　会L3
すわる　座る　to sit down [u]　会L6

せいかつ　生活　life; living　会L10
せいけいげか　整形外科　orthopedic
　　surgeon　会L12(e)
せいじ　政治　politics　会L1, 会L12
せいせき　成績　grade (on a test, etc.)
　　　　会L12
せいぶつがく　生物学　biology　会L1
せいり　生理　period　会L12(e)
せかい　世界　world　会L10
せがたかい　背が高い　tall (stature)
　　　　会L7
せがひくい　背が低い　short (stature)
　　　　会L7
せき　cough　会L12
せきがでる　せきが出る　to cough [ru]
　　　　会L12
せなか　背中　back (body)　会L7(e)
ぜひ　是非　by all means　会L9
せまい　狭い　narrow; not spacious　会L12
せんげつ　先月　last month
　　　　会L4(e), 会L9
せんこう　専攻　major　会L1
せんしゅう　先週　last week
　　　　会L4, 会L4(e)

せんせい　先生　teacher; Professor . . .
　　　　会L1
ぜんぜん + negative　全然　not at all
　　　　会L3
せんたくする　洗濯する　to do laundry
　　[irr.]　会L8
せんぱつ　先発　departing first　会L10(e)

そう　(I think) so　会L9
そうじする　掃除する　to clean [irr.]
　　　　会L8
そうです　That's right.　会L1
そうですか　I see.; Is that so?　会L1
そうですね　That's right.; Let me see.
　　　　会L3
そこ　there　会L2
そして　and then　読L9-II, 会L11
その　that . . .　会L2
それ　that one　会L2
それから　and then　会L4
それに　moreover, . . .　会L12

ダイエットする　to go on a diet [irr.]
　　　　会L11
たいおんけい　体温計　thermometer
　　　　会L12(e)
〜だい　〜代　charge; fee　会L12
だいがく　大学　college; university　会L1
だいがくいんせい　大学院生　graduate
　　student　会L1
だいがくせい　大学生　college student
　　　　会L1
だいきらい (な)　大嫌い　to hate　会L5
だいじょうぶ　大丈夫　It's okay.; Not
　　to worry.; Everything is under control.
　　　　会L5
だいすき (な)　大好き　very fond of; to
　　love　会L5
たいてい　usually　会L3
だいとうりょう　大統領　president of a
　　country　会L11
たいへん (な)　大変　tough (situation)
　　　　読L5-II, 会L6
たかい　高い　expensive; high　会L2
だから　so; therefore　会L4
たくさん　many; a lot　会L4
〜だけ　just . . . ; only . . .　会L11
ただいま　I'm home.　会G
たつ　立つ　to stand up [u]　会L6
たとえば　例えば　for example　会L11(e)
たのしい　楽しい　fun　会L5
たのしみにする (〜を)　楽しみにする
　　to look forward (to) [irr.]　読L7-II

たばこをすう　たばこを吸う　to smoke
　　[u]　会L6
たぶん　多分　probably; maybe　会L12
たべもの　食べ物　food　会L5
たべる　食べる　to eat [ru]　会L3
たまご　卵　egg　会L12
たまねぎ　onion　会L8(e)
だれ　who　会L2
たんご　単語　word; vocabulary　会L9
たんざく　strip of fancy paper　読L12-II
たんじょうび　誕生日　birthday　会L5

ちいさい　小さい　small　会L5
ちかく　近く　near; nearby　会L4
ちかてつ　地下鉄　subway　会L10
チケット　ticket　会L9
ちこくする　遅刻する　to be late (for an
　　appointment) [irr.]　会L11
ちち　父　(my) father　会L7
ちゃ　茶　green tea　会L3
ちゃいろい　茶色い　brown　会L9(e)
ちゅうごく　中国　China　会L1, 会L2
ちゅうしゃ　注射　injection　会L12(e)
ちょっと　a little　会L3

ツアー　tour　会L10
ついたち　一日　the first day of a month
　　　　会L4(e)
つかう　使う　to use [u]　会L6
つかれている　疲れている　to be tired
　　　　読L8-II
つかれる　疲れる　to get tired [ru]
　　　　会L11
つぎ　次　next　会L6
つぎに　次に　secondly　読L8-II
つぎは〜　次は〜　next (stop), . . .
　　　　会L10(e)
つくえ　机　desk　会L2(e), 会L4
つくる　作る　to make [u]　会L8
つける　to turn on [ru]　会L6
つまらない　boring　会L5
つめたい　冷たい　cold (things/people)
　　　　会L10
つり　fishing　会L11
つれてかえる　連れて帰る　to bring (a
　　person) back [u]　読L12-II
つれてくる　連れてくる　to bring (a
　　person) [irr.]　会L6

て　手　hand; arm　会L7(e)
〜で　by (means of transportation); with (a
　　tool)　会L10

Tシャツ (ティーシャツ)　T-shirt　会L2
ていきけん　定期券　commuter's pass　会L10(e)
ていねいないいいかた　ていねいな言い方　polite expression　会L11(e)
デート　date (romantic, not calendar)　会L3
でかける　出かける　to go out [ru]　会L5
てがみ　手紙　letter　会L9
できるだけ　as much as possible　会L12
でぐち　出口　exit　会L10(e)
～です　I am ....　会G
テスト　test　会L5
てつだう　手伝う　to help [u]　会L6
テニス　tennis　会L3
では、おげんきで　では、お元気で　Take care.　読L5-II
デパート　department store　会L7
てぶくろ　手袋　gloves　会L10
でも　but　会L3
てら　寺　temple　会L4
でる　出る　to appear; to attend; to exit [ru]　読L6-I, 会L9
テレビ　TV　会L3
てん　天　the heavens; the sky　読L12-II
～てん　～点　...points　会L11
てんき　天気　weather　会L5
でんき　電気　electricity; light　会L2(e), 会L6
てんきよほう　天気予報　weather forecast　会L8
でんしゃ　電車　train　会L6
てんてき　点滴　intravenous feeding　会L12(e)
てんぷら　天ぷら　tempura　会L10
でんわ　電話　telephone　会L1
でんわする　電話する　to call [irr.]　会L6

と　戸　door　読L10-II
～と　together with (a person); and　会L4
～ど　～度　...degrees (temperature)　会L8
ドア　door　会L2(e)
トイレ　toilet; restroom　会L2
どう　how　会L8
どうして　why　会L4
どうぞ　Please.; Here it is.　会L2
どうですか　How about ...?; How is ...?　会L3
どうぶつえん　動物園　zoo　会L10
どうも　Thank you.　会L2
どうやって　how; by what means　会L10
とお　十　ten　会L9
とおか　十日　the tenth day of a month　会L4(e)

とき　時　when ...; at the time of ...　会L4
ときどき　時々　sometimes　会L3
とけい　時計　watch; clock　会L2
どこ　where　会L2
ところ　所　place　会L8
ところで　by the way　会L9
とし　年　year　読L10-II
としうえ　年上　someone older　会L10
としょかん　図書館　library　会L2
どちら　which　会L10
とっきゅう　特急　super express　会L10(e)
どっち　which　会L10
とても　very　会L5
となり　隣　next　会L4
どの　which ...　会L2
どのぐらい　how much; how long　会L10
トマト　tomato　会L8
とまる　泊まる　to stay (at a hotel, etc.) [u]　会L10
ともだち　友だち　friend　会L1
どようび　土曜日　Saturday　会L3, 会L4(e)
ドライブ　drive　会L11
とりにく　鶏肉　chicken　会L8(e)
とる　撮る　to take (a picture) [u]　会L4
とる　取る　to take (a class); to get (a grade) [u]　読L7-II, 会L11
とる　to take off [u]　読L10-II
どれ　which one　会L2
とんかつ　pork cutlet　会L2
どんな　what kind of ...　会L5

ないか　内科　physician　会L12(e)
なか　中　inside　会L4
ながい　長い　long　会L7
なく　泣く　to cry [u]　読L12-II
なくす　to lose [u]　会L12
なす　eggplant　会L8(e)
なつ　夏　summer　会L8
～など　and so forth　読L12-II
ななつ　七つ　seven　会L9
ななふん　七分　seven minutes　会L1(e)
なにか　何か　something　会L8
なにも + negative　何も　not ... anything　会L7
なのか　七日　the seventh day of a month　会L4(e)
なまえ　名前　name　会L1
ならう　習う　to learn [u]　会L11
なる　to become [u]　会L10
なん/なに　何　what　会L1

にかげつまえ　二か月前　two months ago　会L4(e)
にがつ　二月　February　会L4(e)
にぎやか (な)　lively　会L5
にく　肉　meat　会L2
にさんにち　二三日　for two to three days　会L12
にし　西　west　会L6(e)
にじ　二時　two o'clock　会L1(e)
にじっぷん　二十分　twenty minutes　会L1(e)
にじはん　二時半　half past two　会L1
にしゅうかんまえ　二週間前　two weeks ago　会L4(e)
にじゅうよっか　二十四日　the twenty-fourth day of a month　会L4(e)
にじゅっぷん　二十分　twenty minutes　会L1(e)
にちようび　日曜日　Sunday　会L3, 会L4(e)
～について　about ...; concerning ...　会L8
にっき　日記　diary　読L9-II
にふん　二分　two minutes　会L1(e)
にほん　日本　Japan　会L1
にほんご　日本語　Japanese language　会L1
にほんじん　日本人　Japanese people　会L1
にもつ　荷物　baggage　会L6
～にん　～人　[counter for people]　会L7
にんきがある　人気がある　to be popular [u]　会L9
にんじん　carrot　会L8(e)

ねがい　願い　wish　読L12-II
ねこ　猫　cat　会L4
ねつがある　熱がある　to have a fever [u]　会L12
ねむい　眠い　sleepy　会L10
ねる　寝る　to sleep; to go to sleep [ru]　会L3
～ねん　～年　...years　会L10
～ねんせい　～年生　...year student　会L1

ノート　notebook　会L2
のど　throat　会L12
のどがかわく　のどが渇く　to become thirsty [u]　会L12
のぼる　登る　to climb [u]　会L11

のみもの　飲み物　drink　会L5
のむ　飲む　to drink [u]　会L3
のりかえ　乗り換え　transfer　会L10(e)
のる　乗る　to ride; to board [u]　会L5

は　歯　tooth　会L7(e), 会L12
パーティー　party　会L8
バーベキュー　barbecue　会L8
はい　yes　会L1
はいいろ　灰色　gray　会L9(e)
ばいてん　売店　shop; stand　会L10(e)
はいゆう　俳優　actor; actress　会L11
はいる　入る　to enter [u]　会L6
はく　to put on (items below your waist) [u]
　　会L7
はく　吐く　to throw up　会L12(e)
はし　chopsticks　会L8
はじまる　始まる　(something) begins
　[u]　会L9
はじめて　初めて　for the first time
　　　　会L12
はじめまして　How do you do ?　会G
はじめる　始める　to begin [ru]　会L8
はしる　走る　to run [u]　会L11
バス　bus　会L5
バスてい　バス停　bus stop　会L4
パソコン　personal computer　会L6
はたけ　畑　farm　読L12-II
はたらく　働く　to work [u]　会L7
はたをおる　はたを織る　to weave [u]
　　　　読L12-II
はちがつ　八月　August　会L4(e)
はちじ　八時　eight o'clock　会L1(e)
はちふん　八分　eight minutes　会L1(e)
ばつ　×（wrong）　会L11(e)
はつおん　発音　pronunciation　会L11(e)
はつか　二十日　the twentieth day of a
　month　会L4(e)
はっしん　発疹　rash　会L12(e)
はっぷん　八分　eight minutes　会L1(e)
はな　鼻　nose　会L7(e)
はな　花　flower　会L4
はなし　話　story; talk　読L8-II
はなしをする　話をする　to have a talk
　[irr.]　読L9-II
はなす　話す　to speak; to talk [u]　会L3
はなみず　鼻水　runny nose　会L12(e)
はは　母　(my) mother　会L7
はやい　早い　early　会L3
はやい　速い　fast　会L7
はやく　早く / 速く　(do something)
　early; fast　会L10
はらう　払う　to pay [u]　会L12
ハラルフード　halal　会L8(e)

はる　春　spring　会L10
はれ　晴れ　sunny weather　会L8
はん　半　half　会L1
パン　bread　会L4
〜ばん　〜番　number...　会L1, 会L11(e)
ばんごう　番号　number　会L1
ばんごはん　晩ご飯　dinner　会L3
〜ばんせん　〜番線　track number...
　　　　会L10(e)
バンド　band　読L11-II
ハンバーガー　hamburger　会L3

ピアノ　piano　会L9
ピーナッツ　peanut　会L8(e)
ビール　beer　会L11
ひがし　東　east　会L6(e)
ひく　弾く　to play (a string instrument or
　piano) [u]　会L9
ひこうき　飛行機　airplane　会L10
ピザ　pizza　読L6-III, 会L9
ひさしぶり　久しぶり　it has been a long
　time　会L11
ビジネス　business　会L1, 会L2
びじゅつかん　美術館　art museum
　　　　会L11
ひだり　左　left　会L4
ひだりがわ　左側　left side　会L6(e)
びっくりする　to be surprised [irr.]
　　　　読L10-II
ひと　人　person　会L4
ひとつ　一つ　one　会L9
ひとつめ　一つ目　first　会L6(e)
ひとびと　人々　people　読L12-II
ひとり　一人　one person　会L7
ひとりで　一人で　alone　会L4
ひふか　皮膚科　dermatologist　会L12(e)
ひま（な）　暇　not busy; free (time)　会L5
びよういん　美容院　beauty parlor　会L10
びょういん　病院　hospital　会L4
びょうき　病気　illness; sickness
　　　　会L9, 会L12(e)
ひる　昼　noon　読L9-II
ひるごはん　昼ご飯　lunch　会L3
ひろい　広い　wide; spacious　会L12
ピンク　pink　会L9(e)

フィリピン　Philippines　会L1
ふく　服　clothes　会L12
ふくろ　袋　bag　会L8(e)
ふたつ　二つ　two　会L9
ふたつめ　二つ目　second　会L6(e)
ぶたにく　豚肉　pork　会L8(e)
ふたり　二人　two people　会L7

ふたりずつ　二人ずつ　two people each
　　　　会L11(e)
ふつう　普通　local (train)　会L10(e)
ふつか　二日　the second day of a month
　　　　会L4(e)
ふつかよい　二日酔い　hangover　会L12
ぶどう　grape　会L8(e)
ふとっています　太っています　to be
　on the heavy side　会L7
ふとる　太る　to gain weight; overweight
　[u]　会L7
ふね　船　ship; boat　会L10
ふゆ　冬　winter　会L8
ふる（あめ / ゆきが）　降る（雨 / 雪が）
　(rain/snow) falls [u]　会L8
ふるい　古い　old (thing)　会L5
プレゼント　present　会L12
ふろ　風呂　bath　会L8
ふろにはいる　風呂に入る　to take a
　bath [u]　会L8
ぶんか　文化　culture　読L11-II
ぶんがく　文学　literature　会L1, 読L7-II
ぶんぽう　文法　grammar　会L11(e)

へいじつ　平日　weekday　読L11-II
へた（な）　下手　clumsy; poor at...
　　　　会L8
べつに ＋ negative　別に　nothing in
　particular　会L7
ページ　page　会L6
ベージュ　beige　会L9(e)
へや　部屋　room　会L5
ペン　pen　会L2
べんきょうする　勉強する　to study
　[irr.]　会L3
べんごし　弁護士　lawyer　会L1
へんじ　返事　reply　読L11-II
べんとう　弁当　boxed lunch　会L9
べんぴ　便秘　constipation　会L12(e)
べんり（な）　便利　convenient　会L7

ほうげん　方言　dialect　会L11(e)
ぼうし　帽子　hat; cap　会L2
〜ほうめん　〜方面　serving... areas
　　　　会L10(e)
ホーム　platform　会L10(e)
ホームシック　homesickness　会L12
ホームステイ　homestay; living with a
　local family　会L8
ほかに　anything else　会L11(e)
ぼく　僕　I (used by men)　会L5
ほけんしょう　保険証　health insurance
　certificate　会L12(e)

~ぼしゅう　~募集　looking for . . .
読L11-II

ホストファミリー　host family
読L9-II, 会L11

ホテル　hotel　会L4

ホラー　horror　読L11-II

ボランティア　volunteer　読L11-II

ほん　本　book　会L2, L2(e)

ほんとうですか　本当ですか　Really?
会L6

ほんや　本屋　bookstore　会L4

まあまあ　okay; so-so　会L11

~まい　~枚　[counter for flat objects]
会L5

まいしゅう　毎週　every week　会L8

まいにち　毎日　every day　会L3

まいばん　毎晩　every night　会L3

まえ　前　front　会L4

まがる　曲がる　to turn (right/left) [u]
会L6(e)

まじめ (な)　serious; sober; diligent
読L12-II

まず　first of all　読L8-II

まだ + negative　not . . . yet　会L8

まち　町　town; city　会L4

まつ　待つ　to wait [u]　会L4

まっすぐ　straight　会L6(e), 読L6-I

まつり　祭り　festival　会L11

~まで　to (a place/a time)　会L9

~までに　by (time/date)　読L12-II

まど　窓　window　会L2(e), 会L6

まゆげ　眉毛　eyebrow　会L7(e)

まる　○ (correct)　会L11(e)

まんがか　漫画家　cartoonist　会L11

まんじゅう　sweet bun　読L4-III

みかん　mandarin orange　会L8(e)

みぎ　右　right　会L4

みぎがわ　右側　right side　会L6(e)

みじかい　短い　short (length)　会L7

みず　水　water　会L3

みずいろ　水色　light blue　会L9(e)

みずうみ　湖　lake　会L11

みせ　店　shop; store　読L4-III

みっか　三日　the third day of a month
会L4(e)

みっつ　三つ　three　会L9

みっつめ　三つ目　third　会L6(e)

みどり　緑　green　会L9(e)

みなさん　皆さん　everyone　読L6-III

みなみ　南　south　会L6(e)

みみ　耳　ear　会L7(e)

みやげ　土産　souvenir　会L5

みる　見る　to see; to look at; to watch [ru]
会L3

みんな　all　読L7-II, 会L9

みんなで　all (of the people) together　会L8

むいか　六日　the sixth day of a month
会L4(e)

むかしむかし　昔々　once upon a time
読L10-II

むこう　向こう　the other side; over there
読L12-II

むしば　虫歯　bad tooth　会L12(e)

むずかしい　難しい　difficult　会L5

むすめ　娘　daughter　読L12-II

むっつ　六つ　six　会L9

むね　胸　breast　会L7(e)

むらさき　紫　purple　会L9(e)

め　目　eye　会L7, 会L7(e)

メール　e-mail　会L9

めがね　眼鏡　glasses　会L7

メキシコ　Mexico　読L5-II

メニュー　menu　会L2

めまいがする　to feel dizzy　会L12(e)

もう　already　会L9

もうすぐ　very soon; in a few moments/
days　会L12

もくようび　木曜日　Thursday
会L4, 会L4(e)

もしもし　Hello? (used on the phone)　会L4

もち　rice cake　読L10-II

もちろん　of course　会L7

もつ　持つ　to carry; to hold [u]　会L6

もっていく　持っていく　to take (a
thing) [u]　会L8

もってくる　持ってくる　to bring (a
thing) [irr.]　会L6

もっと　more　会L11

もの　物　thing (concrete object)　会L12

もも　peach　会L8(e)

もらう　to get (from somebody) [u]　会L9

やきゅう　野球　baseball　会L10

やけどをする　to burn oneself　会L12(e)

やさい　野菜　vegetable　会L2

やさしい　easy (problem); kind (person)
会L5

やすい　安い　inexpensive; cheap (thing)
会L5

やすみ　休み　holiday; day off; absence
会L5

やすむ　休む　to be absent (from); to rest
[u]　会L6

やせています　to be thin　会L7

やせる　to lose weight [ru]　会L7

やっつ　八つ　eight　会L9

やま　山　mountain　読L5-II, 会L11

やままち　山道　mountain road　読L10-II

やめる　to quit [ru]　会L11

やる　to do; to perform [u]　会L5

ゆうびんきょく　郵便局　post office
会L2

ゆうめい (な)　有名　famous　会L8

ゆうめいじん　有名人　celebrity　会L10

ゆき　雪　snow　読L10-II, 会L8

ゆっくり　slowly; leisurely; unhurriedly
会L6

ゆび　指　finger　会L7(e)

ゆめ　夢　dream　会L11

ようか　八日　the eighth day of a month
会L4(e)

ようじ　用事　business to take care of
会L12

よかったら　if you like　会L7

よく　often; much　会L3

よじ　四時　four o'clock　会L1(e)

よっか　四日　the fourth day of a month
会L4(e)

よっつ　四つ　four　会L9

よむ　読む　to read [u]　会L3

よやく　予約　reservation　会L10

よる　夜　night　読L5-II, 会L6

よろしくおねがいします　よろしくお願
いします　Nice to meet you.　会G

よんぷん　四分　four minutes　会L1(e)

らいがっき　来学期　next semester
会L11

らいげつ　来月　next month
会L4(e), 会L8

らいしゅう　来週　next week
会L4(e), 会L6

らいねん　来年　next year　会L4(e), 会L6

りゅうがくする　留学する　to study
abroad [irr.]　会L11

りゅうがくせい　留学生　international
student　会L1

りょう　寮　dormitory　読L9-II
りょうり　料理　cooking; dish
　　　　　読L6-III, 会L10
りょうりする　料理する　to cook [irr.]
　　　　　会L8
りょこう　旅行　travel　会L5
りょこうする　旅行する　to travel [irr.]
　　　　　会L10
りんご　apple　会L8(e), 会L10

ルームメイト　roommate　会L11

れい　例　example　会L11(e)
れきし　歴史　history　会L1, 会L2
レストラン　restaurant　会L4
レポート　(term) paper　会L4
れんしゅう　練習　exercise　会L11(e)
れんしゅうする　練習する　to practice
　　[irr.]　会L10
レントゲン　X-ray　会L12(e)

ろ

ろくがつ　六月　June　会L4(e)
ろくじ　六時　six o'clock　会L1(e)

ろっぷん　六分　six minutes　会L1(e)

ワイン　wine　読L6-III
わかい　若い　young　会L9
わかる　to understand [u]　会L4
わかれる　別れる　to break up; to
　　separate [ru]　会L12
わすれる　忘れる　to forget; to leave
　　behind [ru]　会L6
わたし　私　I　会L1
わたしたち　私たち　we　読L12-II
わたる　渡る　to cross [u]　会L6(e)
わるい　悪い　bad　会L12

A B C D E F G H I J K L M N O P Q R S T U V W X Y Z

単語さくいん2　Vocabulary Index (E-J)

会……会話・文法編
　　(Conversation and Grammar section)
読……読み書き編
　　(Reading and Writing section)
G……あいさつ (Greetings)
(e)……Useful Expressions
I・II・III……問題番号（読み書き編）
　　(number of exercise in the
　　Reading and Writing section)
[u] u-verb　[ru] ru-verb　[irr.] irregular verb

A

about (approximate measurement)
　〜ぐらい　会L4
about...　〜について　会L8
absence　やすみ　休み　会L5
absent (from)　やすむ　休む [u]　会L6
actor　はいゆう　俳優　会L11
actress　はいゆう　俳優　会L11
adult　おとな　大人　読L12-II
after...　〜ご　〜後　会L10
after (an event)　（〜の）あと　（〜の）
　後　読L8-II, 会L11
after meals　しょくご　食後　会L12(e)
air conditioner　エアコン　会L6
airplane　ひこうき　飛行機　会L10
alcoholic drink　（お）さけ　（お）酒
　　会L3
all　みんな　読L7-II, 会L9
all (of the people) together　みんなで
　　会L8
allergy　アレルギー　会L8(e), 会L12
alone　ひとりで　一人で　会L4
already　もう　会L9
always　いつも　読L6-III, 会L8
A.M.　ごぜん　午前　会L1
and　〜と　会L4
and so forth　〜など　読L12-II
and then　そして　読L9-II, 会L11
and then　それから　会L4
(get) angry　おこる　怒る [u]　読L12-II
answer　こたえ　答　会L11(e)
answer　こたえる　答える [ru]　読L8-II
antibiotic　こうせいぶっしつ　抗生物
　質　会L12(e)
anything else　ほかに　会L11(e)
appear　でる　出る [ru]　会L9
apple　りんご　会L8(e), 会L10
April　しがつ　四月　会L4(e)
arm　て　手　会L7(e)
art museum　びじゅつかん　美術館
　　会L11
as far as (a place)　〜まで　会L5
as much as possible　できるだけ　会L12

Asian studies　アジアけんきゅう　アジ
　ア研究　会L1
ask　きく　聞く [u]　会L5
astronaut　うちゅうひこうし　宇宙飛
　行士　会L11
at about...　〜ごろ　会L3
at the time of...　とき　時　会L4
athlete　スポーツせんしゅ　スポーツ
　選手　会L11
attend　でる　出る [ru]　会L9
August　はちがつ　八月　会L4(e)
Australia　オーストラリア　会L1, 会L11
avocado　アボカド　会L8(e)

B

back　うしろ　後ろ　会L4
back (body)　せなか　背中　会L7(e)
bad　わるい　悪い　会L12
bad tooth　むしば　虫歯　会L12(e)
bag　かばん　会L2
bag　ふくろ　袋　会L8(e)
baggage　にもつ　荷物　会L6
bamboo hat　かさ　会L10-II
band　バンド　読L11-II
bank　ぎんこう　銀行　会L2
barbecue　バーベキュー　会L8
baseball　やきゅう　野球　会L10
bath　（お）ふろ　（お）風呂　会L8
beautiful　きれい（な）　会L5
beauty parlor　びよういん　美容院
　　会L10
become　なる [u]　会L10
beef　ぎゅうにく　牛肉　会L8(e)
beer　ビール　会L11
begin　はじめる　始める [ru]　会L8
(something) begins　はじまる　始まる
　[u]　会L9
beige　ベージュ　会L9(e)
best　いちばん　一番　会L10
between　あいだ　間　会L4
biology　せいぶつがく　生物学　会L1
bicycle　じてんしゃ　自転車　会L2
birthday　たんじょうび　誕生日　会L5
black　くろい　黒い　会L9, 会L9(e)
black and white　しろくろ　白黒
　　会L9(e)
blackboard　こくばん　黒板　会L2(e)
blue　あおい　青い　会L9, 会L9(e)
board　のる　乗る [u]　会L5
boarding ticket　じょうしゃけん　乗車
　券　会L10
boat　ふね　船　会L10
book　ほん　本　会L2, 会L2(e)
bookish expression　かたいいいかた
　かたい言い方　会L11(e)
bookstore　ほんや　本屋　会L4

boring　つまらない　会L5
borrow　かりる　借りる [ru]　会L6
bound for...　〜いき　〜行き　会L10(e)
boxed lunch　（お）べんとう　（お）弁当
　　会L9
boyfriend　かれ／かれし　彼　会L12
bread　パン　会L4
break (a bone)　こっせつする　骨折す
　る　会L12(e)
break up　わかれる　別れる [ru]　会L12
breakfast　あさごはん　朝ご飯　会L3
breast　むね　胸　会L7(e)
bright　あたまがいい　頭がいい　会L7
bring (a person)　つれてくる　連れて
　くる [irr.]　会L6
bring (a person) back　つれてかえる
　連れて帰る [u]　読L12-II
bring (a thing)　もってくる　持ってく
　る [irr.]　会L6
Britain　イギリス　会L1, 会L2
brothers and sisters　きょうだい　兄弟
　　会L7
brown　ちゃいろい　茶色い　会L9(e)
Bullet Train　しんかんせん　新幹線
　　会L10
burn oneself　やけどをする　会L12(e)
bus　バス　会L5
bus stop　バスてい　バス停　会L4
business　ビジネス　会L1, 会L2
business to take care of　ようじ　用事
　　会L12
busy (people/days)　いそがしい　忙し
　い　会L5
but　でも　会L3
..., but　〜が　読L5-II, 会L7
buttocks　（お）しり　会L7(e)
buy　かう　買う [u]　会L4
by (means of transportation)　〜で
　　会L10
by (time/date)　〜までに　読L12-II
by all means　ぜひ　是非　会L9
by the way　ところで　会L9
by what means　どうやって　会L10

C

cabbage　キャベツ　会L8(e)
cafe　カフェ　会L3
cafeteria　しょくどう　食堂　会L7
cake　ケーキ　会L10
call　でんわする　電話する [irr.]　会L6
camera　カメラ　会L8(e)
camp　キャンプ　会L11
Canada　カナダ　会L1
cap　ぼうし　帽子　会L2
car　くるま　車　会L7
Car No. 1　いちごうしゃ　一号車　会L10(e)

A B C **D** E F G H I J K L M N O P Q R S T U V W X Y Z

---

carrot にんじん 会L8(e)

carry もつ 持つ [u] 会L6

cartoonist まんがか 漫画家 会L11

castle （お）しろ （お）城 読L5-II

cat ねこ 猫 会L4

catch a cold かぜをひく 風邪をひく [u] 会L12

celebrity ゆうめいじん 有名人 会L10

chair いす 会L2(e), 会L4

charge 〜だい 〜代 会L12

cheap (thing) やすい 安い 会L5

cheerful あかるい 明るい 読L11-II

Cheers! (a toast) かんぱい 乾杯 会L8

chef シェフ 会L11, 読L6-III

chicken とりにく 鶏肉 会L8(e)

child こども 子供 会L4

chill out at home ごろごろする [irr.] 会L10

China ちゅうごく 中国 会L1, 会L2

Chinese character かんじ 漢字 会L6

chopsticks はし 会L8

city まち 町 会L4

class クラス 会L4

class じゅぎょう 授業 会L11

clean きれい（な） 会L5

clean そうじする 掃除する [irr.] 会L8

clever あたまがいい 頭がいい 会L7

climb のぼる 登る [u] 会L11

clock とけい 時計 会L2

close (something) しめる 閉める [ru] 会L6

clothes ふく 服 会L12

cloudy weather くもり 曇り 会L8

club activity サークル 会L7

clumsy へた（な） 下手 会L8

coffee コーヒー 会L3

cold かぜ 風邪 会L12

cold (things/people) つめたい 冷たい 会L5

cold (weather) さむい 寒い 会L5

college だいがく 大学 会L1

college student だいがくせい 大学生 会L1

colloquial expression くだけたいいかた くだけた言い方 会L11(e)

color いろ 色 会L9

come くる 来る [irr.] 会L3

coming from しゅっしん 出身 会L11

common language きょうつうご 共通語 会L11(e)

commuter's pass ていきけん 定期券 会L10(e)

company かいしゃ 会社 会L7

composition さくぶん 作文 会L9

computer コンピューター 会L1, 会L2

concerning... 〜について 会L8

concert コンサート 会L9

constipation べんぴ 便秘 会L12(e)

convenience store コンビニ 会L2

---

convenient べんり（な） 便利 会L7

cook りょうりする 料理する [irr.] 会L8

cooking りょうり 料理 読L6-III

cool (weather) すずしい 涼しい 会L10

corner かど 角 会L6(e)

correct (○) まる 会L11(e)

cough せき 会L12

cough せきがでる せきが出る [ru] 会L12

(counter for flat objects) 〜まい 〜枚 会L5

(counter for people) 〜にん 〜人 会L7

country くに 国 会L6

cow うし 牛 読L12-II

cram school じゅく 塾 読L7-II

cross わたる 渡る [u] 会L6(e)

cry なく 泣く [u] 読L12-II

cucumber きゅうり 会L8(e)

cuisine りょうり 料理 会L10

culture ぶんか 文化 読L11-II

curtain カーテン 会L2(e)

cut きる 切る [u] 会L8

cut (classes) サボる [u] 会L11

cute かわいい 会L7

---

dance おどる 踊る [u] 会L9

date (romantic) デート 会L3

daughter むすめ 娘 読L12-II

day after tomorrow, the あさって 会L4(e), 会L8

day before yesterday, the おととい 会L4(e)

day off やすみ 休み 会L5

deadline しめきり 締め切り 会L11(e)

December じゅうにがつ 十二月 会L4(e)

decide きめる 決める [ru] 会L10

...degrees (temperature) 〜ど 〜度 会L8

delicious おいしい 会L2

dentist しか 歯科 会L12(e)

departing first せんぱつ 先発 会L10(e)

departing second じはつ 次発 会L10(e)

department store デパート 会L7

dermatologist ひふか 皮膚科 会L12(e)

desk つくえ 机 会L2(e), 会L4

dialect ほうげん 方言 会L11(e)

diarrhea げり 下痢 会L12(e)

diary にっき 日記 読L9-II

dictionary じしょ 辞書 会L2(e)

die しぬ 死ぬ [u] 会L6

difficult むずかしい 難しい 会L5

---

diligent まじめ（な） 読L12-II

dining commons しょくどう 食堂 会L7

dinner ばんごはん 晩ご飯 会L3

disgusted with きらい（な） 嫌い 会L5

dish りょうり 料理 読L6-III

dislike きらい（な） 嫌い 会L5

do する [irr.] 会L3

do やる [u] 会L5

do laundry せんたくする 洗濯する [irr.] 会L8

doctor いしゃ 医者 会L1, 会L10

dog いぬ 犬 会L4

don't look well げんきがない 元気がない 会L12

door と 戸 読L10-II

door ドア 会L2(e)

dormitory りょう 寮 読L9-II

dream ゆめ 夢 会L11

drink のみもの 飲み物 会L5

drink のむ 飲む [u] 会L3

drive うんてんする 運転する [irr.] 会L8

drive ドライブ 会L11

E

ear みみ 耳 会L7(e)

early はやい 早い 会L3

(do something) early はやく 早く／速く 会L10

east ひがし 東 会L6(e)

easy かんたん（な） 簡単 会L10

easy (problem) やさしい 会L5

eat たべる 食べる [ru] 会L3

economics けいざい 経済 会L1, 会L2

egg たまご 卵 会L12

eggplant なす 会L8(e)

Egypt エジプト 会L1

eight やっつ 八つ 会L9

eight minutes はっぷん／はちふん 八分 会L1(e)

eight o'clock はちじ 八時 会L1(e)

eighteen minutes じゅうはっぷん／じゅうはちふん 十八分 会L1(e)

eighth day of a month, the ようか 八日 会L4(e)

electricity でんき 電気 会L2(e), 会L6

eleven minutes じゅういっぷん 十一分 会L1(e)

eleven o'clock じゅういちじ 十一時 会L1(e)

eleventh day of a month, the じゅういちにち 十一日 会L4(e)

e-mail メール 会L9

(something) ends おわる 終わる [u] 会L9

energetic げんき（な） 元気 会L5

English (language) えいご 英語 会L2

ENT doctor じびか 耳鼻科 会L12(e)

enter はいる 入る [u] 会L6
entrance いりぐち 入口 会L10(e)
erase けす 消す [u] 会L6
eraser けしゴム 消しゴム 会L2(e)
essay さくぶん 作文 会L9
every day まいにち 毎日 会L3
every night まいばん 毎晩 会L3
every week まいしゅう 毎週 会L8
everyone みなさん 皆さん 読L6-III
Everything is under control. だいじょ
　うぶ 大丈夫 会L5
exam しけん 試験 会L9
example れい 例 会L11(e)
excellent food ごちそう 読L9-II
Excuse me. すみません 会G
exercise うんどうする 運動する [irr.]
　会L9
exercise れんしゅう 練習 会L11(e)
exit でぐち 出口 会L10(e)
exit でる 出る [ru] 読L6-I, 会L9
expensive たかい 高い 会L2
express きゅうこう 急行 会L10(e)
extremely すごく 会L5
eye め 目 会L7, L7(e)
eyebrow まゆげ 眉毛 会L7(e)

F

face かお 顔 会L7(e), 会L10
fall あき 秋 会L10
(rain/snow) falls （あめ／ゆきが）ふる
　（雨／雪が）降る [u] 会L8
family かぞく 家族 会L7
famous ゆうめい（な）有名 会L8
farm はたけ 畑 読L12-II
fast はやい 速い 会L7
(do something) fast はやく 早く／速
　く 会L10
father おとうさん お父さん
　会L1, 会L2
(my) father ちち 父 会L7
February にがつ 二月 会L4(e)
fee 〜だい 〜代 会L12
feel dizzy めまいがする 会L12(e)
festival （お）まつり （お）祭り 会L11
fifteen minutes じゅうごふん 十五分
　会L1(e)
fifth day of a month, the いつか 五日
　会L4(e)
finger ゆび 指 会L7(e)
firefighter しょうぼうし 消防士
　会L11
first ひとつめ 一つ目 会L6(e)
first day of a month, the ついたち 一
　日 会L4(e)
first of all まず 読L8-II
first-year student いちねんせい 一年
　生 会L1
fish さかな 魚 会L2
fishing つり 会L11

five いつつ 五つ 会L9
five minutes ごふん 五分 会L1(e)
five o'clock ごじ 五時 会L1(e)
flower はな 花 会L4
fond of すき（な）好き 会L5
food たべもの 食べ物 会L5
foot あし 足 会L7(e), 会L12
for example たとえば 例えば
　会L11(e)
for…months 〜かげつ 〜か月
　会L10
for the first time はじめて 初めて
　会L12
for two to three days にさんにち
　二三日 会L12
for…weeks 〜しゅうかん 〜週間
　会L10
foreign country がいこく 外国 会L11
forget わすれる 忘れる [ru] 会L6
four よっつ 四つ 会L9
four minutes よんぷん 四分 会L1(e)
four o'clock よじ 四時 会L1(e)
fourteen minutes じゅうよんぷん
　十四分 会L1(e)
fourteenth day of a month, the じゅう
　よっか 十四日 会L4(e)
fourth day of a month, the よっか 四
　日 会L4(e)
free (time) ひま（な）暇 会L5
Friday きんようび 金曜日
　会L4, 会L4(e)
friend ともだち 友だち 会L1
frightening こわい 怖い 会L5
from… 〜から 読L7-II, 会L9
from now on これから 読L11-II
front まえ 前 会L4
fruit くだもの 果物 会L5
fun たのしい 楽しい 会L5
funny おもしろい 面白い 会L5
future しょうらい 将来 会L11

G

gain weight ふとる 太る [u] 会L7
game ゲーム 会L4
game しあい 試合 会L12
gate かいさつ 改札 会L10(e)
general admission seat じゆうせき
　自由席 会L10(e)
get (a grade) とる 取る [u] 会L11
get (from somebody) もらう [u] 会L9
get angry おこる 怒る [u] 読L12-II
get off おりる 降りる [ru] 会L6
get to know しる 知る [u] 会L7
get up おきる 起きる [ru] 会L3
Get well soon. おだいじに お大事に
　会L12
girlfriend かのじょ 彼女 会L12
glasses めがね 眼鏡 会L7
gloves てぶくろ 手袋 会L10

go いく 行く [u] 会L3
go back かえる 帰る [u] 会L3
go on a diet ダイエットする [irr.]
　会L11
go out でかける 出かける [ru] 会L5
go to sleep ねる 寝る [ru] 会L3
God かみさま 神様 読L12-II
gold きんいろ 金色 会L9(e)
gold ゴールド 会L9(e)
good いい 会L3
Good afternoon. こんにちは 会G
good at… じょうず（な）上手 会L8
good child いいこ いい子 会L9
good deed いいこと 読L10-II
Good evening. こんばんは 会G
Good morning. おはよう／おはようご
　ざいます 会G
Good night. おやすみ（なさい）会G
Good-bye. さようなら 会G
good-looking かっこいい 会L5
grade (on a test, etc.) せいせき 成績
　会L12
graduate student だいがくいんせい
　大学院生 会L1
grammar ぶんぽう 文法 会L11(e)
grandfather おじいさん 会L7
grandmother おばあさん 会L7
grape ぶどう 会L8(e)
gray グレー 会L9(e)
gray はいいろ 灰色 会L9(e)
green グリーン 会L9(e)
green みどり 緑 会L9(e)
green light あおしんごう 青信号
　会L9(e)
green tea （お）ちゃ （お）茶 会L3
guardian deity of children じぞう／お
　じぞうさん 読L10-II
guitar ギター 会L9

H

hair かみ 髪 会L7, L7(e)
halal ハラルフード 会L8(e)
half はん 半 会L1
half past two にじはん 二時半 会L1
hamburger ハンバーガー 会L3
hand て 手 会L7(e)
hangover ふつかよい 二日酔い
　会L12
happy しあわせ（な）幸せ 読L10-II
hat ぼうし 帽子 会L2
hate だいきらい（な）大嫌い 会L5
have a fever ねつがある 熱がある [u]
　会L12
have a fight けんかする [irr.] 会L11
have a talk はなしをする 話をする
　[irr.] 読L9-II
hay fever かふんしょう 花粉症
　会L12(e)
he かれ 彼 会L12

looking for... 〜ぼしゅう 〜募集 読L11-II

L

lose なくす [u] 会L12
lose weight やせる [ru] 会L7
lot, a たくさん 会L4
love だいすき (な) 大好き 会L5
lunch ひるごはん 昼ご飯 会L3

M

magazine ざっし 雑誌 会L3
major せんこう 専攻 会L1
make つくる 作る [u] 会L8
man おとこのひと 男の人 読L5-II, 会L7
mandarin orange みかん 会L8(e)
many たくさん 会L4
March さんがつ 三月 会L4(e)
(get) married けっこんする 結婚する [irr.] 会L7
match しあい 試合 会L12
matters こと 読L11-II
May ごがつ 五月 会L4(e)
maybe たぶん 多分 会L12
meal ごはん ご飯 会L4
mean-spirited いじわる (な) 意地悪 会L9
meaning いみ 意味 会L11(e), 会L12
meat にく 肉 会L2
medicine くすり 薬 会L9
meet あう 会う [u] 会L4
memorize おぼえる 覚える [ru] 会L9
menu メニュー 会L2
Mexico メキシコ 読L5-II
milk ぎゅうにゅう 牛乳 会L10
Milky Way, the あまのがわ 天の川 読L12-II
mobile スマホ 会L2
Monday げつようび 月曜日 会L4, 会L4(e)
money (お)かね (お)金 会L6
month after next, the さらいげつ 再来月 会L4(e)
more もっと 会L11
moreover,... それに 会L12
morning あさ 朝 会L3
mother おかあさん お母さん 会L1, 会L2
(my) mother はは 母 会L7
mountain やま 山 読L5-II, 会L11
mountain road やまみち 山道 読L10-II
mouth くち 口 会L7, 会L7(e)
movie えいが 映画 会L1
Mr./Ms.... 〜さま 〜様 読L5-II
Mr./Ms.... 〜さん 会L1
much よく 会L3
music おんがく 音楽 会L3
my place うち 会L3

N

name なまえ 名前 会L1
narrow せまい 狭い 会L12
navy こんいろ 紺色 会L9(e)
near ちかく 近く 会L4
near future こんど 今度 会L9
nearby ちかく 近く 会L4
neck くび 首 会L7(e)
need いる [u] 会L8
neighborhood きんじょ 近所 読L11-II
(get) nervous きんちょうする 緊張する [irr.] 会L12
new あたらしい 新しい 会L5
New Year's (お)しょうがつ (お)正月 読L10-II, 会L11
newspaper しんぶん 新聞 会L2
next つぎ 次 会L6
next となり 隣 会L4
next (stop),... つぎの〜 次は〜 会L10
next month らいげつ 来月 会L4(e), 会L8
next semester らいがっき 来学期 会L11
next week らいしゅう 来週 会L4(e), 会L6
next year らいねん 来年 会L4(e), 会L6
nice すてき (な) 素敵 会L12
Nice to meet you. よろしくおねがいします よろしくお願いします 会G
night よる 夜 読L5-II, 会L6
nine ここのつ 九つ 会L9
nine minutes きゅうふん 九分 会L1(e)
nine o'clock くじ 九時 会L1(e)
nineteen minutes じゅうきゅうふん 十九分 会L1(e)
ninth day of a month, the ここのか 九日 会L4(e)
no ううん 会L8
No. いいえ 会G
noon ひる 昼 読L9-II
north きた 北 会L6(e)
nose はな 鼻 会L7(e)
not... anything なにも + negative 何も 会L7
not at all ぜんぜん + negative 全然 会L3
Not at all. いいえ 会G
not busy ひま (な) 暇 会L5
not to feel well きぶんがわるい 気分が悪い 会L12(e)
not much あまり + negative 会L3
not spacious せまい 狭い 会L12
Not to worry. だいじょうぶ 大丈夫 会L5

O

not... yet まだ + negative 会L8
notebook ノート 会L2
nothing in particular べつに + negative 別に 会L7
November じゅういちがつ 十一月 会L4(e)
now いま 今 会L1
number ばんごう 番号 会L1
number... 〜ばん 〜番 会L1, 会L11(e)
nurse かんごし 看護師 会L1

O

obstetrician and gynecologist さんふじんか 産婦人科 会L12(e)
occupation しごと 仕事 会L1, 会L8
o'clock 〜じ 〜時 会L1
October じゅうがつ 十月 会L4(e)
of course もちろん 会L7
office worker かいしゃいん 会社員 会L1, 会L8
often よく 会L3
okay まあまあ 会L11
old (thing) ふるい 古い 会L5
old man おじいさん 会L7
old woman おばあさん 会L7
older brother おにいさん お兄さん 会L1, 会L7
(my) older brother あに 兄 会L7
older sister おねえさん お姉さん 会L1, 会L7
(my) older sister あね 姉 会L7
on うえ 上 会L4
on foot あるいて 歩いて 会L10
(be) on the heavy side ふとっています 太っています 会L7
once a year いちねんにいちど 一年に一度 読L12-II
once upon a time むかしむかし 昔々 読L10-II
one ひとつ 一つ 会L9
one... ある〜 読L12-II
one hour いちじかん 一時間 会L4
one minute いっぷん 一分 会L1(e)
one o'clock いちじ 一時 会L1, 会L1(e)
one person ひとり 一人 会L7
one way かたみち 片道 会L10(e)
oneself じぶん 自分 読L10-II
onion たまねぎ 会L8(e)
only... 〜だけ 会L11
open (something) あける 開ける [ru] 会L6
operation しゅじゅつ 手術 会L12(e)
ophthalmologist がんか 眼科 会L12(e)
or 〜か〜 会L10
orange オレンジ 会L9(e)
orthopedic surgeon せいけいげか 整形外科 会L12(e)

thirteen minutes　じゅうさんぷん　十三分　会L1(e)

thirty minutes　さんじゅっぷん／さんじっぷん　三十分　会L1(e)

this . . .　この　会L2

this month　こんげつ　今月　会L4(e), 会L8

this morning　けさ　今朝　会L8

this one　これ　会L2

this person (polite)　こちら　会L11

this semester　こんがっき　今学期　会L11

this week　こんしゅう　今週　会L4(e), 会L6

this year　ことし　今年　会L4(e), 会L10

three　みっつ　三つ　会L9

three minutes　さんぷん　三分　会L1(e)

three o'clock　さんじ　三時　会L1(e)

throat　のど　会L12

throw away　すてる　捨てる [ru]　会L8

throw up　はく　吐く　会L12(e)

Thursday　もくようび　木曜日　会L4, 会L4(e)

ticket　チケット　会L9

(boarding) ticket　じょうしゃけん　乗車券　会L10(e)

ticket vending area　きっぷうりば　切符売り場　会L10(e)

till (a time)　〜まで　会L5

time　じかん　時間　会L10

(be) tired　つかれている　疲れている　読L8-II

(get) tired　つかれる　疲れる [ru]　会L11

to (a place/a time)　〜まで　会L9

today　きょう　今日　会L3, 会L4(e)

together　いっしょに　一緒に　会L5

together with (a person)　〜と　会L4

toilet　トイレ　会L2

tomato　トマト　会L8

tomorrow　あした　明日　会L3, 会L4(e)

tonight　こんばん　今晩　会L3

tooth　は　歯　会L7(e), 会L12

tough (situation)　たいへん（な）　大変　読L5-II, 会L6

tour　ツアー　会L10

town　まち　町　会L4

toy　おもちゃ　会L11

track number . . .　〜ばんせん　〜番線　会L10(e)

traditional Japanese theatrical art　かぶき　歌舞伎　会L9

traffic light　しんごう　信号　会L6(e)

train　でんしゃ　電車　会L6

train ticket　きっぷ　切符　会L12

transfer　のりかえ　乗り換え　会L10(e)

travel　りょこう　旅行　会L5

travel　りょこうする　旅行する [irr.]　会L10

T-shirt　Tシャツ（ティーシャツ）　会L2

Tuesday　かようび　火曜日　会L4, 会L4(e)

turn (right/left)　まがる　曲がる [u]　会L6(e)

turn off　けす　消す [u]　会L6

turn on　つける [ru]　会L6

TV　テレビ　会L3

twelve minutes　じゅうにふん　十二分　会L1(e)

twelve o'clock　じゅうにじ　十二時　会L1(e)

twentieth day of a month, the　はつか　二十日　会L4(e)

twenty minutes　にじゅっぷん／にじっぷん　二十分　会L1(e)

twenty-fourth day of a month, the　にじゅうよっか　二十四日　会L4(e)

two　ふたつ　二つ　会L9

two minutes　にふん　二分　会L1(e)

two months ago　にかげつまえ　二か月前　会L4(e)

two o'clock　にじ　二時　会L1(e)

two people　ふたり　二人　会L7

two people each　ふたりずつ　二人ずつ　会L11(e)

two weeks ago　にしゅうかんまえ　二週間前　会L4(e)

U

uh-huh　うん　会L8

uh-uh　ううん　会L8

um . . .　あのう　会L1

umbrella　かさ　傘　会L2

under　した　下　会L4

understand　わかる [u]　会L4

unhurriedly　ゆっくり　会L6

university　だいがく　大学　会L1

U.S.A.　アメリカ　会L1

use　つかう　使う [u]　会L6

usually　たいてい　会L3

V

various　いろいろ（な）　読L9-II

vegetable　やさい　野菜　会L2

very　とても　会L5

very fond of　だいすき（な）　大好き　会L5

very soon　もうすぐ　会L12

vocabulary　たんご　単語　会L9

voice　こえ　声　読L10-II

volunteer　ボランティア　読L11-II

W

wait　まつ　待つ [u]　会L4

walk　あるく　歩く [u]　会L12

wallet　さいふ　財布　会L2

warm　あたたかい　暖かい　会L10

wash　あらう　洗う [u]　会L8

watch　とけい　時計　会L2

watch　みる　見る [ru]　会L3

water　みず　水　会L3

watermelon　すいか　会L8(e)

we　わたしたち　私たち　読L12-II

weather　てんき　天気　会L5

weather forecast　てんきよほう　天気予報　会L8

weave　はたをおる　はたを織る [u]　読L12-II

Wednesday　すいようび　水曜日　会L4, 会L4(e)

week after next, the　さらいしゅう　再来週　会L4(e)

weekday　へいじつ　平日　読L11-II

weekend　しゅうまつ　週末　会L3

Welcome (to our store).　いらっしゃいませ　会L2

Welcome home.　おかえり（なさい）　会G

west　にし　西　会L6(e)

what　なん／なに　何　会L1

what kind of . . .　どんな　会L5

when　いつ　会L3

when . . .　とき　時　会L4

where　どこ　会L2

which　どちら／どっち　会L10

which . . .　どの　会L2

which one　どれ　会L2

white　しろい　白い　会L9, 会L9(e)

who　だれ　会L2

why　どうして　会L4

wide　ひろい　広い　会L12

window　まど　窓　会L2(e), 会L6

wine　ワイン　読L6-III

winter　ふゆ　冬　会L8

wish　ねがい　願い　読L12-II

with (a tool)　〜で　会L10

woman　おんなのひと　女の人　読L5-II, 会L7

word　たんご　単語　会L9

work　しごと　仕事　会L8

work　はたらく　働く [u]　会L7

world　せかい　世界　会L10

worry　しんぱいする　心配する [irr.]　会L12

write　かく　書く [u]　会L4

writer　さっか　作家　会L11

wrong (×)　ばつ　会L11(e)

X

X-ray　レントゲン　会L12(e)

Y

year　とし　年　読L10-II

year after next, the　さらいねん　再来年　会L4(e)

year before last, the　おととし　会L4(e)

. . . year student　〜ねんせい　〜年生　会L1

...years ～ねん ～年 会L10
...years old ～さい ～歳 会L1
yellow きいろい 黄色い 会L9(e)
...yen ～えん ～円 会L2
yes うん 会L8
yes ええ 会L3

yes はい 会L1
yesterday きのう 昨日 会L4, 会L4(e)
you あなた 会L4
young わかい 若い 会L9
younger brother おとうと（さん） 弟
　（さん） 会L1, 会L7

younger sister いもうと（さん） 妹（さ
　ん） 会L1, 会L7

Z

zoo どうぶつえん 動物園 会L10

日本地図
にほんちず

Map of Japan

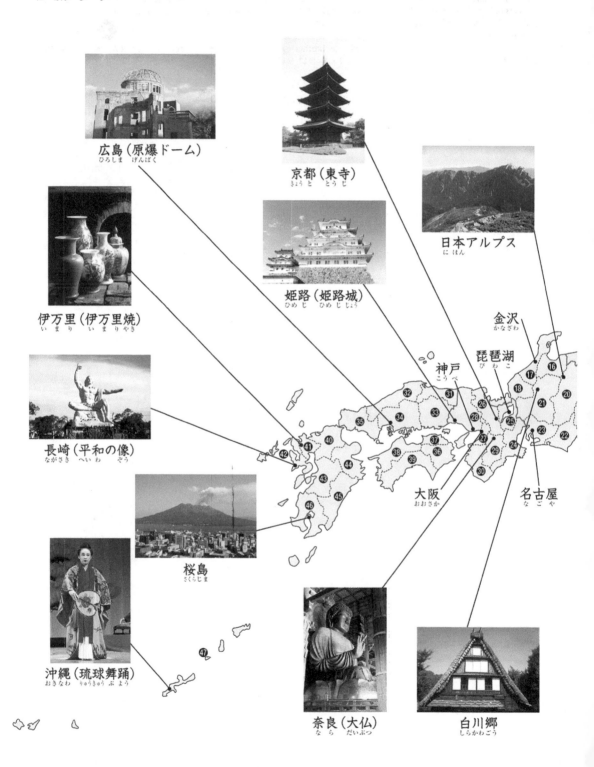

広島（原爆ドーム）
ひろしま げんばく

京都（東寺）
きょうと とうじ

日本アルプス
にほん

姫路（姫路城）
ひめじ ひめじじょう

伊万里（伊万里焼）
いまり いまりやき

金沢
かなざわ

琵琶湖
びわこ

神戸
こうべ

長崎（平和の像）
ながさき へいわ ぞう

大阪
おおさか

名古屋
なごや

桜島
さくらじま

沖縄（琉球舞踊）
おきなわ りゅうきゅうぶよう

奈良（大仏）
なら だいぶつ

白川郷
しらかわごう

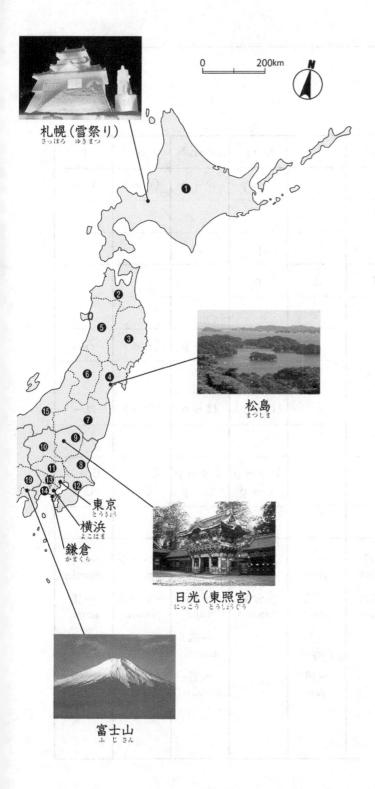

0 ── 200km

北海道地方
ほっかいどうちほう
❶北海道
ほっかいどう

東北地方
とうほくちほう
❷青森県
あおもりけん
❸岩手県
いわてけん
❹宮城県
みやぎけん
❺秋田県
あきたけん
❻山形県
やまがたけん
❼福島県
ふくしまけん

関東地方
かんとうちほう
❽茨城県
いばらきけん
❾栃木県
とちぎけん
❿群馬県
ぐんまけん
⓫埼玉県
さいたまけん
⓬千葉県
ちばけん
⓭東京都
とうきょうと
⓮神奈川県
かながわけん

中部地方
ちゅうぶちほう
⓯新潟県
にいがたけん
⓰富山県
とやまけん
⓱石川県
いしかわけん
⓲福井県
ふくいけん
⓳山梨県
やまなしけん
⓴長野県
ながのけん
㉑岐阜県
ぎふけん
㉒静岡県
しずおかけん
㉓愛知県
あいちけん

近畿地方
きんきちほう
㉔三重県
みえけん
㉕滋賀県
しがけん
㉖京都府
きょうとふ
㉗大阪府
おおさかふ
㉘兵庫県
ひょうごけん
㉙奈良県
ならけん
㉚和歌山県
わかやまけん

中国地方
ちゅうごくちほう
㉛鳥取県
とっとりけん
㉜島根県
しまねけん
㉝岡山県
おかやまけん
㉞広島県
ひろしまけん
㉟山口県
やまぐちけん

四国地方
しこくちほう
㊱徳島県
とくしまけん
㊲香川県
かがわけん
㊳愛媛県
えひめけん
㊴高知県
こうちけん

九州地方
きゅうしゅうちほう
㊵福岡県
ふくおかけん
㊶佐賀県
さがけん
㊷長崎県
ながさきけん
㊸熊本県
くまもとけん
㊹大分県
おおいたけん
㊺宮崎県
みやざきけん
㊻鹿児島県
かごしまけん
㊼沖縄県
おきなわけん

札幌（雪祭り）
さっぽろ　ゆきまつ

松島
まつしま

日光（東照宮）
にっこう　とうしょうぐう

東京
とうきょう

横浜
よこはま

鎌倉
かまくら

富士山
ふじさん

写真提供・協力：東寺／東大寺（撮影：矢野建彦）／奈良市観光協会／姫路市／伊万里市観光戦略課

数 Numbers
かず

	regular				h→p	h→p/b	p	k
1	いち				いっp	いっp	(いっ)	いっ
2	に							
3	さん				p	b		
4	よん	し	よ	よ	p			
5	ご							
6	ろく				ろっp	ろっp	(ろっ)	ろっ
7	なな	しち	しち					
8	はち				(はっp)	はっp	(はっ)	はっ
9	きゅう	く	く					
10	じゅう				じゅっp じっp	じゅっp じっp	じゅっ じっ	じゅっ じっ
how many	なん				p	b		
	～ドル dollars ～枚 sheets ～度 degrees ～十 ten ～万 ten thousand	～月 month	～時 o'clock ～時間 hours	～年 year ～年間 years ～人 people ～円 yen	～分 minute ～分間 minutes	～本 sticks ～杯 cups ～匹 animals ～百 hundred	～ページ page ～ポンド pounds	～か月 months ～課 lesson ～回 times ～個 small items

This chart shows how sounds in numbers (1-10) and counters change according to their combination.

1. *Hiragana* indicate the sound changes in numbers, and letters show the changes in the initial consonant of counters.
2. ( ) means that the change is optional.
3. An empty box means no sound change occurs.

k→g	s	s→z	t	special vacabulary for numbers			
いっ	いっ	いっ	いっ	ひとつ	ついたち	ひとり	1
				ふたつ	ふつか	ふたり	2
g		z		みっつ	みっか		3
				よっつ	よっか		4
				いつつ	いつか		5
ろっ				むっつ	むいか		6
				ななつ	なのか		7
はっ	はっ	はっ	はっ	やっつ	ようか		8
				ここのつ	ここのか		9
じゅっ じっ	じゅっ じっ	じゅっ じっ	じゅっ じっ	とお	とおか		10
g	z			いくつ			how many
～階 *kai* floor ～軒 *ken* houses	～セント *cents* ～週間 *shūkan* weeks ～冊 *satsu* books ～歳 *sai* years of age	～足 *soku* shoes ～千 *sen* thousand	～通 *tsū* letters ～丁目 *chōme* street address	small items years of age cf. はたち (20 years old)	date cf. じゅうよっか (14) はつか (20) にじゅうよっか (24) なんにち (how many)	people cf. ～人 *nin* (three or more people)	

活用表 Conjugation Chart
かつ よう ひょう

verb types	dictionary forms	long forms (*masu*) (L3)	*te*-forms (L6)	short past (L9)	short present neg. (L8)	short past neg. (L9)
irr.	<u>する</u>	します	して	した	しない	しなかった
irr.	<u>くる</u>	きます	きて	きた	こない	こなかった
ru	たべ<u>る</u>	～ます	～て	～た	～ない	～なかった
u	か<u>う</u>	～います	～って	～った	～わない	～わなかった
u	ま<u>つ</u>	～ちます	～って	～った	～たない	～たなかった
u	と<u>る</u>	～ります	～って	～った	～らない	～らなかった
u	あ<u>る</u>	～ります	～って	～った	*ない	*なかった
u	よ<u>む</u>	～みます	～んで	～んだ	～まない	～まなかった
u	あそ<u>ぶ</u>	～びます	～んで	～んだ	～ばない	～ばなかった
u	し<u>ぬ</u>	～にます	～んで	～んだ	～なない	～ななかった
u	か<u>く</u>	～きます	～いて	～いた	～かない	～かなかった
u	い<u>く</u>	～きます	*～って	*～った	～かない	～かなかった
u	いそ<u>ぐ</u>	～ぎます	～いで	～いだ	～がない	～がなかった
u	はな<u>す</u>	～します	～して	～した	～さない	～さなかった

The forms with * are exceptions.

著者紹介

坂野 永理（ばんの えり）
テンプル大学で教育学博士号取得。南山大学、関西外国語大学を経て、現在、岡山大学教授。著書に『日本語コミュニケーションゲーム80』『Kanji Look and Learn』（共著／ジャパンタイムズ出版）がある。

池田 庸子（いけだ ようこ）
ペンシルベニア州立大学で比較文学修士号取得。イースタン・ニュー・メキシコ大学、ペンシルベニア州立大学、関西外国語大学を経て、現在、茨城大学教授。著書に『Kanji Look and Learn』（共著／ジャパンタイムズ出版）がある。

大野 裕（おおの ゆたか）
上智大学で言語学修士号を取得後、マサチューセッツ大学アムハースト校で博士コースに在籍。同校および関西外国語大学、名古屋大学留学生センターを経て、現在、立命館大学大学院言語教育情報研究科教授。

品川 恭子（しながわ ちかこ）
ウィスコンシン大学マジソン校で日本語学修士号取得。カリフォルニア大学アーバイン校、関西外国語大学を経て、現在、カリフォルニア大学サンタバーバラ校講師。著書に『Kanji Look and Learn』（共著／ジャパンタイムズ出版）がある。

渡嘉敷 恭子（とかしき きょうこ）
オハイオ州立大学で日本語言語学修士号取得。コネチカット・カレッジ、オハイオ州立大学を経て、現在、関西外国語大学教授。著書に『Kanji Look and Learn』（共著／ジャパンタイムズ出版）がある。

About the Authors

Eri Banno is a professor at Okayama University, and has previously taught Japanese at Nanzan University and Kansai Gaidai University. She earned her Ed.D. in education at Temple University. Her publications include the co-authored works *80 Communication Games for Japanese Language Teachers* and *Kanji Look and Learn* (both published by The Japan Times Publishing).

Yoko Ikeda is a professor at Ibaraki University, and has previously taught Japanese at Eastern New Mexico University, Pennsylvania State University, and Kansai Gaidai University. She earned her M.A. in comparative literature at Pennsylvania State University. Her publications include the co-authored *Kanji Look and Learn* (The Japan Times Publishing).

Yutaka Ohno is a professor at Ritsumeikan University's Graduate School of Language Education and Information Science (LEIS), and has previously taught Japanese at the University of Massachusetts Amherst, Kansai Gaidai University, and Nagoya University. He earned his M.A. in linguistics at Sophia University, and enrolled in a doctoral program at the University of Massachusetts-Amherst.

Chikako Shinagawa teaches Japanese at the University of California, Santa Barbara, and has previously taught Japanese at the University of California, Irvine, and Kansai Gaidai University. She earned her M.A. in Japanese at the University of Wisconsin, Madison. Her publications include the co-authored *Kanji Look and Learn* (The Japan Times Publishing).

Kyoko Tokashiki is a professor at Kansai Gaidai University, and has previously taught Japanese at Connecticut College and Ohio State University. She earned her M.A. in Japanese linguistics at Ohio State University. Her publications include the co-authored *Kanji Look and Learn* (The Japan Times Publishing).

OTO Navi — Sound Navigator
Audio Player for The Japan Times Publishing's books

The audio material for GENKI is available through **OTO Navi — Sound Navigator**, an app for listening to audio material provided with books published by The Japan Times Publishing.

How to Use OTO Navi

1. Scan the QR code below and download OTO Navi from App Store or Google Play.

2. Search for **GENKI Vol. 1** [**3rd Ed.**] within the app.

3. Download the audio material and play it!

ジャパンタイムズの音声アプリ 「OTO Navi」のご案内

『げんき』の音声は、ジャパンタイムズ出版の音声再生アプリ「**OTO Navi**」でご利用いただくことができます。

ご利用方法：

1. 下のQRコードで、App Store または Google Play から「OTO Navi」をダウンロード。

2. アプリ内で『**初級日本語げんき1**［**第3版**］』を検索。

3. 音声をダウンロードして、再生してください。

App Store

Google Play